Chinese Women
YESTERDAY & TODAY

A DA CAPO PRESS REPRINT SERIES

China
in the 20th century

Chinese Women
YESTERDAY & TODAY

By

FLORENCE AYSCOUGH

DA CAPO PRESS • NEW YORK • 1975

Library of Congress Cataloging in Publication Data

Ayscough, Florence Wheelock, 1878-1942.
    Chinese women, yesterday and today.

    (China in the 20th century)
    Reprint of the ed. published by Houghton Mifflin,
Boston.
    Bibliography: p.
    Includes index.
    1. Women—China.   2. China—Social life and customs.
I. Title.
HQ1737.A97   1975   301.41'2'0951   74-32095
ISBN 0-306-70700-4

THIS DA CAPO PRESS EDITION OF *CHINESE WOMEN* IS AN UNABRIDGED
REPUBLICATION OF THE FIRST EDITION PUBLISHED IN BOSTON IN 1937.

COPYRIGHT 1937 BY FLORENCE AYSCOUGH MACNAIR.

PUBLISHED BY DA CAPO PRESS, INC.
A SUBSIDIARY OF PLENUM PUBLISHING CORPORATION
227 WEST 17TH STREET, NEW YORK, N.Y. 10011

Chinese Women
YESTERDAY & TO-DAY

T he conduct of women, in China, is patterned on Confucian standards. After the introduction of Buddhism, however, the gentle Bodhisattva, Kuan Yin, became the Patron Saint of women. To her they turn when in grief, of her they beg progeny. She has been for many centuries the central figure in the inner apartments. This portrait of her is a rubbing from a stone stele in the Shêng Yin Ssŭ, a monastery on the West Lake Hangchow.

Chinese Women
YESTERDAY & TO-DAY

By

FLORENCE AYSCOUGH

Illustrations from the Chinese

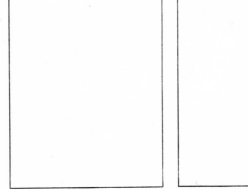

BOSTON

HOUGHTON MIFFLIN COMPANY

The Riverside Press Cambridge

1937

The Riverside Press
CAMBRIDGE · MASSACHUSETTS
PRINTED IN THE U.S.A.

Contents

PART THREE

Introduction

BOOKS, like children, choose their own roads. Was ever a work, in completion, that which its author, at inception, intended? My Chinese women, with true feminine persistence, have chosen their own way — and their own company. That last is an interesting point. As I wrote I realized that certain types would not mingle. The ladies of China who lived according to the *Record of Rites*, who formed links between dead ancestors and unborn descendants, who exemplified the instincts and philosophy of their race, would not admit to their company those sisters who had, in dishonorable ways, broken the mould of pattern.

In studying the women of China I was amazed and overwhelmed at the numbers whose names have been preserved to posterity. I doubt if the annals of any country can be compared, in this respect, to those of China. Obviously I must set limits to my scheme. I chose, therefore, as mandrel to the work, Ch'iu Chin, the remarkable character who bridges the chasm between the Old World and the New. She, it is true, broke the mould of pattern: she put duty to her country, duty to her sex, before the more obvious duty to husband and children. She sacrificed her life in attempting to rouse to patriotism, and to emancipate from alien rule, her 'companions of the womb,' both women and men. Many of the qualities she evinced had been manifested in earlier days by her atavic ancestors, each typical of a quality highly prized by the Chinese. They form the company of those who have chosen to attend her.

Various ladies, more fair than virtuous, are famous in Chinese records. Their lives are easily matched in other parts of the world, nor do they reveal the peculiar instincts and philosophy of their race. Imperial favorites have brought monarchs to their doom under skies both bright and dull. Details differ; the results, in royal circles, have been the same.[1]

Powerful Empresses, Regents such as Tzŭ Hsi, the Manchu Ruler, or Usurpers like Wu Tsê T'ien, who for twenty-five years and more interrupted the rule of the T'ang, have issued Edicts from the Dragon Throne; and pattern Consorts have assisted many Sons of Heaven.

A number of love stories exist which deal with civilian life and which are characteristically Chinese — albeit the chief actresses shatter moulds of pattern. These one day I hope to assemble.

The study just made has crystallized in my mind the appreciation of various Chinese qualities heretofore dimly apprehended. What people have so great a power of acceptance? What people in accepting so preserve self-respect? I recollect a trivial incident illustrating this statement: North of the Great River it was a year of difficulty. Floods? Drought? Who knows which? — had deprived the peasants of their harvest. Refugees thronged Shanghai. A little hovel, mud-walled, straw-roofed, sprang up at the threshold of my Grass Hut. In this hovel there lived, throughout the winter months, a family. Father, mother, two little sons. An iron rice-pan, mounted on an earthen oven, and a straw pallet seemed to be their only possessions. The dialect the family spoke was unknown to me, but each day we greeted each

[1] A Chinese writer, Shu Chiung (Mrs. Wu Lien-teh), has handled with great charm the lives of two royal favorites: *Beauty of Beauties* (Shanghai, 1931) is the life of Hsi Shih. *The Most Famous Beauty of China* (Shanghai and New York, 1924) is the biography of Yang Kuei-fei, whose story is also given by Maude Meagher in *White Jade* (London and Boston, 1930). In *Beauty in Exile*, Shu Chiung gives the life of the 'Bright Concubine' whose name is a synonym for homesickness.

other and each day I was struck afresh by the calm beauty of the woman's face, by her perfect poise, self-possession and self-respect. I discussed their condition with Amah, my kindly maid, who for many years directed my movements. I suggested that help be given the refugee family 'because they were so poor.' Amah shook her head. 'He no b'long poor man,' she replied. 'He have got ground.' She then explained that they were landowners from North of the River, driven South by hard times, that when Spring came they would return to cultivate their fields, and that it would be very tactless on my part to treat the family as beggars. Obedient to her advice I confined offerings to trifles for the children. Spring came. The family vanished. I have never forgotten their calm acceptance and have never ceased to ask myself: 'Could you live under such conditions and preserve self-respect?' The answer, I may state, is in the negative.

This quality of acceptance will help the Chinese in the ordeal now before them. It is their greatest strength. As these lines go to press, events in North China crowd: invasion has occurred; advance by a powerful enemy will, perhaps, soon eventuate. Mrs. Chiang Kai-shih, wife of the Generalissimo, herself secretary to the air forces, calls upon the women of China to fight Japan 'according to their ability.' In addressing them she says:

> In the world war the women of every country gave their best. The women of China are no less patriotic or capable of physical endurance than the women of other lands. This we shall show the world. Our final victory, no matter how belated it may be, will erase forever the days of humiliation which for so long have crowded our calendar, and will remove the sorrow which for years has bent our heads and bowed our hearts.

> China is facing the gravest crisis in its history. This means we must sacrifice many of our soldiers, masses of our innocent people, much of the nation's wealth and see ruthlessly destroyed the results of our reconstruction.

I think of the woman who lived uncomplainingly throughout the winter in a mud hovel and realize that the Chinese capacity for suffering will enable her people to face the trial which seems imminent. Mrs. Chiang Kai-shih will not call upon her countrywomen in vain.

During this study I realized, too, more clearly than heretofore, that the theory of Chinese discipline is erected on a framework of imitation. A 'mould of pattern' is created for every imaginable eventuality. Children are seldom troubled by the verb 'to do,' or its inverse. A mirror of behavior is held before them. It has puzzled me, this matter of discipline. How is it that children who, when small, are allowed to do what they please, as they please, when they please, suddenly at the age of twelve or thirteen become abnormally obedient — and remain obedient throughout their lives? I tried to elicit the theory of discipline from Nung Chu *hsien shêng* — Mr. Cultivator-of-Bamboos — my teacher. He looked at me pityingly, as one would look at an uncomprehending infant, then picked up a paper-weight which lay on the table before us, saying, as he moved its position: 'If you *tell* a child not to move this paper-weight, of course the child moves it.' That was all he said. I nodded, and realized that to attain perfect obedience one should avoid command; I realized too that a child should be *shown* that paper-weights 'are not moved.' This method, effective with the Chinese, who are collective by nature, is less successful with the more individualistic Occidental. A friend of mine chid her small son, who broke some rule of table ritual: 'Douglas, we don't do it that way.' Douglas aged four, a thorough Westerner, replied firmly: '*I* do.' Such an incident is inconceivable in a Chinese family of pre-Republican days.

A number of folksongs have been included in this work because I feel, rightly or wrongly, that folksongs betray the heartbeats of a people. Furthermore, five indigenous words are worth a ream of description.

A word in regard to translation: Unless otherwise attributed, the translations in this book are, in every case, my own. I have tried to render the Chinese idiom as closely as possible, and have, moreover, worked on the method of translation which I describe in the introductions to both *Fir-Flower Tablets, Poems translated from the Chinese*, and *Tu Fu, the Autobiography of a Chinese Poet*.

The illustrations, with the exception of Ch'iu Chin's photograph given to me by her daughter, and the frontispiece, which is taken from a rubbing in the possession of my husband, are from Chinese books: *Lieh Nü Chuan*, the *Kuei Fan*, and *Ku Chin Pai Mei T'u*, this last being the work of the great nineteenth-century illustrator Wu Yu-ju.

To a number of friends acknowledgments are due: To my teacher Nung Chu *hsien shêng* whose sympathetic interpretation illumines every page we read; to Mr. Lindsay Lieu, of the Chinese Salt Gabelle, a keen student of literature, who kindly gave me the printed edition of *Kuei Fan* which I have used; to Doctor Wu Yi-fang, President of Gin Ling College, who has shown great interest in this study of her sisters; to Doctor Lin Yutang, author of *My Country and My People*, who called my attention to *The Sacrificial Prayer for Ah Chên* and the *Ballad of the Little Nun*; to Mrs. Lin Yutang who has talked sympathetically about the life of women in China; to Doctor Chên Shou-yi of the National University, Peking, for his helpful suggestions in connection with the translation of Pan Chao's *Seven Precepts*; to Mr. Chang Tsung-ch'ien at the University of Chicago for his kind assistance; to Doctor and Mrs. Han of St. John's University, Shanghai; to Wang Tsan-chih for the portrait of her heroic mother, Ch'iu Chin, and to my husband Harley Farnsworth MacNair who has been ever ready to 'lend me his ears' and to 'give me his advices' — be they bitter or sweet.

A month has passed since I wrote the above. Disaster envelops China. A ruthless enemy has blockaded her coasts and is attempting by the aid of every modern weapon to obtain mastery of her people and break her national spirit. Noncombatants and refugees, as well as soldiers, are being slaughtered.

That the spirit of Ch'iu Chin and her atavic ancestors, Hua Mu-lan and other Women Warriors, survives is proved by a United Press message, of September 11, from Shanghai which reads:

'Thousands of Chinese girls fought in the front lines to-day against the Japanese.

'They fought side by side with the regular army forces. Others were engaged in militia duties in the rear or were assisting in first-aid relief in the battle zones.

'The ''peach-bloom'' maidens participated in some of the heaviest battles along the Shanghai front. Several were killed in action and many were wounded.'

FLORENCE AYSCOUGH

AT THE HOUSE OF THE WUTUNG TREES
  CHICAGO, *September*, 1937

Part One

Chinese Ladies

Men decide laws, women morals.
French saying

IN VISION a long line of ladies seems to issue from behind the baton-door. Ladies who, for centuries, have lived in seclusion practising only the domestic arts; who, for centuries, have spoken only with those men to whom they were nearly related. Now they stand eyes wide open, under the fold of Mongolian eyelids, gazing at the outer world of which they have become a part.

The baton-door, so called because its original shape — round above, square below — resembled the *kuei* or small stone baton given as a sign of rank to nobles, led to the 'running-horse two-storied building' occupied by women in a typical Chinese household. It is the door to inner apartments, a world in themselves. Until a few years ago the only world known to Chinese women.

The breath-taking change that has taken place in the Central Flowery State can be appreciated only by realizing contrasts. Whereas heretofore opportunity outside the baton-door was nil, to-day it stretches to the horizon. In theory and in law, sons and daughters of Han now stand shoulder to shoulder on level ground, before the selfsame road. In truth and in custom, the difference between them is still Heaven-high. It is amazing, however, to measure the distance these ladies have progressed.

In 1905 government education of women was non-existent; fifteen years later over four hundred thousand girls were studying in various schools. Shortly afterward several hundred university chairs were occupied by women. Before 1905, broadly speaking, none but the 'oldest profession' was open to a woman; now none is closed. In the old days a young girl was governed by the following rules: 'When walking do not turn the head, when speaking do not show the teeth, when sitting keep the legs immobile, when standing prevent all movement of the skirt.' To-day young girls enter the realm of athletics, become 'scouts,' play basket-ball, do unheard-of things. Before me lie two pictures; both are newspaper clippings. One shows four girls, in the shortest bathing suits, the tank champions of China at a Shanghai swimming meet. I gasp. Yes, I know that Miss Beauty Fish competed in the Olympic Games in Berlin, that her name was in every Chinese newspaper, I suppose she wore a swimming suit, but to see portraits of these undressed Chinese girls in public print — makes the incredible credible! The other picture shows a feminine atom hurtling through the air left leg forward, right leg back, right hand grasping tennis racket stretched forward, left hand holding tennis ball stretched back. A veritable spread-eagle pose. Mouth is open, all teeth show, bobbed hair is literally 'all over the place.' The caption reads: 'She beat them all.' The legend: 'Miss Gem Hoahing, the Chinese girl from Hongkong, won the schoolgirls' tournament at Queen's Club, beating Miss Rowe, junior champion of England and holder of the Yatman cup, by 6–2, 6–3. Miss Rowe will be too old to play at Junior Wimbleton in September, 1935, while the Chinese girl cannot compete because she is not old enough.' If the energy and determination displayed by Miss Gem Hoahing are criteria, little wonder that people say, 'The future of China lies in the hands of her women.'

Nor is this idea strange. The world behind the baton-door was ruled by a matriarchy formed on strict lines in which every individual occupied her allotted post and behaved according to *kuei chü*. Literally *kuei*, the circle enclosing right conduct, *chü* the square of right action. The term is in use throughout the Chinese social structure and controls correct behaviour under all circumstances. It includes our term 'social convention' but is stretched to comprise moral action. One speaks of 'old *kuei chü*'; new *kuei chü* is not, as yet, definitely fixed.

Following the lead of Nature herself all civilizations have differentiated the position of men and women. The reason why in China this differentiation is so sharply marked is to be found in the requirements of the cult of ancestor-worship. A cult, by no means abandoned, lying at the roots of Chinese civilization. It is connected with belief in the Yin or Shadow World, a realm stretching the other side of death where spirits, thin ghosts of former years, have the same needs which they felt here in the Yang or Light World. These needs can be met by male descendants only. The unfortunates who have not provided for posterity, by either sons of the body or adoption, become lonely hungry ghosts who, at different seasons of the year and special hours of the day, invading the World of Light do harm. It is logical that a woman cannot perform these sacrifices. Until the day of her marriage she is only a guest in her father's house, and when she leaves must undertake the responsibilities of her husband's clan. Much has been made of the preference in Chinese families for boy children. The same preference is found in Western lands for boys, to carry on the family name, but in the West this fearful responsibility to the Yin World does not exist, therefore sons are not essential. That Chinese parents love sons more dearly than daughters, provided that the care of ancestors is assured, I do not believe. Chinese fathers, especially, dote on their little girls, carry them about, decorate their foreheads with peach-blossom marks, dress them up like dolls, and, according to our ideas, spoil them shockingly. Read Po Chü-i's poems to Golden Bells, his little girl who died.

Birthday of Golden Bells

March   of my years   is about to reach   four   tens;
Have   a daughter   called   Golden   Bells.

Since her birth a complete year has revolved,
She learns to sit, cannot talk.

I blush, have garnered no wisdom,
Cannot avoid commonplace affection, love.

From now on is my body bound to outer things;
Can console myself only with what is before my eyes.

If there be not the distress of her untimely death,
Shall be involved in finding a groom, sending the bride
   to his home!

This will cause my planned retirement to the hills
To be delayed for ten years and five!

THINKING OF GOLDEN BELLS

My person worn and ill has seen four tens;
Petted, doted on, a three-year-old daughter.

Not a boy, still a triumph over nothing;
To soothe my affection sometimes fondled her.

One dawn, released as a bird she left me;
Her soul's shadow has no place to rest.

I think of when, untimely, she was transformed in
   death,
Of her confused prattle when she learned to speak.

First realize that flesh and bones love
Is focused only by sorrow, grief.

Thoughts echo from time before I had her;
Use reason to banish pain, bitterness.

Forget   treasured thoughts;   the day   is already   long past,
Three   times   have cold,   heat,   interchanged.

This   day   my heart   is   wounded
Because   I met,   face to face,   the nurse   who gave her
    breast.

Read also the sacrificial prayer to Ah Chên written by her
father, noted among the *literati* of his day, and burnt at the
scene of her childish games.

On the third day of the last decade in *i wei* year, during
reign of Wan Li — December 23, A.D. 1619 — Ah Chên,
elder daughter of Shên Chün-lieh, died, untimely, because smallpox did not come out. She was buried in
a mat near the rest-house at Northern Mounds. In order
to bring her happiness in the Dark World her mother —
of the Po Clan — chanted daily, repeating Buddhist
sutras, and later urged that I write a sacrificial prayer.
I could not endure to bring down my writing-brush on
paper.

When Ah Chên had been dead three times seven days,
we offered up well-cooked food and I wrote a literary
piece mourning her. This we burned on the level ground
where, in life, she had skipped and tossed about her playthings. It ran:

ming hu, alas! grief intense!
Your name Ah Chên.
Born during *ping chên* year. (A.D. 1616)
Using characters *ping* and *chên*
We chose your name Chên.
At first when you were born
Truly, I did not rejoice.
A man aged three tens and more,
Had, not a man-child, but a girl!
When you were not yet a year old,

You were already very lovable.
If I snuggled you in my neck, or beckoned,
You smiled, laughed aloud.
At this time, your nurse,
Chou Yu strapped you on her back in a swaddling cloth.
Once dressed, she did not loosen girdle,
But, ten times in a night, would rise.
You hungered? At once had mother's milk,
You were satisfied — slept with Yu.
On your account she suffered bitterness
Sometimes, also blame and wrong.
Moved you from wet place to a dry one,
'Pared good flesh to patch your sores.'
If she were too attentive, your mother scolded,
If not enough, you cried.
Last year — *mou wu* —
My luck was not complete,
It was urgent that I attend literary examinations,
Dreading to leave you, I went.
Chou Yu died;
My examinations were unsuccessful.
When I returned you pulled my sleeve,
Demanding things to play with.
With you at my side,
In spite of disappointment, I had joyful thoughts.
Your teeth increased daily;
Your quick wit was daily more.
Called 'Da,' called 'Ma,'
The sounds improved not a little.
Often knocking with your own hand on door,
You asked: 'Who is it?'
At the time my nephew came
You called him *ko ko* — elder brother.
He playfully seized your toys,
Much ruffled you ran, hid.
When your maternal uncle came,

You pulled his robe;
Called aloud, saying: 'Ma,'
Forthwith laughed 'ha ha.'
When your paternal uncle came,
Greeting him, you played the host;
Lifting wine-cup said '*ch'ing*' — pray drink';
Everybody laughed like thunder.
Your grandfather went to the country;
You also went to Soo.
A year passed you did not see him;
We asked: 'Do you know him or not?'
You answered: 'Know him,
White cap, white beard.'
You had maternal grandfather,
Face to face had not met.
Asked you: 'Guest whence comes he?'
At once replied: 'Pei Ching.'
Maternal grandmother
Loved you as if her body had given you birth.
In all, three, five, times,
Carrying you, travelled to Soo.
Third watch — midnight — you demanded toys,
Fifth watch — day-dawn — you demanded fruit.
Father, mother wanted you,
You refused, 'not can.'
Turning spoke to me saying:
'Ah P'o — granny — thinks of me.'
This year, Sixth Moon,
You had disastrous boils.
I travelled to Soo,
Would fetch you home.
Brushed lightly afflicted place,
Your face very mournful.
Did not dare to cry,
Fearing to cry be not right.
When you took fruit, or boiled dumplings with meat,

You peeped, to see how we felt.
If our faces did not show approval,
It was not instantly put between the teeth.
Tossing playthings about, if
They were accidentally broken, spoilt,
And we looked displeased,
You withdrew hand, slapped and hid it.
Your mother, severe with faults,
At times, exercised strict control,
Fearing that, grown tall,
You would ripen practised habits.
My idea not the same.
In private said to her:
'How should girl baby know?
Does right to follow her wishes.'
Once when you were in Soo.
Father, mother returned home to Lou.
Asked you inclination:
'Desire go, desire remain?'
Reply was undecided.
Thought in your heart at two extremes.
Presently you returned home,
So joyful we could not hold ourselves.
We enticed you, made you jump,
Pulled idiotic false faces.
In little basket you carried dates,
Sat on tiny chair, ate rice-gruel;
Mouth chanted the Great Learning;
Raised hands in reverence to Buddha.
You played game of forfeits, guessed, conquered;
Encircled house galloping like a horse.
Laughed *hai hai*, clapped hands,
Rejoiced in your own cleverness.
In not even half a Moon,
We reached time of your death.
Heaven is it? Fate is it?

Spirits? Immortals? we do not know.
Before you died
Called doctor to examine, observe.
Said: 'Perhaps cold from vicious wind,'
Said: 'Perhaps blotches preceding smallpox.'
Cold? We are not certain.
Blotches? Have regular symptoms.
Until this moment, in thinking of the illness,
We cannot estimate what it was.
You who loved to say words
During this time did not speak.
Breathed with hoarse crashing sound, panted,
Eyes stretched, stared about you.
Standing in a ring, all wept silent tears,
Your tears, too, flowed, clear as water.
wu hu, alas! can grief endure words *tsai!*
Discussing ordinary emotions of this world
A girl dies, why weep?
Computing years of my life
Am in my prime, am poor, alone.
You were most intelligent.
Although a girl, you were enough.
Who could know that demons-below-the-earth, spirits above,
Would thus use tiger claws of cruelty?
Ten days earlier,
Your younger sister Ah Shun,
Smaller than you by two years,
Had the same illness,
Died in three days.
You know her well.
Being now without comrades
Should depend on little sister.
You can already walk,
Little sister cannot stand firmly.
Going, coming, lead each other by the hand,
Love each other, do not quarrel.

Should you meet Nurse Yu
Enquire of her, saying:
'Father had a wife called Ku;
Father has dead mother, Min.
Would only go and be with them.'
She will surely lead you.
Stay there for the present
Near the side of Ku.
Younger sister is small, you must lead;
Under-Earth Prefecture
Is not like home.
I write this prayer, but
You cannot read characters.
I only call, 'Ah Chên,
Your father is here.'
Cry aloud for you,
Call you by name.

Verses from the *Classic of Poetry*, often quoted to show the contempt in which the Chinese hold women, read:

(The Ruler said:) 'Divine for me my dreams.
What dreams portend good-fortune?
Of bears and yellow-spotted bears,
Of snakes and venomous serpents (have I dreamed).'

The Chief Diviner interpreted them: (saying)

'Bears, yellow-spotted bears,
Harbingers of prosperity, predict birth of sons.
Snakes, venomous serpents,
Harbingers of prosperity, predict birth of daughters.'
Thou shalt bring to birth sons,
They shall be cradled on beds,
Shall be clothed in robes,
Shall toy with jade symbols of rank.

Their   cries   *huang huang*   shall   be strong.
Grand   the vermilion   knee-pads   they   will wear when
     sacrificing,
Of   household,   of state,   they   the lordly   Rulers.

Thou   shalt   bring to birth   daughters;
They   shall be   cradled   on the earth,
Shall be   wrapped   in froths;
They   shall   toy   with   tiles   used in weaving.
Theirs   no responsibility   for right,   for wrong,
Theirs   only   to follow rules   regarding   sacrificial food
     and wines.
Theirs   to behave   so as not to be despised,   nor imprison
     sorrow   in hearts   of father,   mother.[1]

As Legge, Giles, and other sinologues point out, contempt
should not be understood. The tile is an emblem of weaving
because women prepare for the loom the fibres of the nettle-
hemp and grass-cloth by rubbing them on tiles. The tile is
therefore a mark of woman's craft, not a symbol of inferiority.

The theoretical position of women is clearly set forth in
the ancient learning: Chinese philosophy, based on belief
in the interaction of the principles Yin and Yang, which by
this interaction produce everything in the visible palpable
world, postulates equal importance of the functions pertaining
to each.

Yin, the Negative Essence, corresponds to darkness, to
water, to the moon, to weakness, to depth, to all things
feminine; Yang, the Positive Essence, corresponds to light,
to hills, to the sun, to strength, to height, to all things

[1] *Classic of Poetry*, Part II, Book IV, Ode v, Stanzas 7, 8, 9, translation by Florence
Ayscough.
A *froth* is a square piece of cloth in which a baby is wrapped. One corner of the
cloth is left free and extends beyond the child's head, serving as a convenient holder
by which the bundled baby may be carried.

masculine. Interlocking they are shown forming a circle, symbol of entirety. Yin, Yang; Woman, Man: each necessary to the other. Neither superior, neither inferior; antithetical, indispensable. From their union, within the circle, life proceeds endlessly.

Antithesis in their mutual functions is the point stressed by Chinese in the relations of men and women. From the Emperor on his Dragon Throne down to the lowliest boatman in his mat-roofed craft the same rules held; they are expressed in the chapter *Hun I*, the *Record of Rites*:

> Hearken to the Son-of-Heaven regarding tenets for men. Hearken to Her-who-is-equal-to-the-Sovereign regarding compliance required of women. Son of Heaven directs inherent principle of Yang essence, She-who-is-His-equal regulates Yin qualities. Son of Heaven rules all without, She-who-is-His-equal directs all within. If tenets of men be not cultivated functions of Yang essence will not evolve, their opposition will be manifest in the sky, sun will suffer eclipse as though consumed by a living creature. If compliance of women be not cultivated Yin qualities will not develop, their opposition will be manifest in the sky, moon will suffer eclipse. When the sun vanishes Son of Heaven puts on plain robes of raw silk, rectifies government within Six Palace Halls, purifies Yang essence in All-below-the-sky. When the moon is consumed, She-who-is-equal-to-the-Sovereign dresses in plain robe of raw silk, regulates administration of Six Palace Halls, purifies Yin qualities in All-below-the-sky. Son of Heaven is to His Consort as sun to moon, as Yang to Yin. Each essential to the other, she perfects the whole.[1]

Although ladies to-day have breached the circle, finding the rôle of compliance which entailed the Three Dependences

[1] *A Chinese Mirror*, by Florence Ayscough.

— to father, to husband, to son — no longer to their taste, the ancient philosophy preserves its influence in Chinese life. The society which China is evolving will be its own. Many foreign scions are being grafted on the old trunk; it, if it will survive, must remain rooted in its past. I return to the study of contrasts.

CHILDHOOD: THEN AND NOW

Dawn till dark weed fields,
By night spin thread.
Boys, girls, of country village
Know well household needs.

Tiny   children   not yet   able
To drive   plough   or throw   loom,
Learn   to sow   melon   seed
In shade   of mulberry   trees.

A Chinese Folksong

SMALL Chinese children were, in the old days, all-pervading. No upper story nursery in charge of a severe starched female for them. They participated in all functions, which, following the course of a lunar year, were varied and colorful.

At dawn on New Year's Day, having been up all night, they watched the installation of Ts'ao Chün's portrait. Patron Saint of the Kitchen Stove, supposed to have been away for five days, reporting the doings of the family to the Jade Emperor, he now returned with watchful eye to his accustomed place. The First Moon was one of many festivities and small children generally accompanied their mothers. Babies often wore tiger caps and shoes, girls looked very smart with ear-rings, tiny bracelets, and many braids of hair, while boys, small replica of their fathers, were apt to wear suspended from their necks a potent amulet. Second Moon saw the Flowers' Birthday and small fingers helped to tie red congratulatory tags on plants and bushes. Third Moon, corresponding to our April, when warmth is in the air, when wild geese flying South write the character *jên* — man — upon the sky, brought Ch'ing Ming, festival of Clear Brightness. Tombs must be swept. The family often made an outing of such occasion and tiny boys bowed before ancestral graves while their sisters solemnly watched. Fifth Moon, fifth day, saw artemisia and sweet flag leaves hung by doorways, children wore tiger coats and dots of artemisia juice on their foreheads as protection against evil spirits. And so through the Bright Year one festival followed the other until, five days before its ending, preparations were made to dispatch Ts'ao Chün upon his celestial journey. A series of incidents amusing to young and old. Chinese children still go about far more than do ours though the modern mother frequently arranges to leave them at home.

Education in the earliest years was simply a question of influence and imitation on the part of a child. Discipline, with a capital D, did not exist. Boys and girls by the age of six were treated differently; a little girl of seven was separated from her brothers and at the age of ten he was supposed to leave the inner apartments while she began an exclusively feminine training within the baton-door. Nowadays kindergartens and primary schools are springing up. They are as yet far too few, the lack of sufficient teachers being a major handicap. Discipline, on Western lines, is discussed as being desirable, but I question whether Chinese children will ever be submitted to severe forms of doubtful value.

GIRLHOOD : THEN AND NOW

Ten and three, could weave silk threads;
Ten and four, learned to cut-out clothes;
Ten and five, swept strings of *k'ung hou* lyre;
Ten and six, hummed lines of Classics: *Poems, Writings.*
Ten and seven, became wife of my Lord.

Chinese Ballad

No OTHER section of Chinese society has been as profoundly affected by twentieth-century modernization as has that of young girls; for the vast majority the world is transformed.

'Then' a daughter of an official family *might* receive instruction in the Four Arts: music, playing hedged-in-checkers, calligraphy, painting. She might even, at the risk of becoming a *ts'ai nü*, a talented woman, be instructed in literature and poetry. There have been many *ts'ai nü* in Chinese history, but their lives have often been unhappy; in general parents preferred, for their daughters, happiness to fame. A husband she must have. No Chinese father can commit a more serious sin of omission than to neglect his daughter's betrothal. Everyone knows that men seek, in their wives, knowledge of the domestic arts rather than proficiency in those of the scholar; therefore the average road is the safer.

Behind the baton-door young girls learned to sew, to weave, to supervise a household, and to embroider. This last art was most important. All the articles connected with her trousseau, not only those for her own use but those to be given as presents to her husband's family, must be embroidered by herself. Girlhood was preparation for marriage: the rites of politeness must be learned and her young fancy, as she sat stitching plum blossom or bird of happiness, must be fixed on the unknown and unseen person of her betrothed who was, she hoped, a brilliant scholar. To him she was linked by an unbreakable cord. Had this not been tied before birth by the old man who arranges marriages? Of this she was convinced, every step in her training emphasized the fact. Even the dark valley of foot-binding, where suffering was intense, led to bright heights of conjugal admiration for three-inch golden lilies shod in exquisitely embroidered shoes.

Behind the baton-door, in the garden or the courtyards, busy days passed for the young girl, a guest in her father's household. Tasks were performed: when crickets sang in the Seventh Moon winter clothes were taken out and mended; on the seventh day she performed rites to enquire of supernatural beings whether or not her needlework and weaving would be successful. On that day too she celebrated the meeting in the sky of the lovers Weaving-Maid and Herdboy who throughout the year live apart one on either side of Silver River, a Chinese name for our Milky Way. To assist their meeting all magpies should hasten at this time to span Silver River with their wings. If one saw a bird of happiness on the Seventh Day of the Seventh Moon one would chide him and tell him to hasten to the skies.

Life was punctuated, too, with the five rites preceding the marriage ceremony. First horoscopes must be compared. The Notes of Eight characters were exchanged. Diviners made elaborate calculations, assured themselves that the cyclical

animals governing the horoscopes of prospective bride and groom were not antipathetic, that no tiger confronted a serpent, that no cock sought alliance with a dog. If so be the animals did not agree the affair was abandoned. Why start life with an impossible handicap? Another bridegroom would be sought and after possibly years of waiting and months of special training a young girl stepped into the scarlet bridal chair and was carried to the home of her husband who, lifting her red silk veil, for the first time saw her face.

Cases have occurred when the strict seclusion, ideal for Chinese maidenhood, has been violated. Love-stories in actuality and in fiction have shaken Chinese households. Youths and maidens have seen each other, love has resulted.

Assisted by waiting-maid, or some other sympathetic individual, assignations have been made and the lovers have met
in a courtyard or some secluded spot. Lovesickness and
clandestine meeting are indeed favorite themes for story-
tellers and dramatists. How frequent they were in actuality
it is impossible to say. A popular folksong throws light on
such happening:

OLD DAME WANG

Opening

Outside   gauze   window-pane,   gauze   window-pane,
ah!

Is sound   of calling,   tapping;   'tis she   who lives beyond
wall.

Lady   of house   asks,   'What sound is that?   who is that?
ah!'

'It is I,   old   Dame   Wang,   who lives beyond   wall.'

Old   Dame   Wang,   entered   door   seated   herself   on
high   round   stool;

ee-e   ho;   ee-e   ho;   hai!

Lady sings:

'You think   lightly   of me,   disregard me,   *ya!*   do not
come   to   this   my   contemptible   place.'

ee-e   ho;   ee-e   ho;   hai!

Dame Wang   pulled open,   lifted,   rose   hibiscus   curtain,
ah!

Perceived,   inhaled,   scent   of rouge,   powder,

Threw back,   lifted,   shining   red silk   quilt,   *ah!*

Peered,   peered,   whispered   'Oh! Second   Young
Lady!'

Second   Young   Lady   was   thin,   did not   indeed
resemble   form   or figure   of a   girl!

ee-e   ho;   ee-e   ho;   hai!

Verse 1

Spoken: 'How has Second Young Lady felt these last few days, eh?'

Sung: 'I, slave, for these several days, *ah!*
Have been bound in languor, bound in languor.
Tea indeed, dislike, am too listless to drink, *ah!*
Rice, too, cannot bear to eat.
Tea, rice, *ya!* I have aversion to taking, verily it is difficult for me to use them.'
   ee-e ho; ee-e ho; hai!

Verse 2

Spoken: 'Shall I on your account call a doctor to come,
    look at you, look at you?'

Sung: 'I, slave, will not call him, *ya!*
I, slave, do not want him indeed!
If a doctor is called to come, *ya!*
He will pinch, pinch; pound, pound!
Pinched, pinched, *ya;* pounded, pounded;
   I fear that possibly I, the slave, would be
   hurt!'
     ee-e ho; ee-e ho; hai!

Verse 3

Spoken: 'Shall I on your account call a Buddhist Priest
    to come then?'

Sung: 'I, slave, will not call him, *ya!*
I, slave, do not want him indeed!
If a Buddhist Priest is called, comes, *ya!*
He will tinkle, tinkle, again tinkle,
Tinkle, tinkle, *ya,* tinkle, tinkle; then will
   slave fear retribution!'
     ee-e ho; ee-e ho; hai!

Verse 4

Spoken: 'Shall I on your account call a La Ma Priest
    to come then?'

Sung: 'I, slave, will not call him, *ya!*
I, slave, do not want him indeed!
If a La Ma Priest is called, comes, *ya,*
He will chitter, chatter, then whine and wail;
Chitter, chatter, *ah!* whine and . wail; then
   will slave fear retribution!'
     ee-e ho; ee-e ho; hai!

Verse 5

Spoken: 'Shall I on your account call an Exorcist
of Demons to come then?'

Sung: 'I, slave, will not call her, *ya!*
I, slave, do not want her indeed!
If Exorcist of Demons is called, comes, *ya,*
She will cast spells, make incantations, chant,
mutter;
Cast spells, make incantations, chant, mutter;
then will slave feel terror.'
ee-e ho; ee-e ho; hai!

Verse 6

Spoken: 'This one not wanted! that one not wanted!
this illness of yours how did you get
it, *eh?'*
Sung: 'In Third Moon, Third Moon, *ya!*
In Third Moon is Clear Brightness Feast;
On peach trees flowers have opened, *ya!*
Willow trees also have brought forth green;
A descendant of Wangs, *ah!* he, young gentleman, was strolling about enjoying Spring
scene!'
ee-e ho; ee-e ho; hai!

Verse 7

Spoken: 'Strolling in Spring, not strolling in Spring,
what has it to do with you, *eh?'*
Sung: 'He indeed loved household slave,
With red rouge, white powder, am a lovely
girl.
Household slave also loved him, *ya!*
His years few, he is student of books.
Have spoken with him several times, spoken
peach flower words — words of passion.'
ee-e ho; ee-e ho; hai!

Verse 8

Spoken: 'Peach-flower passion, no peach-flower passion!
do you not fear father, mother will
know, *eh?'*

Sung: 'Slave's father, father, *ya,*
          Is aged seven times ten and eight more.
          Slave's mother, mother, *ya,*
          Has dragon ears,   deaf ears; has   flower eyes,
              dim eyes.
          They, these two people! surely I can have
              no fear of them!'
                   ee-e ho; ee-e ho; hai!

Verse 9

Spoken: 'You do not fear elder brother, elder brother's
              wife will know, *eh?'*
Sung: 'Slave's elder brother, *ya!*
          Often, often is not in household;
          Slave's elder brother's wife, *ah!*
          Often, often goes to mother's household.
          They, these two people! surely I can have
              no fear of them!'
                   ee-e ho; ee-e ho; hai!

Verse 10

Spoken: 'You do   not   fear elder sister, younger sister
              will know, *eh?'*
Sung: 'Slave's elder sister, elder sister, *ya!*
          Is not very different from slave;
          Slave's younger sister, younger sister, *ah!*
          Years few, does not comprehend anything;
          What you and I say is same pattern of
              words.'
                   ee-e ho; ee-e ho; hai!

Verse 11

Spoken: 'What shall I do on your account, *eh?'*
Sung: 'Honoured, revered Old Dame Wang, *ah!*
          Considering you her venerable adopted mother,
          This girl hurriedly kneels before you, *ah!*

Telling her misery to venerable adopted mother.
This affair, can you arrange it for me,
  indeed?'
        ee-e ho; ee-e ho; hai!

Verse 12
Spoken: 'And if I cannot arrange it, *eh?*'
Sung: 'If you cannot arrange it — I will probably
  die of bitterness.'
        ee-e ho; ee-e ho; hai!

To-day 'official families' in the old sense no longer exist.
In 1905 the literary examinations, gate to officialdom and all
it meant, were abolished. Well-to-do families there are in
plenty and among the quiet hills away from the hurry of
modernity young girls may still lead secluded lives. In urban
centres, however, they have plunged into modern life. Avid
for learning they attend school: kindergarten, primary school,
secondary school, the university. They train as nurses, prepare for the teaching profession, study science.

In 1935 an enchanting young person dressed in a long blue
velvet coat said to me: 'Yes, I used to know much T'ang
poetry, my grandmother taught me. Now I have no time to
read. I am doing research on that parasite which attacks the
ears of mice.' No longer are young girls trained for matrimony alone.

Athletics are popular; foot-binding, except in backward
districts, and among the poor, who so generally are conservative, has been abolished. Girls develop their bodies and
walk on untrammelled feet. Radio keeps them in touch with
the humming world and many aspire to foreign education.

Betrothal is still of greater importance than the actual
marriage ceremony but according to the new code both

parties must be consulted and give consent. The most fashionable bridal conveyance is now a bedecked motor car — preferably one painted red — the bride therein no longer wears a scarlet robe or hides her face behind an opaque silken veil. The great majority of wedding dresses are pale pink; the veil, made of tulle, is blush rose and flowers are worn in the hair. A few ultra-smart young women, overcoming the age-old aversion to white, color of mourning, wear dresses and veils in Western style.

If life for the well-to-do maiden has been altered, for her poor sister it has been transformed. 'Then' no respectable girl could work for a wage. Girl singers there were, and in travelling troupes of various kinds daughters did their share. Girl acrobats were popular: the tiny things stood on upturned feet of adults and allowed themselves to be bundled about in the air. Daughters of the very poor, often sold as slaves, during girlhood performed domestic work of every kind; it was, however, the business of their owners to arrange for marriage, and with marriage slavery ceased. Otherwise daughters of the poor remained at home, assisted in household tasks, shared household joys awaiting the day when, seated in the red bridal chair, they would go out from their own family, to enter that of a husband. For them foot-binding was of vital importance. It was the patent of gentility. What mother would condemn her child to go through life marked as a 'big-footed' woman of the coolie class when by binding the feet a door to advancement in the social scale might be opened? And indeed what girl would desire that such door remain closed? At the cost, therefore, of long-drawn agony feet were bound and slowly crushed.

Now a thousand avenues to material betterment are open.

Mechanical industry has invaded the Central Flowery State. Monster factories have opened. Hands in their millions are needed. Hands of Chinese girls are remarkably deft. What more natural than that the monsters should swallow willing maidens? And willing they are.

Cotton mills, silk filatures, match and cigarette factories, knitting mills, printing works, rug factories, embroidery and lace industries all absorb thousands of children and girls.

Wages are low, hours long, conditions in many cases bad; but even limited economic independence is sweet and in urban centres children throng at factory doors begging employment.

The West has experienced years of struggle regarding the conditions of employees; the expression 'child labor' is to us a contradiction in terms. Ideally children and labor should have no connection. Children should study, should play, should enjoy the breath of Heaven. But what if they cannot study because the necessary schools do not yet exist? What if their families are so poor that both food and clothing are insufficient? What if their only playground is a street?

Education in China has made immense strides, but primary schools are still lamentably few. Many families are so poor that food and clothing are scarce. In crowded cities children have no place to play; the breath of Heaven is often tainted. Their earnings certainly ameliorate home conditions, workers have better food and clothing than they would otherwise enjoy. The questions are most difficult to answer. Hundreds of earnest men and women are pondering these problems. The government is trying to enforce regulations protecting those who toil. Meanwhile little girls tend spindles, brush cocoons — that is, plunging a cocoon into hot water they loosen an end of fine silk to facilitate its being reeled, their

little hands suffering cruelly as a result. They dabble too
with white sulphur in match factories as no little girl should
do.

Slavery is to-day illegal, but children still serve in rich
families, and are often well treated. Foot-binding is forbidden
but people of the old school still admire tiny feet. Amah, an
old woman who has been with me a long time, does not care
for modern ways. Two years or so ago she criticized the new
in stinging terms: nowadays no one can write a decent letter.
Everyone uses common everyday words, not beginning a letter
with proper terms of respect. She remarked that there was
no use in taking her little niece to the theatre because the
child understood nothing about the story, only cared to see
the sparkling clothes and nimble tumblers. Amah herself,
I may interpolate, although illiterate knows all the historical
tales which lie behind the drama and when she hears a tune
realizes instantly what play is to be performed. I attempted
feeble dissent, saying: 'At all events girls can *walk* better
nowadays; they don't have small feet.' 'No handsome,' replied Amah and proceeded to stamp about the room in a
ridiculous way imitating the stride of a modern young woman.

To-day youths and maidens meet with a good deal of freedom. One even sees them walking about in approved Western
style, manly arm encircling girlish waist. On the whole,
however, separation of the sexes is still more general than
with us.

Like their rich sisters, the poor await their wedding day.
Rites are in principal the same, in degree widely different.
The daughter of the masses must often approach her husband's
home in the old-style chair but her hopes are set on a modern
motor car — one as smart as possible!

MARRIAGE: THEN

Natural affinities are, at dawn of time, bound in an indissoluble knot.

IT IS truly said that in China a woman marries not an individual but a family. She goes out from her father's house to become a link binding the Clan of her husband to his forebears and to his descendants. The cult of ancestors requires that the spirits of the dead shall be cared for by sons and grandsons in unending succession. Posterity must be assured, therefore the position of wife was one of supreme importance. Should she bear no sons, it was her duty not only to acquiesce in but to further the choice of concubines. Should they also bear no sons, then adoption of a nephew, a collateral relative, or even some boy not connected with the Clan must be resorted to. Mencius declares that of the three unfilial acts the greatest is the leaving of no descendants. It shows supreme ingratitude to parents to leave them with none to perform ancestral rites.

Marriage in the olden days was no indulgence of personal preference for this man, or that; it was the fulfilling of a contract made in the beginnings of time by cosmic forces, a contract governed by the stars, a contract by which individuals became one with the cosmos. This idea accounts, I think, for the extraordinary stress laid by Chinese on chastity and the devotion, by a woman, to even the thought of one man. An illuminating tale told at greater length by an authority of note is the following: [1] A girl of eighteen, Chang Shih by name, was shortly to be married. Her bridegroom, to whom she had been betrothed in early childhood, suddenly died. The parents dreaded to tell her of this sad fact, but Chang

---

[1] *Lion and Dragon in Northern China,* by R. F. Johnson, p. 232.

Shih, sensing that something was wrong, asked what the trouble might be. Her mother replied, weeping, that he, who was to have become son-in-law of the house, had closed his eyes in death.

The young girl turned quietly and left the room, expressing no emotion. Presently she reappeared. Gold hair ornaments, powder, and rouge had been laid aside. She wore, instead of silk-gauze skirt and brocaded jacket, a long white coarse cotton gown. Black hair hung loose upon her shoulders; her pale face was strained and set. The mother horrified exclaimed: 'How is it that you, who are still a maid, appear thus as a widow?' She tried then to comfort her daughter explaining that a new marriage would shortly be arranged. Chang Shih replied: 'My mother's voice speaks, the thoughts are not my mother's. Can I, your daughter, give myself to another man when my husband has gone, all lonely, to the Yellow Springs?' Continuing she begged that the wedding be not cancelled, that at the time appointed, seven days later, she might sit in the bridal chair and, escorted by the spirit of her husband, go to his home.

Marriage of two spirits or of living girls to the spirits of dead men are not rare in China and always bring renown to the families concerned. In this case everyone was delighted and preparations for the wedding were completed.

In Shantung, where these events took place, it is customary for the groom to proceed to the house of the bride seated in the scarlet bridal chair. This is followed by a green official chair which he uses on the return journey. The groom is received with great ceremony and is introduced to everyone present except the bride whom he is not allowed to see. When she is ready to start the farewell ceremony is accomplished, the red sedan containing the bride is carried first, the green, now occupied by the groom, follows, and the procession returns to the house of the groom where the marriage ceremony takes place.

On Chang Shih's wedding day all was accomplished according to ritual, the only difference being that, instead of a living bridegroom, the *p'ai wei*, a strip of white paper, bearing his name and age and the important words *ling wei* — seat of the soul — was placed in the red chair for the first journey, and occupied the green chair on the way back. Arrived at the groom's house the *p'ai wei* was placed in the great hall, where family and friends were waiting to receive the young girl, and the wedding ceremony joining the living to the dead was performed. Chang Shih, elaborately dressed as a rich young bride, paid the necessary reverence to Heaven, Earth, to the ancestral tablets of her new family, and finally to the living members of that family in order of seniority. Then, retiring to what should have been her bridal chamber, she laid off the wedding dress and appeared in the sackcloth of a widow.

Weeks filled with sad and onerous duties passed. They were devotedly performed by the virgin widow of a man whom she had never seen. Finally the burial day dawned. A long file of white-clad mourners accompanied by the widow threaded the fields to a newly made grave. The coffin was lowered. To the surprise and horror of all the widow threw herself into the grave and lay face down upon the coffin. Puzzled, the mourners stood at first in silence, respectful of grief; finally relatives urged the young woman to arise. She merely replied: 'My place is by my husband. Fill up the grave.' Thinking to humor her each mourner, according to custom, sprinkled a handful of earth upon the coffin and the prostrate form. Having done this everyone went away leaving the widow to her strange vigil.

An hour or two later relatives returned to supervise the filling of a grave which they expected now to find occupied by the coffin only. They were mistaken. Chang Shih, prone in the grave, lay dead.

In many countries widows follow their husbands to the other world; many forms of conjugal suicide are reported. The intensity of feeling, however, that caused a beautiful young girl to will death that her spirit might accompany to the World of Shade that of a man she did not even know, can, I believe, be explained only by a realization of the cosmic side to Chinese union. Even heavenly bodies joined in planning such union. The Chinese say: 'If there be affinity those, one thousand *li* parted, will meet. If there be no affinity, those face to face, know each other not.'

The first step to be taken in any intended marriage was a comparison of horoscopes. Should these not harmonize proof was seen that prospective bride and groom were not destined to be mated and the matter forthwith was dropped. A development of this principle, followed during the last few centuries, provides that each individual, according to the hour of his birth, lives under the influence of some animal. In the case of marriage, these must not be antipathetic. Legend moreover has it that an old man who sits under a tree in the moon turns the leaves of a huge book in which are inscribed names of all intended to wed. He carries a great bag full of red cords and with these he loops together feet of bride and groom.

Six ceremonies were required to legalize marriage which should not be entered into by those of the same surname. The most important, and the only one involving a written contract, was the betrothal. A go-between, generally a woman, has, since proto-historic days, been considered essential. The *Classic of Poetry* contains an ode noting the importance of this functionary:[1]

HEWING AXE-HANDLE

To hew wood for an axe-handle, how can it be done?
Without axe it cannot be attained to.
To 'seize a woman by the ear' — make her a wife — how
    can it be done?
Without a go-between it cannot be accomplished.

The go-between was first commissioned by the young man's family to learn the girl's name and hour of birth. These were given to a geomancer who cast the horoscope. If this were favorable the second ceremonial, the sending of the go-between with an offer of marriage, was accomplished. Assent in writing, the betrothal contract, formed the third rite. The fourth consisted of sending presents to the girl's family. These presents were called 'geese and silks,' the ceremony itself being referred to as 'sending the goose.' This bird, which is believed to pair but once, is supposed to act in conformity with the female and the male principles, the Yin and Yang. It flies toward Yin, the North, in Summer and returns to Yang, the South, for cold weather. The go-between in the fifth ceremony requested the bride's parents to set a lucky day 'to spread out embroidered tester.' The sixth

[1] *Classic of Poetry*, Part I, Book XV, Ode 5, 'Odes of Pin.'

rite was the delivery of the bride to the groom or his repre-
sentative. An infinite number of local variants are found in
the ritual accompanying these ceremonies. Woman was not
supposed to have a regular *dot* but her family often gave
furniture and presents in kind, while she carried gifts of her
own handiwork to her new family. The betrothal contract,
solemn in character, was difficult to break but legal codes of
different dynasties provided, under exceptional circumstances,
for its dissolution.

The bride, spoken of as the 'oriole mate,' spent three or
four days before marriage in seclusion. In Chinese parlance
she 'waited in the hall.' Expenses borne by the family of
the groom were often vast. Feasts for the neighborhood,
gifts for the bride, new clothes for the groom, these and a
hundred other expenses often sank a family in debt. The
ceremony, itself, was simple. The bride, unaccompanied by
relatives but generally attended by maid-servants, arrived in
a magnificent scarlet chair, and stepped into her husband's
home over a saddle, called *an*, the word being a homonym of
'peace.' There she and the groom prostrated themselves before a table upon which stood a tablet to Heaven and Earth,
a pair of lighted candles, and a bronze incense-burner emitting
fragrant fumes. Wine-cups joined by red cords were exchanged;
the couple performed obeisance to the ancestral tablets, to
the parents of the groom, and to his relatives in order of
seniority. The bridegroom, walking backwards and leading
his wife by a strip of silk, then conducted her to the nuptial
chamber where he sat beside her upon the wedding bed. The
saying was that whoever was first seated would be dominated,
throughout life, by the other. Natural hesitation, therefore,
takes place. This matter settled, the red silk bridal veil covered

with many strings of pearls was parted and the bridegroom had his first sight of the bride's face. Presently he departed to join his guests at a feast and the bride, alone in a strange house, was submitted to an obnoxious performance called *nao hsin fang* — tumult in bridal room. This was primarily to test her self-control. I would remark, parenthetically, that self-control is a virtue strongly stressed in China. A little nurse once said to me: 'Our women never cry out in childbirth. In so doing they would, very much, lose face.' When self-control does fail and a Chinese gives way to what is called *ch'i* — literally: exhalation of breath — the result is appalling. In case of the bride, guests were allowed to inspect her, to tease her, and to make remarks upon her appearance while she uttered no word, and betrayed no annoyance.

On the third day after marriage, counting the wedding day as one, the bride prepared a meal for her parents-in-law and offered sacrifice to the Ancestral Tablets. This ceremony marked her acceptance by the Clan. Should she happen to die in this interim, though marriage were consummated, her body would be returned to her own home for burial.

Once married a woman 'has gone out from the home'; the same term is used when a boy enters the Buddhist priesthood; she can return only on rather formal terms. In some places a married daughter is not supposed to go upstairs in her father's house, lest, it is said, she should bring bad luck. A superstition; but significant. The *Record of Rites* describes a woman's marriage in the following phrase: 'Woman has her return home place.' Could the clan idea be better expressed?

☯

Life behind the baton-door was, for a young woman, a succession of duties. Privacy was hers only behind the curtains of the huge marriage bed which, with its little portico, seemed a room in itself. The wooden bed was often painted scarlet and had many panels of gilded carving showing scenes from the lives of famous people. Fame alone did not qualify individuals to appear in this pantheon, as I learned one day when trying to decipher the legends shown on an ancient marriage bed which Amah, my maid, had bought for me in the interior. Here, with his wife, sat the aged and virtuous Kuo Tzŭ-i receiving birthday congratulations; here Chiang T'ai Kung, who gives protection against demons; here the great poet Li T'ai-po; at this point I exclaimed, 'Is Yang Kuei-fei there?' T'ai-po had sung the charms of Yang Kuei-fei, one of the most beautiful women in Chinese history. She had a pernicious influence upon the Emperor Ming Huang whose favorite she was. Their love-story, universally known, is popularly considered to reflect small credit on any of those concerned. Number Two Boy, who always helped me in matters connected with folklore, replied, 'No — oh, no' and hastily left the room. In a few moments he returned, a deprecatory look on his gentle face. He spoke quietly as one would do in correcting a child. Pointing to the bed he said: 'Missisee, Yang Kuei-fei never can puttee this side. No b'long proper woman.' Illumination came to me: the wedding-bed inculcated virtue by means of example. Here surrounded by effigies of 'pattern' men and women a couple began married life. Here, only, could they show each other the mutual affection which marriage should bring. Before other members of the family, man and wife were always formal, any sign of love being considered indecent. Kissing in public was unheard of. In fact, the term for kissing did not exist. Displays of affection, spoken of as 'to smell the face,' only took place in private. Even on the stage love scenes are so delicate and so restrained as to be, to the uninitiated, scarcely recognizable. A Chinese couple lived according to the folk-saying: 'Ascend bed, husband and wife; descend from bed, reserved gentlefolk.'

☯

Mr. Cultivator-of-Bamboos, my teacher, once described to me a young wife's day:

> She rose very early, put on shoes and adjusted skirt before stepping out from curtained portico of bed. Could not appear before even the most devoted maid-servant without her outer skirt, nor could she appear before anyone in sleeping-clothes. She quickly washed, coiled her hair, then, followed by a serving-maid who carried tea, hurried to her mother-in-law's room herself to serve the tea. If her father-in-law were still alive she poured it out and set it down outside the curtained bed. Returned then to her room, prepared a little food for herself and husband. Serving-maids reported as soon as the mother-in-law had risen, whereupon the daughters-in-law all hurried to superintend her hair-dressing; offered to do it for the old lady with their own hands, handed her her garments, and so on. Sons, also, paid an early visit. Then came breakfast. Lao T'ai T'ai, as the old lady was called, seated herself facing South and might ask a daughter-in-law to sit facing East and breakfast with her. Serving-maids brought in the dishes but did not serve Lao

T'ai T'ai. Daughters and sons' wives performed such office.

When dismissed after breakfast the younger women occupied themselves in various ways. Richer people did embroidery, painted, practised various musical instruments, superintended the large staff in the fulfilment of duties. In larger houses there were two kitchens, one where general food was cooked, the other where special dishes for Lao T'ai T'ai were prepared. If she were pleased she would direct that gifts of money be presented to servants at the end of the month, such gifts to be tied with red strings. The last thing at night, all daughters-in-law assembled in her room to see that Lao T'ai T'ai had everything she needed.

Servants were not engaged for a short term but grew up in a household, men-servants often marrying maid-servants in a properly arranged manner. They lived on the premises and often took the surname of the family they served. Their children were educated with those of the family and had exactly the same advantages. In studying, servants' children sat on the lower side of the table facing North, while children of the household faced South. The clever son of a domestic could attend official examinations, provided he left the service of the family and gave up the use of their surname. There was a head man-servant and a head woman-servant who had great authority, who considered themselves and their children as members of the family.

'That,' concluded Mr. Cultivator-of-Bamboos, 'is the way great families lived.'

☯

In poorer families women had yet more responsibility. Farmers' wives, although small-footed, often helped in the fields besides performing household tasks such as cooking, weaving, and making clothes. Their peculiar function was the rearing of silk-worms and spinning of silk.

The consort of the legendary Yellow Emperor is supposed to have invented the process, and has been created Patron Saint of Silk. She was worshipped annually in Spring by the reigning Empress who, as an example to the people, herself opened the sericulture season ... Silkworms are temperamental insects. They cannot endure noise, nor do they like light. The eggs spread on paper must be kept cool, after worms are hatched they must be kept warm; when moulting they must hunger, between sleeps be well fed. They may not be placed too close together nor too far apart; there are an infinite number of rules. In some places women hatch the worms by the warmth of their bodies, wearing the papers on which eggs are spread under their coats. It is a most complicated process requiring infinite care and patience. Men gather mulberry leaves needed to nourish the worms but women perform the remaining work.

Folksongs, most popular in China, interpret vividly thoughts of the people. An ideal marriage according to Chinese ideas is described in

TWELVE MOONS

FIRST MOON

During First Moon is New Year,
During First Moon is New Year.
My good man goes to war; goes out to sweep
frontier passes.

I have no heart to light flower lamps.
He collects bows, also arrows.

Busy, busy, have no leisure,
Busy, busy, have no leisure.
Tiger feelings are roused; hear on street in front sound
     of drums, clamor of brass gongs.
Must prepare travelling bags for my husband.
How arrange work, to have time to go and gaze?

Have made ready many sorts of clothing,
Have made ready many sorts of clothing.
Long inner robe; short outer jacket; thick, thick,
     the padded cotton.
In my eyes tears, a wide pool, a wide pool!
In my hand needle and thread to sew.

Sorrows of parting, ten thousand times
     ten thousand thousands!
Sorrows of parting, ten thousand times
     ten thousand thousands!
In this peaceful village wind and waves snap apart
     silk cord of lover's union.
This dawn I am beside my husband,
Cannot tell the day when we shall meet again.

SECOND MOON
Spring is cut in half at heart of Second Moon,
Spring is cut in half at heart of Second Moon.
My good man goes out to war; I, his slave, am
     deeply wounded in my affection;
I fill to brim, hand up a cup of wine,
When it is finished go out to see him leave.

You go to seek name and fame,
You go to seek name and fame.

Deserted   slave,   deep   in   home of your ancestors,
        will tend   the lamp   of solitude,
Desiring   only   that   you   may quickly   win   renown,
Unfurl   your flag,   instantly   know   victory.

My   husband,   you   must   listen,
My   husband,   you   must   listen.
Write   many   many   letters   that will bring me   peace;
        I will examine   each one   minutely.
On   frontier   passes   dark North Wind   is cold,
I desire   that you   protect   yourself   carefully.

My words   ended,   he   starts   on journey,
My words   ended,   he   starts   on journey.
His person   astride   decorated   saddle;   in   his heart
        unwillingness   to go.
Moving   ten paces   he nine times   turns   his head:
In   our hearts   both   feel   acid grief.

THIRD MOON
Clear   Brightness   comes always   in Third   Moon,
Clear   Brightness   comes always   in Third   Moon.
Red   peach-flowers,   green   willow-leaves,   are beautiful
        seen   in shining   Spring.
My   man!   he   is not   at   home;
Who   will undertake   to worship at,   to put in order
        the graves?

His slave   herself   bears   the responsibility,
His slave   herself   bears   the responsibility.
And makes offerings   to Spirit   tablets   of   Clan   An-
        cestors   arranged together   in the Central   Hall.
It is a necessity;   there can   be no negligence   in offering
        the paper   coins,
Burnt in order to   prevent   the   forebears   from for-
        getting.

Heart   of Lowly One   is deeply   wounded   by anxiety!
Heart   of Lowly One   is deeply   wounded   by anxiety!
Sound   of her wailing   rises to tablets   of husband   and
      wife,   the father   and mother   who died   in old
      age.
'Your   boy   is   at   the frontier   passes;
'Protect,   safeguard   his   body   from all   illness.'

I   turn,   enter   my embroidered   chamber,
I   turn,   enter   my embroidered   chamber.
Look   at my reflection   in the mirror;   my face,   which
      has been rosy as a water-caltrop   bloom,   is dried,
      yellow.
The   day   when we   were   cut apart   cannot   be reck-
      oned   as long past,
But I am   thin;   the mould,   the pattern   of my beauty
      is cracked!

FOURTH MOON

Summer   stands   when Fourth   Moon   comes,
Summer   stands   when Fourth   Moon   comes.
Not   cold,   not   hot   is the weather,   but settled,   mild,
      agreeable;
And   in   this   time   of beautiful   light
My   husband   is forced   to be   without.

I live in solitude,   silence;   I suffer,   endure,
I live in solitude,   silence;   I suffer,   endure.
Bending down   my head,   I look at,   examine   my red,
      flower-embroidered   shoes, saying:
'My   good   man   is not   at   home;
'Who   will come   and regard   you   lovingly?'

My   body   is thin   as   split firewood,
My   body   is thin   as   split firewood.
Do not   drink tea;   do not   eat food;   my eyebrows
      will   not   open.

Throughout   the days   my Lord   mocked   at other
    people.
Now,   my Lord   and   his slave   know   the thinking
    of each other suffering.

This is within   my Fate;   it accords   with what should be,
This is within   my Fate;   it accords   with what should be.
I fear   yellow   dusk;   and   the moon   lighting   flowers
    on the terrace;
I feel   chilly,   miserable;   lie down   to sleep   in my
    clothes,
Too languid   to loosen   scented   girdle   of openwork
    silk gauze.

FIFTH MOON

During Fifth Moon comes Tuan Yang, the Day of
    South Principle;
During Fifth Moon comes Tuan Yang, the Day of
    South Principle.
Last year, I remember, we drank *hsiung huang* wine
    together,
When we had taken it, exhilaration transported,
    transported us.
Together we gazed at pomegranate flowers as they
    bloomed.

This day, how cold and dreary!
This day, how cold and dreary!
I do not hang a spirit charm of artemisia leaves,
    but wear a sprig of cedar.
This very year, this very season,
Are patterned on the Buddhist model of asceticism.

Alone I keep watch in empty bedroom,
Alone I keep watch in empty bedroom.
I sleep wrapped in my clothes, and going out into
    the dream-world, effect union with you.
Suddenly I come back to realm of waking;
I lie alone within the openwork red curtain.

Moon is shining on gauze-silk window-panes,
Moon is shining on gauze-silk window-panes.
Others are annoyed that nights are so short: I feel re-
    sentment that they are so long.
Do not sleep until hour of yellow dusk preceding
    dawn
When I hear cockerels chant their song.

SIXTH MOON

During Sixth Moon fiery heat is difficult to bear,
During Sixth Moon fiery heat is difficult to bear.

My good man has gone to war; my heart is the
reverse of care-free.
We have been separated, cut apart for half a year;
Nor have I seen a single letter, a writing of harmony
and love.

I take incense to burn before the Sainted Figure,
I take incense to burn before the Sainted Figure.
'Kuan Yin, Goddess of Mercy who saves the world
from bitterness, who relieves misery,
'Protect and hold him precious, bring him soon from
his journey.
'His slave will offer sacred books and cause them
to be printed.'

I question divining-slips, I implore the spirits;
I question divining-slips, I implore the spirits.
According to divining-slips, undisturbed peace should
be with him who travels.
I entreat bamboo-tallies hanging on the pillar:
'The separation of husband and wife shall be ended.'

Heart sinks; I sigh deeply,
Heart sinks; I sigh deeply.
I know this questioning of divining-slips, this
entreating of bamboo-tallies is all not true.
I believe the man who is away deceives me; he is
not faithful!
In the end bad luck will surely last.

SEVENTH MOON
Autumn stands in Seventh Moon skies,
Autumn stands in Seventh Moon skies,
For Oxherd and Weaving-Maid it is once more
a year.
When to-day sun rose from sea-mist they crossed
Silver River;

At   its setting   they   see   each other   once again.

This   day   they unite   in circle of marriage,
This   day   they unite   in circle of marriage.
At   clear   dawn   on   bright   morrow   they   return
        to either   side.
They are certainly   like   my   husband   and his Unworthy
        One,   whose
Love   and passion   are   snapped off,   scattered!

Affairs   in this world   do not   attain   perfection,
Affairs   in this world   do not   attain   perfection.
Spirits   and immortals   also   suffer   sorrows,   joys;
        separation,   union;
How   much more   we   people   of this   world!
Should   we not   have   the sorrow   of cutting apart,
        division?

I sleep   then   but do not   sleep   in peace,
I sleep   then   but do not   sleep   in peace.
Eyes   gazing   towards Heaven's   River,   I   say   these
        words:
'Weaving-Maid,   come   down   from your star   in Heaven;
'Let us suffer   the resentment of chilly solitude   to-
        gether.'

EIGHTH MOON
During   Eighth   Moon   is   Mid-Autumn,
During   Eighth   Moon   is   Mid-Autumn.
Crowds   of people,   who celebrate   harvest   moon,
        are, as they should be,   high   in   upper stories;
So too, am I,   my Lord's   slave;   but I endure   solitude,
        isolation,
My   eyebrows   are   often   wrinkled.

Wild geese   fly past   Southern   Pavilion,

Wild geese   fly past   Southern   Pavilion.
Golden   wind   blows in gusts,   blows in gusts;   cold as
ice,   cold as ice,   its sound the whirring of an arrow,
whirring of an arrow.
My   man   is   at   the frontier   passes;
Its   blowing   will   penetrate   his fighting   coat.

Melancholy   pervades   my   heart,
Melancholy   pervades   my   heart.
Heart   and mind   filled with thoughts   of my husband,
each   day   am anxious,   grieved.
Stealthily,   stealthily,   my gold buttons   loosen   on their
silk loops;
I know   therefore   that   my   body   is thinner.

This silent   solitude,   when   will it   cease?
This silent   solitude,   when   will it   cease?
Thoughts   and emotions   of a man   do not   flow   in
same   channels   as do those   of a woman;
Yet   it cannot,   must not be   that he   is tied in knot of
affection   to a new wife,
That doting on   fresh   flower   he   forgets   the old...

NINTH MOON
Day of Repeated   Yang Principle   falls in   Ninth   Moon,
Day of Repeated   Yang Principle   falls in   Ninth   Moon.
My good   man   went out   to war;   I have not   seen him
turn,   come back.
Circle   of our marriage   but completed,   we were suddenly
cut   apart.
Who   can become   inured   to this   bitterness?

My   eyes,   by their   watching,   are bored through,
My   eyes,   by their   watching,   are bored through.
Heat   has gone,   cold   has come,   to be united   in circle
of marriage   would be rapture.

Days grow shorter, nights grow longer,
Distracted thoughts and longings are not within
    my control.

Thinking of each other suffering is wearisome, is
    wearisome,
Thinking of each other suffering is wearisome, is
    wearisome.
ling tan, magic antidote from the Jade-Grey Sea,
    is not sufficient;
How is my illness to be cured
Unless I see him once again?

My fair face is not as it was before,
My fair face is not as it was before.
A flower denied rain and dew must also wither,
    die.
How much more the charm and beauty of a woman
If she see not her lover, her good man?

TENTH MOON

Tenth Moon, the Little Glowing Springtime,
Tenth Moon, the Little Glowing Springtime.
Yet Earth is frozen, skies are cold, snow of good
    fortune flies, flies.
My good man is at frontier passes;
Is he cold? is he hot? Not a soul enquires.

Hills are high; waters deep,
Hills are high; waters deep.
I suffer sorrow on your account; the flame of my
    spirit is being quenched.
If you have been forgetful of my passion
Will Heaven not be angered?

I remember the woman of long ago who went forth,

I remember the woman of long ago who went forth.
The Unworthy One of Mêng who sought her hus-
    band; everyone, everyone has heard of, knows
    about her;
Weeping at the Long Wall, she presented cold-
    weather clothes;
A thousand *li* she travelled with much exertion and
    distress.

That heart was like my heart,
That heart was like my heart.
Hearts and bowels of people nowadays do not com-
    pare with those of long ago.
If I should seek my good man
I fear people would utter fiery words of scorn.

ELEVENTH MOON
Eleventh Moon has come, is here,
Eleventh Moon has come, is here.
Dripping water becomes ice; snow flowers whirl,
    whirl.
I light a warm and friendly little hand-stove
To embrace instead of 'him who makes me submit.'

Grief has killed the many charms of this woman,
Grief has killed the many charms of this woman.
Who can accomplish with me union of love-pheasant,
    blending of firebird?
Fire in hand-stove is friendly; it warms, it warms,
But it is not like the wonder of 'him who makes me
    submit.'

Who is it who beats upon the door?
Who is it who beats upon the door?
It is the man who brings letters, calling: 'Elder
    sister, elder sister.'

I receive in my two   hands   that which comes,
A wrapping covering words of harmony and love.

I snap, and open the envelope,
I snap, and open the envelope.
Within   is   written   'My honored   wife   must   not
    weary   her heart;
'But behind   gate   and inner door   exert   thoughtful
    care;
'I strive,   must surely   arrive   at Year's   End.'

TWELFTH MOON

Twelfth   Moon   is   before   our eyes,
Twelfth   Moon   is   before   our eyes.
Last   night's   lamp   flower,   knotted   in five colors of
    happiness,   formed   a lotus blossom;
Magpies   of good fortune   called   *cha*   *cha*.
I think   it must be   that   we shall see   each other   once
    again.

Outside   door,   in market-place,   a hubbub,   a clamor!
Outside   door,   in market-place,   a hubbub,   a clamor!
My good   man   has returned   home;   dismounts   from
    horse;   leaves   saddle.
He   is   good,   he does not   break   faith;
He is   a true,   upright   son   of Han.

Once   again   broken   mirror   is round,
Once   again   broken   mirror   is round.
Not only   does my good   man   return,   come back   to
    house   and garden:
'Thinking   of each other   suffering'   has also   been   cut
    short
By   two-edged sword   from   Dragon   Spring.

Happiness,   delight,   cannot   be   expressed!

Happiness, delight, cannot be expressed!
Together within bed-curtains of transmuted gold, we
    confide our inmost thoughts.
A saying runs: 'Return from far distance
Is better than joy of new marriage.'

                       ☯

Officials, not being allowed to serve in their home districts,
carried out governmental work in various parts of the empire.
Their wives, often left in charge of the family home with its

many inhabitants, where births and deaths succeeded each other, became accustomed to authority and responsibility. A responsibility which could not be casually deputed. The wife, chief of the Yin principle, was essential to her position. In the *Record of Rites*, it is expressly stated that men shall not concern themselves with matters behind the doors and that women shall not concern themselves with those beyond the doors. There was as much to do within as without.

The young wife who became the mother of a son felt that destiny was fulfilled. Ancestral rites were provided for, and a potential official who, by his learning, might bring fame to the family lay in her arms. Now she was like the moon in the sky, everlasting. Having no son, she would resemble a comet flashing across the heavens. Her every effort was expended to bring up her son in a manner creditable to family and ancestors. Nor were her own children the sole care. Those of the husband's concubines were legitimate and looked upon as children of the *ti*, the legal wife; she was referred to by her husband's children, or the servants as *ti mu*, mother of the house. Probably this emphasis upon the wife as chief of the Yin principle accounts for the reverence and devotion shown by Chinese men throughout her life to the household mother, an indispensable link in the continuity of the clan.

Concubinage in China has been much misunderstood. It was a logical outgrowth of the family system and the social structure; by no means mere pandering to lust. Ancestors required male descendants. If one woman did not produce them, another should be given opportunity to do so. Furthermore an official required a companion when he left home to fulfill his duty at far-away posts. First Lady could not throw off the responsibilities to parents-in-law, to children, to the assembled household; a Second Lady generally accompanied the Master. Her position was legal, she could not be deserted, but no one suggested that hers was the position of wife. Various formalities were observed on her entrance to the household, but no betrothal contract was made nor did she ride in a red chair.

In the Imperial harem ladies were divided into definite classes. First came the consort, the Empress; then followed three concubines of the first rank, nine of the second, twenty-seven of the third, eighty-one of the fourth, and any number of lesser ladies.

In private households there were two grades of concubines: the first, those acquired with legal formality, and the second, those purchased — possibly from a brothel.

The *Record of Rites* gives rules in regard to lesser ladies:

> Therefore concubines, although old, if years have not overflowed five tens, must wait on Lord each fifth day. When about to do so shall purify self, rinsing mouth and bathing. Shall straighten dress and garments, comb hair, draw on fillet, lay broad hairpin across back of head, draw some hair into shape of a horn and brush dust from the remainder. Shall put on tasselled throat band and adjust shoestrings. In dress, garments, drinking, and eating, although a favorite concubine, she shall come after her superior. If wife be not there, concubine in waiting shall not venture to remain whole night with her Lord.[1]

Whether this form of polygamy made for happiness, or the contrary, is a debatable point. Doubtless jealousy often tore a household, but a position regularized is strong and ladies

[1] *Li Chi*, Vol. 5, Leaf 63.

of the side-chambers probably accepted their fate, for the most part, with grace.

The codes of different dynasties have divers rules regarding concubines. The Ming code, for instance, allowed but one. The Ch'ing code permitted an indefinite number. Liaison with a woman neither wife nor concubine is described as *yeh ho* — union in the wilds; children springing therefrom are illegitimate.

An important part of a wife's duty was connected with the ancestral sacrifices. To quote once more the *Record of Rites*:

> Lord and his wife join in presenting offerings to delight bright soul which, ascending, unites with Yang principle, as well as dark soul which, descending, unites with Yin principle. This is called union with those who are no more.[1]

Eigh terms describe the degrees of Maternal Relationship, besides those of natural mother, which were recognized: *provide-for mother*, she who has brought up a child not of her own household; *legal mother*, the relation in which a wife stands to children of her husband's concubines; *continue-on-the-duties mother*, the term for stepmother; *merciful mother*, relation of a concubine who brings up child of the wife; *married mother*, a child's own mother who after the death of the father has married again; *gone-out mother*, one who is divorced; *concubine mother*; and *milk mother*, one who gives the breast to an infant of the wife.[2]

[1] *Li Chi*, Vol. 4, Leaf 48.
[2] *Chinese Reader's Manual*, by W. F. Mayers.

☯

Slavery is reported from proto-historic days. The oracle bones found on the site of Anyang, capital of the Shang Dynasty, which reigned some fourteen hundred years before our era, mention slaves. If men were then enslaved it is more than probable that women shared the same fate. Succeeding dynasties recognized slavery. Under the Han at the beginning of our era it is reported that 'slave girls were kept in the seraglio, that they were taught to sing and dance as entertainers, and that women were employed as servants and as wet-nurses.'[1] The custom has persisted down the ages in a mild form, as far as women are concerned. Owners arrange the marriage of slaves who then attain freedom.

☯

Domestic discord — lute and lyre not being in accord — was not sufficient cause for divorce, but for the following seven reasons a man might put his wife away: barrenness, lasciviousness, jealousy, talkativeness, thieving, disobedience to her husband's parents, and leprosy. These conditions were, however, almost nullified by the provision that no woman might be divorced whose parents were not living to receive her back. Furthermore, no wife who had mourned three years for her parents-in-law, nor one who had borne poverty in a family which later became rich, could be put away. For three reasons a woman might demand her freedom from

[1] From a paper on 'Slavery under the Han Dynasty' read at a session of the American Oriental Society, Cleveland, April 1, 1937, by Mr. Martin Wilbur of the Field Museum, Chicago.

marriage bonds: if her husband had committed adultery; if he were condemned for some crime; and if he abandoned her for three years. Furthermore, in case of ill treatment she could appeal to her *mu chia* — mother's household — for assistance.

On the whole divorce in ancient China was rare, but a famous case is recorded in early Chinese history. Chiang T'ai-kung, who lived in the eleventh or twelfth century B.C. and who became adviser to the founder of the Chou Dynasty, was in his early youth not only poor but unlucky. Peddling and other undertakings were unsuccessful. His wife Madame Ma lost patience, demanded divorce, and married a carpenter. Later Chiang T'ai-kung, now a duke, passed through the town where she lived. Madame Ma regretting her haste urged that she be reinstated. In reply Chiang T'ai-kung asked her to throw a basin of water into the street. She did so. 'Get the water back,' said the duke, and when she stood impotent before the impossible task he continued: 'As you cannot take back water once thrown on the street, I cannot take back a wife once parted with.' Madame Ma, forthwith, committed suicide. Her former spouse, appalled at this happening, arranged that she be canonized as 'sweeper of the atmosphere.' Her figure, cut out in paper, shows a woman with a broom. It is kept in the women's rooms, hanging under the roof; is brought out when good weather is desired or when, in time of drought, rain is badly needed. Madame Ma's spirit is supposed to inhabit the star 'Brushwood Broom.'

Infidelity carried the severest penalty. In old days a husband had the right to kill an unfaithful wife and her lover. A well-known folksong describes such a case:

The Little Knife

I

Lady of the house, *ya!* is in her room, *ah!*
Is her heart not scorched with fear, *ah?!*
She calls aloud to him she adores:
'You must not come here, *ah!*'
My man knows all, he knows very, very well!
 Too-o ee-e, hoo-o ee-e; hoo-o ee-e, ya!
 Too-o ee-e, hoo-o ee-e; hoo-o ee-e, ya!
 Too-o ee-e, ya!
My man knows all, he knows very, very well!

II

Last night, *ya!* when it was late, *ah!*
I received a most distressing beating, *ya!*
In the clear dawn he rose early
And seized, and ground, his bright and shining knife,
 his bright and shining knife!
He seeks you and will take revenge! Oh how well he seeks!
 Too-o ee-e, hoo-o ee-e; hoo-o ee-e, ya!
 Too-o ee-e, hoo-o ee-e; hoo-o ee-e, ya!
He seeks you and will take revenge! Oh how well he seeks!

III

Your body is exhausted, *na!* breath of life is thin, *ya!*
How few your years,
That they should now be mourned, *ah!*
Your little life is difficult to save, oh
 very, very difficult to save.
 Too-o ee-e, hoo-o ee-e; hoo-o ee-e, ya!

Too-o ee-e, hoo-o ee-e; hoo-o ee-e, ya!
Too-o ee-e, hoo-o ee-e; hoo-o ee-e, ya!
Your little life is difficult to save, oh
very, very difficult to save!

IV

He whom she adored spoke, said, *ah!*
'Loveliest lady, you must hear me, *ah!*'
The hero Huang Tsao killed men,
Even unto one hundred times ten thousand, *na!*
I need not fear that killing-men bright knife,
that killing-men bright knife,
Too-o ee-e, hoo-o ee-e; hoo-o ee-e, ya!
Too-o ee-e, hoo-o ee-e; hoo-o ee-e, ya!
Too-o ee-e, ya!
I need not fear that killing-men bright knife,
that killing-men bright knife!

V

Man's life, *ya!* is but a hundred years, *ah!*
At the end, it must meet death, *ah!*
That tree is old,
Its leaves withered, faded, *ah!*
My life it will return to the World of Shadows soon,
to the World of Shadows soon.
Too-o ee-e, hoo-o ee-e; hoo-o ee-e, ya!
Too-o ee-e, hoo-o ee-e; hoo-o ee-e, ya!
Too-o ee-e, ya!
And I shall be a ghost, a charming, clever ghost,
a clever, charming ghost!

☯

The law in regard to woman's property was simple — she
had none. No inheritance was hers; she shared the common

purse of her husband's family. From this circumstance has risen the famous Chinese category *san ts'ung*. *San* means 'three'; the word *ts'ung* is generally translated as 'obedience.' 'Dependence' is a better rendering. A woman was thrice dependent: on her father, on her husband, on her son. In my experience, although at the mercy of her mother-in-law's whims, there is very little 'obedience' on the part of Chinese women to their men-folk whom they seem to manage with great efficiency. In fact men often tremble before their wives and faced with some determined old lady are helpless. Among country folk it is a well-known fact that an old woman is at the bottom of every row, and is often found to be implacable. In talking once with a Japanese gentleman regarding women of different countries and their characteristics, I mentioned the Chinese. An expression of terror came over his face. 'But they,' he said, 'are very fierce.'

Widows, although they sometimes did so, were not supposed to remarry. The countryside is dotted with fine stone arches erected in honor of chaste ladies who scorned new ties, and only waited for death to follow their husbands to the Yellow Springs. Continence on the part of widows has been lauded since proto-historic days. An ode in the *Classic of Poetry* [1] reads:

CYPRESS-WOOD BOAT

There floated boat of cypress wood,
There in centre of river.

[1] *Classic of Poetry*, Part I, Book IV, Ode 1. *The Odes of Yung* Text, as given by Legge; translation, my own.

Hair   on his forehead,   dressed   in two filial tufts,
Truly,   he was   my mate!
Until   death,   I swear it,   will have   no other.
Mother,   *ah!*   Heaven,   *ah!*
Do you   not believe me   —   *ah!*

There   floated   boat   of cypress wood,
There   beside   river-bank.
Hair   on his forehead,   dressed   in two filial tufts,
Truly,   he was   my only one!
Until   death,   I swear it,   will not   commit the evil act.
Mother,   *ah!*   Heaven,   *ah!*
Do you   not believe me   —   *ah!*

MARRIAGE: NOW

Days, Moons, go beyond, pass away. Futile to mourn, to grieve.

The Classic of Writings

MANY Chinese of the older generation, bewildered, regret the
passing of the indigenous system which has served their
country for three millennia and more. Its passing was inevitable. Its virtues and its shortcomings were unsuited to international intercourse — in this age unavoidable.   World
shrinkage compels fraternization. The system, with its virtues
and its shortcomings, was condemned in an Imperial Edict
issued, September, 1905. It crumbled during the succeeding
years and new ways slowly crystallized. The Kuomintang
Government came to power in 1927, establishing its capital at Nanking, and China now lives under the legal code it
promulgated on December 26, 1930, and brought into force
May 5, 1931.

Laws regarding the position of women have been basically
altered. On paper, she is on an equality with men. She

shares the family inheritance; is, therefore, no longer subject to the Three Dependences earlier mentioned — those to father, to husband, to son. As a matter of fact the new laws are rather hard on men. Mr. Wang, a Chinese friend of mine, talked eloquently on the subject, declaring that whereas a son is still bound to support his parents throughout their lives, a daughter, although she now shares in the family wealth, does not share this responsibility. The new code allows couples to decide how they will manage their respective properties, in fact it enters into details too numerous to specify. The crux of the matter is that, theoretically, woman has become a legal individual: she is not, to-day, mere daughter, wife, or mother.

Betrothal and marriage are no longer a conventional union of two families, but are contracts freely entered into by individuals. This is not to say that marriages, according to old custom, do not take place. They are many, but marriages in new styles increase daily. Betrothal is still regarded as all-important. The Chinese say: 'When tender stamens begin to unfold, the wasp, a go-between, comes to enquire.' It is now entered into with the consent of youth and maiden; the code, however, cites nine provisions permitting its dissolution.[1] Furthermore it provides that, while no engagement shall be fulfilled under constraint, the individual who lightly breaks such contract shall pay an indemnity. Minimum age for marriage, which has varied during the centuries — under the last dynasty it was sixteen for the man and fourteen for the girl — is now set at eighteen and sixteen respectively. Betrothal can take place earlier.

Details in regard to modern wedding ceremonies are so

[1] *La Femme dans la Société Chinoise,* by Wang Ch'ang-pao.

varied that generalization is impossible. A few weddings are completely foreign in style — smart brides, clad in white satin, followed by pages and bridesmaids, sweep up the aisles of churches to plight their troth. They are showered with confetti and wound in paper ribbons at wedding receptions.

Country girls marry in accordance with ancient custom and in place of the red silk veil, worn formerly, put on smoked glasses, thus preserving their modesty. Country people are still apt to spend big sums on the weddings of their sons. In 1934 a youth in my employ, who earned eighteen Chinese dollars a month, was married. His people, landowners in a near-by village, feasted their friends from far and near. I, who happened to be in hospital, received a charmingly arranged selection of delicacies. The sum expended by the family, I was informed, exceeded twelve hundred Chinese dollars. Yet their house was a humble edifice with a mud floor.

A Japanese domestic science research bureau has assembled some interesting statistics in regard to wedding expenses in different countries. A man of moderate income spends, of his annual income: in Great Britain, France, and Germany one per cent; in the United States two per cent; in Italy four, Spain seven, Russia eight; Japan fifteen to twenty-five, and China twenty-five to thirty per cent.

During the last three years the New Life Movement, inaugurated and actively sponsored by Generalissimo and Mrs. Chiang Kai-shih, has, following the examples of Italy and Germany, encouraged mass marriages. The first ceremony on these lines took place in Hangchow on March 15, 1935, nine couples participating, a witness to the ceremony being a Mr. Lee Fong-hsiao, reputed to be one hundred and thirteen years of age. The aura of his longevity enveloped brides and grooms.

On April 3 of the same year, fifty-seven couples were married before Mayor General Wu Teh-chên at the magnificent new Civic Centre of Greater Shanghai. A brass band played the bridal march from 'Lohengrin' and ten thousand people pressed against police cordons to catch a glimpse of the wedding couples. The brides, carrying bouquets, were dressed in pale pink, with pale pink caplike veils. They proceeded in a long line to meet the grooms who were clad in long blue robes, and short black jackets each decorated with a scarlet badge. Brides filed from the west of the building, grooms from the east, marched around the circular driveway, and up the white stone steps into the great hall. Here on a stage, decorated in scarlet and gold, where stood two immense red candles embossed with Chinese characters reading 'Harmony for One Hundred Years,' waited the witnesses. Two brides and two grooms at a time, coming from left and right simultaneously, mounted the stage, stood before a bas-relief of Doctor Sun Yat-sen, over which the Kuomintang and National flags were crossed, and awaited directions. The announcer indicated that they bow: three times to the flag and the portrait of Doctor Sun, twice to each other, and once to the witnesses. Each couple then received a wedding certificate and a silver crescent engraved with plum blossoms — a gift from the Mayor — and bowing once more, left the stage. When the ceremony had been repeated the necessary number of times brides and grooms, together now, were led from the hall by lantern-bearers.

Various ideas lie behind the adoption of this method, which is rapidly gaining in popularity. A degree of standardization is desirable; the changing of old customs made wedding ceremonies too various. Mass marriages cost about twenty dollars a couple; applicants must be over twenty years old, must pay five dollars for registration, and must appear in simple clothing. Applications are accompanied by six photographs of those who desire passports to matrimony. After an investigation, lasting two weeks, the Social Affairs Bureau notifies applicants whether or not they may proceed with wedding plans.

Naturally those who can afford private ceremonies prefer to have them, the rich will continue on their individual way; but for teachers, students, and people of lesser income Mass Marriage is convenient.

In modern marriage it is necessary only to declare intention and to sign a paper before two witnesses; therefore people of very simple tastes have no ceremony when they decide to wed.

The simplicity, itself, of modern marriage is not very shocking to Chinese, who have always regarded matrimony as a social and religious act entered into by two families, an act with which the law has but little concern. No banns, or license, have been required. In case of later dispute appeal was and is made to the written betrothal contract. Whether or not people of the old school regret the festivities formerly connected with weddings is another question. A certain glamour will doubtless leave the countryside when glittering bridal chairs no more thread their way between fields of jade-green rice.

☯

A revolutionary step taken by many modern couples is their decision to leave the family household. Formerly each son brought home his bride, who tenderly served her mother-in-law. His children were born in the shadow of the family and all shared a common purse. If the son left home to study or to perform governmental work he knew that wife and children were cared for. Husbands and wives of the present generation in many cases prefer homes of their own. A Western-educated Chinese mother has definite ideas regarding the diet, upbringing, and discipline of children. Ideas widely different from those held by an old-fashioned mother-in-law.

In the realm of fiction Miss Buck's heart-rending story 'The First Wife' perfectly describes a situation by no means rare. Each individual is vividly characterized; each behaves with utter sincerity; the sequence of events is logically inevitable; the result — grim tragedy. 'The Old Mother,' another story in the same book, shows the difficulty, of fusing new ideas with old, from another angle. There is much unavoidable pathos in the life of changing China.

Concubinage is no longer legal. It is impossible for anyone who has lived in a strictly monogamous society to realize the revolutionary effect of those five words. Since proto-historic days concubines have been accepted. Now the code ignores their existence, and a wife, if she so chooses, may sue her husband for adultery in case he takes a second lady.

Chinese women demand sex equality in law and in morals, declaring that they will tolerate no 'double standard.' Prophecy is futile but, considering the influence they wield, it is safe to assume that matters will eventually shape themselves in accordance with the women's wishes, especially as, under the new code, only the children of a wife are recognized as legitimate, and only they may inherit property.

Puzzling, difficult situations arise. Article 239 of the Chinese criminal code lists adultery — as do the codes of Austria, Germany, and Switzerland — as crime. Great are struggles over the provisions and revisions of this article. In 1935 a certain Mu Sah-men gave a radio talk in Great Britain which perfectly describes the present situation. It reads in part as follows:

> ... The provision adds a further clause saying, 'Either spouse may apply for a divorce provided the other spouse has committed bigamy.' Does this mean that there shall be no concubinage? Does this mean that a man may no longer take another woman for his pleasure without danger of giving legal grounds of divorce to his first wife? That time-sanctioned social pattern. What is to become of it? Can one simply say, 'And on the third day the new law said there shall be no more concubinage, and there was none'? Our answer is that life does not evolve by this method of lightning change.
>
> The result is that we now find ourselves in a period of transition. This is a period in which there is no right, and yet, there is no wrong. One reads of the struggle everywhere. In the newspaper, there are daily stories; all contemporary novels deal with some phases of it; one sees it in the movies; school girls and boys ponder on it while their parents try to decide what they themselves should do. There is the new. There is the old. The conflict.

A story will illustrate the point; the story of a woman who came to the office of a public women's organization which gives legal advice free to all women who seek to know their rights. This is the woman's problem: Mr. and Mrs. Chang had been married twenty years when Mr. Chang took a concubine. This occurred two years ago. Since then their family life has been unhappy. Now the wife asks the lawyer to get rid of the concubine for her since the new law does not provide for concubinage. In order to help the woman, the lawyer agreed to talk over the matter with other parties concerned to try and bring a peaceful adjustment to this family conflict.

Mr. Chang was called to the office. He told the lawyer that when he took his concubine two years ago he did it with his wife's approval. At that time he thought he was following good social custom. He was ill and needed someone to care for him. His wife was living in another province and unwilling to move to his place of employment. He secured her approval for taking a concubine, and took the concubine by a regular process of buying her some clothes and giving her some money. This was arranged through a middle man.

The concubine was then called to the office of the lawyer for an interview. She told the lawyer that her present rôle of concubine was arranged for her by her mother because of the fact that her own family were extremely poor. Mr. Chang gave her eighty dollars to make clothes and sent an amah and a richshaw to take her to his home. Now she does not wish to have a divorce from him. She feels that the process was legal according to all social custom.

What can a lawyer say to a situation such as this? What can bring happiness and understanding? Can happiness possibly grow out of this? Under the old law the husband has a right to have a concubine, particularly since his wife was not willing to go where he was working when he needed her. Under the old custom the wife's approval would seal the sanctity of such an arrangement. Under old tradition he took her according to approved practices. Conflicts might have occurred in his family, but they would surely have been in whispered terms, but not in an open public courtroom.

Not so under the new. The first wife has heard of this new freedom of women. She is not exactly certain what is involved in this freedom, but she plans now to use it to bring to her and to her children happiness. The concubine has also heard something of this new talk of freedom, and wishes to use it to bring to herself the same happiness. The husband stands perplexed amidst the bantered words of 'freedom,' 'women's rights,' 'a new day for women.' He feels that his wife is unreasonable to bring such a personal matter before the public lawyer. He says that though she calls herself new she is really feudal. He alleges that she would be willing to have a concubine in the home, but that she wishes the concubine to be menial and act as a servant. This is admitted by the wife, for she says that a proper concubine ought to know her place.

What can be the decision of the lawyer? Shall the first wife seek a divorce? She does not wish to be divorced from her husband and has no home to which she can go when she is granted divorce. Shall the concubine be declared to have an illegal relationship with the husband? If so, she also has no other home to which she may go. Shall the concubine follow the conventional status provided by the past? This she is unwilling to do. Shall two wives of equal rank be married to one man? Only miserable conflict can result from such a plan. Through the struggle the husband shakes his head and wonders why there is such conflict: people have always had concubines, he needed a concubine when he was ill. Is the husband living in adultery because there is not now legal provision for concubinage? Is the concubine an adulteress? These are the problems faced by the judge, the husband, the wife, the concubine.

Such problems are inevitable. Confusion arises. Concubinage becomes adultery. Wives threaten husbands as criminals who commit the offence of following social tradition. The concubine who enters in good faith a relationship becomes liable to public censure. This new freedom sought so eagerly by the wife may now become a burden to her. The husband may begin to taste the luxury of freedom and threaten a wife whom he wishes to become rid of until she is forced to divorce him to escape cruelty.

A custom of centuries will not be made into a new way of marriage relationship until a painful period of 'transition' has been passed. Many husbands, many wives, and many concubines will have to suffer the crushing burden of no right and no wrong until a new right and a new wrong has emerged into conventionalized concepts. Some human beings will abuse the efforts to find new ways of life. Some will be bruised. Those who are emerging must bear the burden of that change.

Slavery also has been pronounced illegal. It will be extremely difficult to enforce laws against this rooted custom. In time of famine mouths are too many. Parents sell little girls to keep them alive. Evil men moreover lurk in the streets of country towns and villages, lure little girls with toys and sweetmeats, sweep them away to big cities, and sell them to those who buy domestics or to brothels. Many rescue homes for such children have been founded by the benevolent; the Anti-Kidnapping Society has done much to curb the evil; and the death penalty is now prescribed for kidnappers; nevertheless slavery exists, and must continue its existence until the economic situation improves and active public opinion, especially on the part of women, decrees abolition.

🌑

Divorce is now the simplest matter imaginable and, among the smart set, fashionable. The other day I met a Chinese lady and asked for news of our mutual friends in the Middle Country. She said: 'Oh, yes. So-and-so has got her divorce, she now has a job under the Government. You remember so-and-so?' — mentioning a charming young thing. 'She and so-and-so fell in love with each other. He has several children, you know, but she divorced her husband and made him divorce his wife. The wife was heart-broken; she knelt before him, she wept, she said, "What am I to do? I am forty years old. No one wants me." She begged him to reconsider. He would not. Yes, it is very sad.'

The obstructive ideas, the serious reasons, the consultation with family chiefs required in old days are no more; all now necessary is the agreement of man and woman concerned. They sign a document before two witnesses — and desires of the heart are satisfied. In principle, children belong to their father, but arrangements to suit different cases are made. A woman keeps her own property and a man assumes certain financial responsibilities; again, different cases receive different treatment.

🌑

Will new attitudes of mind eventually destroy the ancient feeling which regarded the marriage rite as predestined union of definite entities representing the principles Yin and Yang? Is such destruction inevitable? Who can say?

In modern China cases of deep devotion to a man unknown are still reported. I heard of one such in 1935: The betrothed of Han Kuei-ching, daughter of a well-to-do family in Shensi, disappeared. Her father urged that she marry another, but Kuei-ching, feeling that the childhood engagement was binding, resigned her post as teacher in a primary school and set out to find Sun Tê-fu, the betrothed whom she had never seen. Attended by an old man-servant, she searched, eight years, in villages, hamlets, and towns. Finally in Tsinan, Shantung Province, Sun Tê-fu was found living as a beggar in a grass-roofed hut. My informant remarked, 'There was no time to tell all the thick and the thin through which she had gone in the eight years; right away she demanded that marriage vows be made.' Sun Tê-fu, a coolie dressed in rags, protested that she should not marry a pauper but Kuei-ching, selling clothing to provide necessary expenses, insisted that there be no delay — nor was there.

Suicide, too, after a husband's death is no thing of the past. In February, 1935, a woman of twenty-seven, secondary wife of Lu Ti-ping, Chairman of the Chêkiang Provincial Government, in despair at her husband's death, threw herself from a high terrace with fatal result. She left a life that was full and sweet: not only had she a son and daughter but she was six months pregnant. More than a hundred leading officials urged the National Government to grant her posthumous honors in recognition of her loyalty to Lu Ti-ping. First Lady also contemplated suicide but was prevented from carrying out her intention by members of the household who caught her by the feet as she was about to take the fatal plunge. It would be interesting to know whether, feeling that the defunct chairman should have company in the Shadow World, the household acquiesced in the leap of Second Lady. The white-clad women seeking death high on a gaze-at-the-moon terrace make a wonderful picture.

In the minds of most Chinese the nearness of Yin World is ever present. They believe, as do those interested in Western psychical research, that for a period, after leaving its earthly envelope, the soul hovers near-by. Intensely logical, the Chinese carry this belief to its ultimate conclusion, and attempt to provide the disembodied soul with things that it may need. In the *Record of Rites* it is written:

> Son of Kung (Confucius) said: 'To tend the dead as if they were dead and gone is not humane: this cannot be done. To tend the dead as if they were still living is not sensible: this cannot be done. That is why bamboo vessels are not perfected for use; earthenware vessels are not fit to be carved; lutes and lyres although strung are not evenly strung; flutes and pandean pipes are not fit to be attuned. Bells there shall be and musical stones but without crossbeams or deer-headed dragon supports. Such are called apparent vessels. The spirits apprehend.'

Near the Grass Hut [1] in Shanghai there stands Jade Buddha Temple, where masses for the dead are held and offerings to spirits are frequently made. The present-day custom is to make these of paper, built up on fine reed supports. The bamboo, earthenware, and other funerary articles mentioned in the *Record of Rites* are no longer used. Such objects to-day, made with amazing skill, are replicas of things in modern use. The window of the shop for Yin World furnishings — it stands opposite the temple — is startling in its realism.

[1] Cf. *A Chinese Mirror*, by Florence Ayscough, Chap. I.

One March day, 1935, the priests of Jade Buddha Temple, with whom I am on friendly terms, sent a message to say that a widow whose husband had died some fortnight earlier was about to offer, by means of fire, a furnished house for the use of his soul. Did I care to see the ceremony? I cared very much to do so, and hurried to the Temple court.

There stood a paper house, large enough to walk about in, perfect in every detail. Outside the great gate waited a jinrickshaw for the master's use. Inside the house the guest hall was charming with table, flower vases, pictures; the library had telephone and radio; the bedroom contained curtained bed, chairs, wardrobe, chest of drawers; the kitchen had stove, meat-block, chopper; the bathroom was modern and complete. At the front door stood a White Russian watchman, such as rich Chinese employ; all was cunningly fashioned from paper. The widow, a serious, middle-aged woman immersed in her preparations, inspected every detail, sending to the Shadow-World furniture shop for this extra article and that. A beautiful clock was one addition, a little hot water bottle which she carefully placed in the bed being the final perfection. She looked gravely at the complete erection. Satisfied with the furnishings, she took handful after handful of paper money, spreading it generously in every possible nook: on the bed, on the floors, in drawers, all over the courtyard. In Yin World her husband's soul should lack nothing that spirit money could buy.

All was ready. Priests wearing grey robes and red overmantles, followed by the widow, filed slowly around the house. The leader purified the air, sprinkling water with a little twig of leaves. Forming a group they all recited a sutra. This completed, straw spread around the foundations of the dwelling was lighted. Swish! With incredible swiftness the edifice blazed. Flames sprang up, licked the walls, consumed the roof, destroyed the furnishings. In the turn of a hand all was gone. The widow remained quite still, on her face an expression of intense concentration. In spirit she stood in Yin World sharing with her husband his joy at her gifts. To her, the ceremony was of deep spiritual significance.

EDUCATION: THEN AND NOW

Human beings at birth naturally good;
Natures much the same, habits widely different;
If, foolishly, no teaching, nature deteriorates;
Right way in teaching, attention to thoroughness.
The Three Character Classic

IN CHINA the twentieth century dawned on a land unprovided, as far as its own Government was concerned, with educational establishments for women. Ladies within the baton-door were schooled, in the domestic arts, by their mothers and the women around them. Mental training, except to a group in the smallest minority, was given by means of example and precept. The lives of worthy daughters, wives, and mothers were held up as 'patterns.' In Chinese belief, human nature, good to start with, should develop on right lines as the natures of great people have developed; therefore it was considered important to know about people of virtue.

The idea of a Pattern runs throughout Chinese thought; Confucius was the comprehensive model on which men tried for over two thousand years to form themselves; since 1912 Sun Yat-sen has largely taken his place. The Son of Heaven on his Imperial Throne was also regarded as a Pattern. Did he not behave according to the accepted standard of kingly conduct he was supposed to abdicate, and has frequently done so. Furthermore, many many 'detailed models,' if I may so express myself, exist. The land is covered with shrines to men who represent some outstanding virtue. Kuan Yü and the patriot Yo Fei are Patron Saints of bravery; the great Yü personifies the ideal official, and so on.

Memories of women are enshrined in books. Hundreds of examples are cited of women whose conduct is worthy of emulation. Indeed the word 'emulation' may be described as the cornerstone of Education in ancient China. Best known among books on women is the *Lieh Nü Chuan — Series of Women's Biographies* — first arranged by Liu Hsiang in the first century of our era. This has been continually added to, re-arranged, and taught from. There is also the *Kuei Fan — Within the Baton-Door Standards* — which, more concise than the *Lieh Nü Chuan*, contains a number of biographies. These are subdivided into classes: those which illustrate the Way of Maidens, the Way of Sisters-in-Law, the Way of Wives, of Mothers, and so on. An interesting point to be noted is that no woman, however famous for beauty and charm, is admitted to this pantheon unless her conduct be above reproach, unless her chastity and devotion secure her a right to pass these portals of fame. Books about the One Hundred Beauties have been written, many ladies fair and frail are celebrated in stories and in verse, but their names are never mentioned within the pages of the *Lieh Nü Chuan* or the *Kuei Fan*.

The biographies recorded have been of immense importance, psychologically, in forming the lives of Chinese women. I have, therefore, as a Postlude to this book, summarized and given extracts from a revision of the *Kuei Fan* published under the Ming Dynasty. The copy I have used comes from an

edition privately reprinted, in memory of his wife, by Li
Hsi-shun during the sixteenth year of the Republic; that is,
in 1927, only ten short years ago, but before the establishment of the Kuomintang at Nanking. There has been a great
change since then. It is doubtful whether, in this era of
streamline education, Chinese gentlemen would be found to
whom the value of ancient virtues would appeal sufficiently
to induce them to order, to-day, such a reprint.

The biographies, naïve, didactic, and highly moral, are accompanied by illustrations, equally naïve and carefully detailed. Eye helped ear in the tuition of ladies within the
baton-door.

In addition to the *Lieh Nü Chuan* and the *Kuei Fan* there was
another and more important work used in connection with
women's education, written by the great Pan Chao instruc-
tress to the Empress Têng during the first century of the
Christian era. This, called *Nü Chieh — Precepts for Women —*
I have translated in connection with Pan Chao's life, given
below. She, an historian and a great scholar, urged that
women study, but did not suggest identical instruction for
men and women.

Progressives of the late eighteen-nineties such as Liang
Ch'i-ch'ao, Tsai Yüan-pei, and Kung-Kuang-yin urged that
women be given learning, that they be taught at least the rudi-
ments of domestic science. Miss Tsêng, a granddaughter of the
famous official Tsêng Kuo-fan, opened a school for girls in
Chang-sha and, denying herself the joys of marriage and
motherhood, devoted her life to teaching. Mission schools
of various types, both Roman Catholic and Protestant,
existed, and statistics, of 1902, show that between four and
five thousand girls were then enrolled as students under

班倢伃

missionary guidance. Roman Catholic schools, for girls, are reported as early as A.D. 1800.

The rôle played by Protestant missionaries in the intellectual 'opening' of China cannot be overestimated. In talking once with a British diplomat I remarked, 'Do you not agree with me in thinking that Protestant missionaries have materially hastened the Revolution?' 'I would go much further,' he replied. 'In my opinion *American* missionaries have been the one most potent factor in bringing about the Revolution.' By the word 'Revolution' a complete change in social structure must be understood. Protestant missionaries, frequently married men and women, taught and exemplified Western ideals of home life. They believed that men and women should be friends, and that boys and girls should play together. Amazing! Horrifying!

Early recruits for mission schools were drawn principally from the poorer classes, the little girls, especially, being for the most part unwanted entities in families where mouths were disproportionate in ratio to rice-bowls.

A quaint oil print, of 1846, exists in the Chater Collection, Hongkong, showing the first Christian boarding-school for women of 'The Society for Promoting Female Education in the East.' The teacher, an old man, sits at a square table. On either side, perched on uncompromising stools, are Ati and Kit, young Chinese women brought from Java by Miss Aldersey, the headmistress. She herself, dressed in Chinese robes, is shown in the foreground of the picture holding a baby in her arms. The other girls, on benches, are placed in demure rows behind long tables.

The educational plan suggested in 1902 — after the distressing defeat by Japan in 1895, and the tragic Boxer Rebellion of 1900 — which combined to buffet Chinese officialdom into a realization that change was essential — made no provision for women's study. A year later came certain revisions in the plan; there was mention of 'unified kindergarten and home education'; a passage read: 'Kindergartens are to supplement home education, home education shall embrace education for women.' During the next few years, especially near the Treaty Ports, privately financed schools for girls increased. By 1905 the Government arranged a program which comprised attention to the domestic arts, for women's studies. In 1907, the year Ch'iu Chin, whose story I give below, was beheaded, an epochal event occurred. The Board of Education issued a series of thirty-six regulations governing girls' normal schools, and twenty-six governing girls' elementary schools. For the first time the existence of women in the general scheme of national education was recognized.

By curious contradiction, in this same year, when their primary education was first recognized, a few girls were allowed to take part in the Kiangsu Provincial Government examination and were sent to study in the United States.

Autumn of 1911 saw the fall of the Manchu Dynasty, alien in race, alien to modern ways of thinking — so far at least as those in power were concerned. Had the tragic Emperor Kuang Hsü been allowed to tread the pathway of reform, as he wished to do, history might have followed a very different course. He, poor wraith, had been swept from actual power in 1898, when his aunt the redoubtable Empress Dowager Tzŭ Hsi had resumed the control of national affairs which had been hers for many years. In 1908 he and she both mounted the dragon and ascended on high, leaving the throne to a child of four supported by regents. Matters seemed hopeless.

A few years later people cried 'Down with the Manchus' and swaying to popular will, as dynasties have ever been supposed to do, the Manchus abdicated.

On January 1, 1912, Sun Yat-sen, whose life had been given to furtherance of Republican ideals, was able to announce to the spirit of Hung Wu, the first Ming Emperor, whose body lay in a crumbling tomb on Purple Mountain, that aliens had been swept from the Dragon Throne. Sun Yat-sen, although elected Provisional President of the new Republic did not hold office long. In truly Chinese spirit of compromise he yielded the presidential seat to Yüan Shih-kai.

Years of struggle ensued. Not until after his death did Sun Yat-sen come into his own — many say that his ideals are not yet carried out. He, however, now spoken of as Chung Shan, Central Mountain, is regarded as the Nation's pivot.[1] His portrait hangs in every school and assembly room, the people bow before it as, formerly, they bowed before the Tablet of Confucius. His tomb, a magnificent structure comprising several buildings of white marble with blue-tiled roofs, is reached by an endless flight of steps, leading up Purple Mountain, to a site near the rose-red hall of death, where lies Hung Wu. A white stone tumulus adjoins the topmost building; under its curved top lie the body and the effigy of Sun Yat-sen.

I have made this long digression into current history because the present-day position of Chinese women is largely the result of Sun Yat-sen's teaching. He believed in equal treatment of the sexes. From the day of its founding, the

[1] September 1, 1937. As this book is in press, newspapers report that in North China the Japanese order all pictures of Doctor Sun Yat-sen to be burned.

Republic of China — if one may personify so vast an entity — has passed one ordinance after another in favor of this equality.

The year 1912 was a turning-point. Until that time the conception of women's education, although it had widened greatly, was that it should make her a good mother and housewife and, possibly, a teacher to train small children. In 1912 she began to be looked on as an individual, as an independent person, who had not only the capacity, but also the right, to develop her talents. Secondary education gained serious consideration from the Government, which introduced regulations regarding middle schools for girls. The period of tuition, four years, was the same as that for boys; the curriculum differed slightly, courses in home management and child care being offered. Popular interest in young women's education was great, even more middle schools for their use being opened by private individuals than by the Government.

The year 1918, when the Teachers' College for Women opened its doors in Peking, saw another step towards higher education. The student movement of 1919 gave a further spur in this direction. Many women took an active part in its development and demanded equality of opportunity in social, political, and educational fields. By 1920 a number of leading universities, both government and private, admitted women on equal footing with men. This occurred only thirteen years after the idea of women's schooling first entered the governmental mind!

In a short time universities and colleges with a few exceptions became co-educational and now higher education, in all its branches, is accessible to women. Nor did they have a struggle to obtain these advantages. Once accepted, the idea that their sisters should share their learning was enthusiastically furthered by men in China. In this the women of China have been fortunate, and in a few years reached a stage which cost women of the West a century of struggle.

That women appreciate the advantages is shown by a few statistics. The Chinese National Association for Advancement of Education states: In 1906, 468,220 students were enrolled in non-missionary schools. Among them 306 (0.07 per cent) were women. In 1916, 172,724 girls (4.35 per cent) were numbered among 3,974,454 students; in 1922, the figures had risen to 417,820 females (6.32 per cent) among 6,615,772 students.

In the years 1931–32 the percentage of women students in colleges and universities was 11.75 per cent. In 1933–34 the proportion had risen to 13.3 per cent; that is, out of a total of 42,933 students in government colleges and universities 5,899 were women.

Four colleges, alone, are for women only: Gin Ling College, Nanking; Hwa Nan College (Methodist), Foochow; Women's Christian Medical College, West Gate, Shanghai; Government Normal College for Women, Tientsin.

The Ministry of Education reported in 1932 on the proportion of females in different kinds of schools:

	Totals	Females	Per cent Females
Kindergarten	43,072	18,274	42.43
Elementary schools	12,179,994	1,827,807	15.01
Secondary schools	547,207	103,055	18.83
Universities	44,167	5,180	11.75

As in other parts of the world, people in China are beginning to find that education of their daughters is a wise economic measure; that, from a financial point of view, education is a sound investment.

Among the institutions for higher learning with a Christian background, Gin Ling College for women, Nanking, is perhaps the most striking. The buildings, in modified Chinese palace style adapted to modern needs, are situated in a beautiful campus. Opened in 1915 with nine students, the college now houses between two and three hundred eager young women who tread the road of higher learning. The President, Doctor Wu Yi-fang, is a striking example of the alert, twentieth-century Chinese woman whose advice is asked on every hand, whose opinion on national, as well as administrative affairs, carries weight.

Provision is even being made in the mass education movement, now seething in the rural districts, to instruct women of the farming and laboring classes. Experimental stations of Ting Hsien — established by Doctor James Yen — and of Tsing Ho, the Rural Service of the Y.W.C.A., the varied projects of the Kiangsu College of Education, are all active in forming clubs and schools. Mothers' clubs, girls' clubs, adult schools, women's schools, training classes for manual work and house economics, now thrive in the tiny hamlets of the Central Flowery State. The people realize that to make women's education a national affair it must spread among the laboring classes, and penetrate farming districts.

I have mentioned mass education. What does the term mean? Mr. George Shepherd, who works in connection with education, replies: 'It is a collection of scattered projects operated by individuals, provinces, and branches of the National Government, all hammering rivets into China's two weakest links: illiteracy and ignorance of national affairs. The unity of all these projects comes firstly from their common purpose, secondly from their exchange of teaching materials, and thirdly from the training of leaders in the older centres to go out as advisers to each new undertaking.'

A late development is the Little Teacher Movement introduced by Doctor T'ao Chi-hsing, a colleague of Doctor Hu Shih and other intellectual leaders. His mother, a charming old lady, was at the age of fifty-seven still illiterate. In a modern establishment this fact was distressing. Doctor T'ao's little son of six had completed the First Reader in a primary school and one day, in 1924, Doctor T'ao suggested that he teach his grandmother, not to suck the proverbial egg, but to read. The child did so. In sixteen days she was able to read a simple letter and in thirty days she had conquered the First Reader. From this beginning a veritable snowball movement has taken place. On every hand children pass on to adults the lessons which they themselves learn at school.

Less academic education is provided for women in the health stations. The Nanking Municipal Health Bureau has opened classes to 'impart common knowledge of public health, and household sanitation, the studying of suitable methods for bringing up children, the building up of good habits, and other important problems relating to home economics. The academic term is set at six months, class hours are scheduled from 2 to 4 o'clock on Saturday afternoons only, amounting to a total of 54 hours for the whole term. Aside from class work, laboratory practice is also emphasized.

'All women with scholastic standing akin to that of Higher Primary School or Junior Middle School, whether married or not, are eligible to join such classes. Aside from paying a guarantee fund of five dollars, no tuition will be charged.'

On every hand, in every way China is struggling with the

monster illiteracy, nor will her women be the last to deal this
monster its death-blow.

PROFESSIONS: THEN

IN THE light of future development, it seems anachronistic
to speak of 'professions' in connection with Chinese women of
prerevolutionary days. The three *ku* — a term of female
address — and the six *p'o* — dames or crones — were recognized. Such were *ni ku*, the Buddhist nun; *tao ku*, the Taoist
nun; *kua ku*, the female professor of divination; *ya p'o*, the
procuress; *mei p'o*, the marriage go-between; *shih p'o*, the
female professor of spiritual manifestations; *ch'ien p'o*, the
professional praying woman; *yo p'o*, the herbalist; and *wên p'o*,
she who brings forth grain from the hull — the midwife.
In a learned Chinese tome is written: 'Whoever has these
mischief-makers about his house is sure to meet trouble.'

Various industries claimed the attention of women, who
in China have never been veiled nor irrevocably confined to an
harem, but one can scarcely designate industrial preoccupation
as a profession. A woman's vocation was the home, her avocation such things as the care of silk-worms and frequently
embroidery. She sat for many hours before her frame creating
flowers, birds, and butterflies in exquisite threads on glimmer-
ing silks and satins. Deftly her delicate fingers executed the
different stitches: the 'enwrapping,' which we call 'satin,'
stitch, both long and short; the 'struck or grass-seed' stitch,
in our nomenclature French knots; the 'oblique' stitch, for
stems of plants; the 'enveloping' or 'couching' stitch; the
'chain,' the 'split,' and the 'man-character' stitches; all these
and more were in her repertory.

Nuns, both Buddhist and Taoist, though especially the

former, are plentiful in China. It is said that at least a hundred thousand are scattered through the provinces of the Central Land. With their shaven heads the Buddhists are scarcely to be distinguished from monks.

Women follow the way of religion for a number of reasons: Poverty drives parents to promise superfluous children of both sexes to this temple or that. Earnest Buddhists disapprove of such action contending that a child is unknowing. A saying runs: 'Halfway along the road of life, may go out from the family; in mid-career is the heart settled.' Illness, too, plays a rôle; parents often dedicate a sick child to celibate life as the price of its recovery. Rich widows become nuns. Little girls run away from brothels and offer themselves to a nunnery, or worn-out prostitutes seek peace within temple walls.

The convents, which are not large, are as a rule under the protection of a monastery, the abbot often officiating at special ceremonies. The nuns themselves are helpful in raising funds. They go about among the women of the rich, who are frequently devout Buddhists. Ordination rites take place in monasteries and culminate, as do those for priests, in scalp-burning, pain being borne 'for the sake of others.' After this has occurred nuns — as do priests — become *ch'u chia jên*: people who have gone out from the family.

In a book of songs appears a poem greatly admired by the Chinese, who especially enjoy the picture evoked of the little nun and her novice lover in the Great Hall. Those familiar with Buddhist temples see in vision the high pillars, the dark heights, the gilded wooden figures which surround the Hall, and the grey-clad human figures of little nun and novice. The poem is written by a little nun who, promised to a temple during an illness, found that she could not endure religious life. The modern poet Hsü Chih-mo revised and published it in order that 'those in the world who love ''the genuine'' may rejoice.'

THE LITTLE NUN

Twice eight is roadway of my years,
'Tis verily time of my green Spring.
Suffered spiritual father to shave, do away with, hair on my
     head.
During each day,
Burn incense, sprinkle water in Buddha's Hall.
See several boy novices
Below, at mountain gate, playing, strolling about.

Hastily their eyes glance at me;
My eyes espy them.
They to me,
I toward them,
We all, feel our hearts drag, take notice.

I am here only because my father liked to con sutras,
My mother loved to study Buddhism.
At dusk she worshipped, at dawn offered prayers,
In Buddha's Hall, each day, burned incense, paid reverence
    to the Saint.
When I came down to this life, many were my ailments,
    disorders.
Because of this was I relinquished, brought up, to enter gate
    of the void;
To pass through life as a nun.
Forgetting spiritual beings I reach toward, regard as before,
    homes of men.
Mouth cannot endure to mutter *mi t'o*, magic formula,
I merely listen to sounds surging from bells and drums.
Hand cannot endure to strike musical stones, ring brass hand-
    bells,
Strike musical stones, ring brass hand-bells, blow spiral
    conch-shells, cause drums to roll like thunder.
Whole day perform meritorious tasks for Shadow-World
    officers in Under-Earth Prefecture.
The Many Hearts Sutra
Must often read through;
The Bright Peacock Sutra
I cannot break apart.
Then there is that *Lotus Sutra*, seven rolls!
It is very difficult to study.
Reverend father haunts my sleep, haunts my dreams; teaches
    much transgression.

Recite several times *mi t'o fu*,

Annoy with my voice go-between dame.
Recite several times: 'Bear patiently, as Kuan Yin does, all
    reproof';
Once make my petition — have nothing to do.
Recite several verses, yawn, hum softly, then yawn.
Why do I realize sadness of my soul is deeply stirred?
Pace encircling gallery; return; strive to allay boredom;
Pace encircling gallery; return; strive to allay boredom.
See again on either hand images of Lo Han, disciples of
    Buddha;
When moulded and shaped were given foolish horns.
A boy sits hugging knees, his mind disburdened of thought:
Lips of the boy speak to me.
A boy sits leaning cheek in his hand:
Heart of the boy treasures thought of me.
A boy opens eyes, idle eyes,
Veiled as setting moon, or rising moon, they peep at me.
Only the cotton-robed Lo Han to laugh ha ha.
Boy smiles at me.
Daylight, plated gold,
Has passed to time of shadows.
To wed me there is a willing mate.
Sainted figures all about us!
That aged old crone, old crone
The deaf one,
She hates me.
The one who leans on a tiger,
Hates me.
That long eye-browed, big image, a Lo Han, grieves for me,
He grieves, wondering what form in old age my life-fruit will
    take.
Lamp before the sainted Figure
Does not equal candles in a bridal chamber.
Case where incense sticks are stored
Does not equal 'precious tortoise-shell' banqueting mat in
    Eastern Pavilion.

Bell tower, drum tower,
Do not equal 'welcome husband terrace.'
Plaited reed-grass praying cushion
Does not equal soft rose-hibiscus wedding mattress.
ho ya! t'ien hsia!
For no cause my heart is hot as fire!
For no cause my heart is hot as fire!
Seize, take, leaden color cotton robe, destroy, tear it to pieces.
Bury them, hide the sutras;
Abandon the wooden fish;
Cast away brass cymbals, little bells for chanting;
From now on and after will flee far, leaving bells, drums, of
    Buddha's Hall.
Will run down the hill, seek a youthful elder brother,
Urge him to beat me — curse me — speak to me — smile at
    me!
This heart is not willing to perfect the Buddha teaching;
I will not recite *mi t'o, pan jo, po lo,* the magic words of in-
    cantation.

Prostitutes described in picturesque terms there have been
since proto-historic days. In close connection with brothels,
singing girls, dancing girls, and professional entertainers have
flourished. As a result, however, of the Chinese social system
courtesans become such by methods somewhat different to
those followed in the West. The great majority of 'mist and
flower' maidens, to use an indigenous term for these ladies, are
sold in early youth to brothel-keepers by poverty-stricken
parents, hard-hearted relatives, or kidnappers. They are
taught singing and dancing, they learn the *p'i-pa,* an instrument rather like a guitar, and are supposed to know the
characters in the Classic of Taoism, the *Tao Tê Ching.*

The *Chronicle of Sundry States* records that in the seventh century B.C. a certain Minister, Kuan Chung by name, developed the practice of prostitution as an addition to the revenues of the land, one of his ideas being to prevent the silver acquired by traders in return for their goods from leaving the country. If these same traders found the mist and flower maidens alluring their gains would be scattered and might eventually filter back to the governmental exchequer. Entertaining the peach-flower ladies certainly were. Probably far more entertaining than their more correct sisters to whom education and social intercourse were denied. Throughout Chinese history, poets and scholars have found the joy of feminine society with ladies trained in the arts of willow lane, many of whom have been famous.

Whatever the way of entry, all courtesans hoped to leave the Green Two-Storied Buildings by the Road of Matrimony. Nor was this an unusual course. Fate often decreed that some guest fall in love with a mist and flower lady whom, desiring to make his concubine, he freed from the 'sweet-scented land' by refunding her purchase price. A delightful scene in a well-known Chinese novelette occurs between the heroine Jade Lute and Liu Shih, an old procuress. Jade Lute who, in time of fighting, has fallen into 'wind and dust,' not wishing to become a 'flower and willow,' begs the old lady to arrange for her some honest union. Liu Shih describes the various sorts of marriage which take place, emphasizes the fact that 'genuine' wedlock is rare, and advises Jade Lute to follow the life of 'poplar blossom' as is urged by her 'pocket mother.' Circumstance forces the girl to 'wed ruin,' but eventually she saves enough money to buy freedom and contracts genuine marriage with an honest oil-vender who loves her passionately.

Such happy fate is not universal. The songs of mist and flower ladies are, as a rule, tragic. The following is an example:

Resent   our meeting   only   in sunset of life;   realize the
       paucity of our connexion.
We   met,   then   parted; my heart   burns with grief.
How   sweet,   beautiful   the time   of fellowship;   our
       life together   had   its limit.
To-day   passing   wild-goose letter   laments   our   friend-
       less   solitude   in two   places.
By what means,   in fleeting day   of girlhood,   could I know
       I should   drop into   this place,   suffer   hardship
       from winds   and flowing waters   of lust?
Nightly,   nightly,   although   mated,   in reality   feel
       solitude.
In first   regret,   listened   not   when you,   my Prince,
       urged reform.
Desiring   to repay   flower   debts,   ill-timed,   fell into
       world   of men;
Because   have fallen   into   world of men,   must   with my
       eyes   girdle caution.
Also   need   ability   to select.
In world   men   who pity   flowers   are   few,
But   those who   would   prop up   a lovely   blossom
       must,   with careful   thought,   enclose it   by ringed
       fence.[1]

Despair weighs down the hearts of those who live in Sell-Smile Village, who feel that only in the life to come will they meet happiness. Buddhism, altered beyond recognition from the original teaching, is their hope; gentle Kuan Yin, Saint of Mercy, their patroness. The thought of old age as a time of honor, respect, and consideration is to Chinese in general

[1] Song VI, *Cantonese Love Songs*, translation by Florence Ayscough.

welcome. To the ladies in the place of flowers and powder it is terrifying. An old folksong vividly describes life in such a place:

MIST AND FLOWERS IN WILLOW LANE

I

Mist and flowers, ah! in Willow Lane
Faces bright with harlots' rouge.
I seem among fairy maidens, *hai, hai.*
I receive official permit, *hai, hai.*
Am imposed on, wronged, by father, mother,
Who, grasping, greedy, covet silver, gold;
They sell me, their slave! Tears stream, *hai, hai,*
Body is lowered, dishonored, *hai, hai.*

Aged ten and three, ten and four,
Ten and five, ten and six.
Slave is compelled to be gay, *hai, hai.*
Selected for lust, studies vice, *hai, hai.*
Ten and seven, *ya!* ten and eight
I play game of forfeits, strive to please;
Lead guests to my bedroom, *hai, hai.*
Am flattered, caressed, receive money, *hai, hai.*

II

Don woman's skirt and hairpin, *ya!*
Bright purple flowers open.
ai ya, i hu, hai, ya.
Heart takes fire, *na!*
Peony flowers open, *ya!*
ai ya, i hu, hai, ya.
Study stringed-instruments, singing, ah!
Moon season flowers open, *ya!*
ai ya, i hu, hai, ya.
Stand by to serve wine, *ya!*
Fair Lady flowers open, *ya!*
ai ya, i hu, hai, ya.

III

Three-inch, gold lotus, feet
Lie upon ivory bed;
Flowers of ecstasy bud, *hai, hai*
Man's lust envelops me, *hai, hai.*

Gifts are bestowed, ah! silver, gold!
If gifts do not come of silver or gold,
Leathern whip descends, *hai, hai*
Tears stream down little face, *hai, hai.*

Years of youth may be bright Spring,
But sad, years of age, of a courtesan!

Everyone, everyone, scorns me, *hai, hai*.
Eyes of contempt regard me, *hai, hai*.

Years pass three tens,
Am aged and worn;
Can withered flower bloom, *hai, hai*?
Old woman returns her permit, *hai, hai*.

IV
Before bed I thrum strings, *ya*
White flowers open, *ya*
ai ya, i hu, hai, ya.

Joy is hidden, gone, *ya*
Nail of Earth flowers bloom, *ya*
ai ya, i hu, hai, ya.

Everyone, everyone, loves, *ya*
Ninth Moon asters open, *ya*
ai ya, i hu, hai, ya.

Face and expression change, *ya*
Gay Ball flowers come, *ya*
ai ya, i hu, hai, ya.

V

Slaves family, *ya*, was poor —
Is indeed still poor.

Where can sons come from, *hai, hai?*

Or little girl children, *hai, hai?*
No sons can I bear,
Nor daughters beget.

For no purpose am I in Bright World, *hai, hai!*
Through Bright World walk in vain, *hai, hai!*
Enraged, resentful is Old Heaven.
Why did two words 'Peach-Flower'
Not drop on another, *ya, ya?*
In former life gained no merit, *ya, ya.*

Desire all day, *ya*, every day,
To be led by the hand, grasped by the wrist,
Desire a pillow in common, desire to share a bed, *chun, chun;*
United behind bridal curtain, *chun, chun.*

VI

Oh! vouchsafe this forthwith!
Moon Season Flowers do not bloom, *ya*
ai ya, i hu, hai, ya.

Incense smoke has ceased, *na*
I am of no repute, *na*
ai ya, i hu, hai, ya.

A heart too desperate, *na*
Has fallen on body of slave, *na*
ai ya, i hu, hai, ya.

Grant a fond bridegroom, *ah!*
To open embroidered chamber, *ah!*
ai ya, i hu, hai, ya.

VII

Great Heaven, *na!* for me the slave
Pray choose a young man!

Would escape, go out, from Mist Flower Lane, *chun, chun;*
Would take Heaven's Hall road, *chun, chun.*

VIII

Would follow a husband, *ah!*
A husband of like mind, *ah!*
ai ya, i hu, hai, ya.

PROFESSIONS: NOW

IN 1935, the woman President of Gin Ling College for Women,
in Nanking, spoke at length on the economic opportunity now
presented to the women of China.   I quote a few of Doctor
Wu Yi-fang's words:

> Economic independence is an easy thing for the modern
> Chinese lady to achieve, these days, provided she wants
> it and is willing to work in preparation for her work.
> If she is well trained and qualified she may compete
> equally with the men for any position from the highest
> government office down. She is not discriminated against,
> neither is there a distinction made between the married
> and unmarried woman. Unlike her American and
> European sisters she does not have to battle opposition
> from members of the other sex.

The world, economically speaking, is hers for the taking. There are, in my opinion, two reasons for this: (1) The liberal men have been encouraging women to become independent individuals. (2) The Chinese are known for being reserved, so even if they did not approve they would not openly oppose. Furthermore, the number of well-trained women is still so small that it has not materially interfered with men workers.

Even now this is a country of extremes: on the one hand young girls talk freely of sex, marriage, and birth control; on the other they are still being married off by their families. This liberating of ideas, among women, is especially noticeable in their attitude toward religion and science. Some students acknowledge science as all-powerful, other modern women still devoutly burn incense sticks in temples. Such anomalies represent the complicated situation here to-day. Only as women become educated can we expect them to step into their places as leaders.

Doctor Wu, one of the leading educators of the day, is an ardent advocate of feminine economic independence but realizes that the choice between marriage and a career looms in China as it does in the West.

A few months ago the following newspaper article appeared in the Chinese Press:

RIGHTS OF CHINESE WIVES TO WORK

Defeat of Advocates of Return to Kitchen

NANKING, *Dec.* 4, 1936

By a large majority, Article 4 of the draft Labor Contract Law, which recognized the right of a husband to cancel his wife's employment when her work proves detrimental to the welfare of the family, was rejected at a regular meeting of the Legislative Yuan this morning. In moving the adoption of the Article, Mr. Shih Wei-huan, a member of the Labor Law Committee, declared that his committee stood for the principle of encouraging housewives to return to the kitchen. As men provided for their families, they ought to have the right to see their homes well managed by their wives.

Bitterly attacking the provision, Mr. Wei Ting-shêng said that not only were the bequeathed teachings of the late party leader for sex equality disregarded, but also the economic status of the average Chinese woman was neglected.

The Article was put to the vote and rejected by a large majority....

It appears that legally Chinese wives shall have complete freedom. I fancy, however, that, practically, they will find two-fold devotion, that to home and to career, as difficult to attain as it is elsewhere.

The great majority of women who choose a professional career become teachers. Demand still far outruns supply. Avid for learning the youth of China requires far more instructors than can, at present, be trained. No young woman of parts need suffer unemployment.

Women medical doctors and midwives, greatly needed, are being trained and find careers awaiting them at every corner. In olden days it was considered incorrect for a medical man to see a woman patient. Ivory figurines of nude women were therefore shown to the doctor, the patient designating on the figure where she felt pain or discomfort. Even to-day a female medical attendant is preferred, by women, to a man. It would seem therefore that for women medicine is an appropriate career. The long and expensive training naturally militates against its general popularity. Between four and five per cent of Gin Ling graduates enter the medical profession.

The history of Western medicine in China is one of great interest. Among the first to appreciate its significance was a lovely Chinese lady who lived at the end of the sixteenth century. She came under the influence of the great Jesuit missionary Père Matteo Ricci who baptized her into the Christian faith under the name of Candida. Married at sixteen she was left a widow at the age of thirty. Père du Halde gives an account of her life; he states:

> During forty-three Years of her Viduity, she exactly imitated those Holy Widows whose character Saint Paul draws, for not contented to edify by her Example, she contributed more than any other Person to advance the infant Church in China... Being sensible that numbers of poor People, for want of necessaries to support Life exposed and abandoned their Children as soon as born, she by the Interest of her Son obtained of the vice-Roy of Sû-chew permission to purchase a large House, where she lodged the Infants thus exposed and provided them with Nurses. The Number of these Children was so great that, notwithstanding all the Care could be taken, upwards of two hundred died every Year.

A marginal note reads: 'Candida erects Hospitals for Found-lings.' I am inclined to think that the word 'asylum' would, in this case, be a better rendering of the French original than the more precise 'hospital.' The benevolent Candida evidently attempted, though without striking success, to aid the foundlings with the knowledge of 'physic' imparted by

Père Ricci to his converts, which knowledge the fathers continued to disseminate until the dissolution of the order in 1773. Early in the nineteenth century, 1805–06, to be exact, Doctor Alexander Pearson, surgeon to the British factory in Canton, introduced the Jenner method of vaccination, which soon sprang into favor among the Chinese 'who,' as he writes, 'though very conservative in their feelings, when once convinced of the benefit of any new method, take it up very readily.' His commentary is heartily endorsed by twentieth-century happenings.

The first person who systematically brought Western medical aid within reach of the Chinese was Doctor John Livingstone, an assistant to Doctor Pearson of whom little else is known. In 1820 he opened a dispensary and sowed seeds which to-day bear abundant fruit in magnificent medical establishments such as the Peking Union Medical College with its Rockefeller Foundation, the Lester Institute in Shanghai, and medical schools missionary and non-missionary, too numerous to mention. The devoted and self-sacrificing work of medical missionaries is vividly and truthfully portrayed in *Yang and Yin*, a novel by Alice Tisdale Hobart.

The treaties of 1842–44 gave foreigners the right to build hospitals and schools as well as places of worship, and by 1858 Doctor Wong Fun, the first Chinese to do so, obtained a medical degree.

Less than thirty years later Doctor Yamei Kin, the first woman aspirant, graduated from Cornell University as doctor of medicine. Even in later life, when I knew her, she kept a subtle, mysterious charm which gave the impression of infinite, if hidden, depths of knowledge. The path she opened has been trodden by a number of courageous women who, to alleviate suffering, braved convention. A few of the pioneers were Doctor Ah-mei Wong, Doctor Ida Kahn, and Doctor Mary Stone. Doctor Stone established a hospital in an old house in Shanghai. It was tumble-down, overrun with rats, and supposedly haunted. Stagnant garden pools bred mosquitoes among the weeds. Hard work and faith had marvellous results; the place was rehabilitated, the pools were drained, fair lotus replaced the choking weeds, and the lamp of science burned brightly within the ghost-ridden walls. Chinese women travelled from far and near, in boats, on squeaking wheelbarrows, or in closed sedan chairs to seek help from their enlightened sister.

To-day the women of China realize their great opportunity and become successful physicians, surgeons, midwives, and dentists. At the graduation exercises of Women's Christian Medical College, Shanghai, a few years ago President Wu Yi-fang of Gin Ling addressed the seven members of the graduating class as follows:

You are expected to render skilled service to the hurts of humanity, but even greater than the duty of skilful performance is that of treating each individual case with the sympathetic attention it deserves. You must remember that you are not experimenting with a technical laboratory problem when you are entrusted with the life of a human being. Regardless of the station of your patient, you must regard him as deserving of your best. In your work in this country you will treat all classes of society. It is your bounden duty to afford all the best of attention without discrimination in social status, creed, or other circumstance of the patient.

The rewards for your work are limitless. The greatest return for your work is the very fact that you are instrumental in prolonging and regenerating life. If you are true to the traditions of your profession you will enjoy the honor that accrues from faithful and valuable service to humanity.

☯

Nurses increase in number each year and find work in many directions. Chinese women with their deft fingers, quiet movements, and controlled habits are delightful sick-room attendants. Personal experience of a number of probationers in a hospital where I spent some months gave me a degree of insight into their varied points of view. All but one looked upon nursing as an avocation prior to marriage; they seemed thoroughly happy.

The exception, Fair Hibiscus, was a quiet little creature from an old-time family in the far North who supported herself. Her hands were marvellously light, she loved massage, was especially interested in hydrotherapy, seemed absorbed in her work, and played the guitar as recreation.

Others were betrothed and looked forward to marriage from various angles. Hidden Orchid-Flower was engaged to a professor of music, her first 'boy friend.' She was an apprehensive type, feared that he had a bad temper and a difficult disposition; wanted to postpone marriage until she was sure of herself — and him; dreaded that marriage might not be a success. Was firm on the point that she did not want to risk divorce.

Ascend to Beauty was quite different. Charming but rather a monkey. Her bright eyes snapped as she told me that she had always had 'boy friends,' that she would shortly marry a youth in Government service, and that, if she were not happy, she would at once seek divorce. At a moment's notice

she went off, summoned by the hypothetical illness of her
well-to-do mother. Nor did she return. The claims of her
trousseau prevented that. Ascend to Beauty was a capable
nurse but the profession suffered no great loss in her defection.

Others there were who had not yet decided whom they
would marry. Meanwhile they earned welcome sums to
augment the family exchequer. As in the West, one meets
women of greatly varied outlook.

The law seems to attract women. Sou Mei-tchêng, trained
in France, attained the judicial bench. A number of others
who have studied abroad or in China are practising in the
courts.

Miss Lily Tie, for instance, is a barrister-at-law of the
Middle Temple, London, who has taken four academic degrees. Born in Jamaica, daughter of a well-known Chinese
merchant of Kingston, she studied in Kingston, as well as at
St. Mary's Hall, Shanghai, and took her B.A. at Newnham
College, Cambridge University. On her return to Jamaica in
1934 she was welcomed at a reception given in her honor.
Her reply to the speeches on that occasion, typical in spirit
of young China, reads in part:

> As Fate will have it, I belong in a way to two countries,
> for besides being born here I received a great deal of my
> early education in this wonderful island, and will always
> regard Jamaica as, in a sense, my motherland. But at the
> same time, I am compelled to share my heart with my
> fatherland, from whom I have felt an urge to go back and
> do my part in the country, for I believe in the greatness of

her past, in the value of the changing present, in the certainty of a great future, and lastly I believe in my own people, in their heritage and in their genius.

So Miss Lily Tie has come back to her fatherland to practise her profession among her own people.

The same idea is expressed by Miss Irene Ho Tung, B.A. Hongkong, M.A. Columbia, Ph.D. University of London, who in 1936 was offered an appointment by the Chinese Government in the Ministry of Education. She returns to China 'with only one purpose in mind: to devote myself entirely in service to my country.' While living in London she started a club for Chinese children in the East End.

The Y.W.C.A. has immense influence in the Central Flowery State. Scores of educated Chinese women, some as secretaries, others as auxiliaries, share with their Western sisters the responsibilities of the organization, which has branches throughout China. It is largely responsible for the striking growth of athletics among girls, an innovation entirely alien to indigenous tradition. The comfortable rooms of Y.W.C.A. centres influence, too, the love of physical comfort in line with Western standards, which is a striking manifestation of modern China.

In measures to ameliorate the conditions of women and children laboring in factories, the Y.W.C.A. has done noble pioneer work. Only in October, 1923, was the Chinese National Y.W.C.A. formally constituted and·at that time there were, in the Association, eighty-five foreign and sixty-five Chinese secretaries. Since the formation of the National

Branch, executive positions tend more and more to be filled by Chinese women who have proved to be most effective officers.

☯

Throughout Chinese history the contribution of women literati has been recorded: Pan Chao, a great historian, lived at the beginning of our era, and poetesses can be named in infinite number. The woman 'writer' in the modern sense and above all the journalist are twentieth-century products. This is not the place to describe the literary renaissance or the Youth Movement of China. In both, women have played an active part. Excellent reporters and columnists have positions on leading newspapers and women writers of talent are at work to-day.

Miss Sophie H. Chên is one of the best known. She uses English as easily as she does her own language, and edited a *Symposium on Chinese Culture* published by the Institute of Pacific Relations.

Miss Ping Hsin, Heart of Ice, is a writer of short stories in modern style; Miss Shih Ming, a Left New Realist, publishes under different pen-names; Miss Lin Shu-hua is a novelist whose main theme is the life of woman and her reactions to society; Miss Ting Ling and Miss Ts'ao Ming, radical writers, have in recent years been arrested and imprisoned; while Miss Fêng Kêng, with two Leftist men writers, was executed on February 7, 1931.

Ardent, courageous, convinced in their beliefs, the writers of modern China are striving to create a new and vital literature written in the vernacular, a language the populace can read. The first collections of their work to appear in English are *Living China*, a vivid little book of stories translated by Edgar Snow, and *Modern Chinese Poetry*, a book of verse, translated by Harold Acton.

Police women, strange as it may seem, function effectively in various big cities. Two pictures of such lie before me. The women-police of Peiping are shown performing their morning exercises at the training school while one, armed with a rifle, stands at attention. Women of the Nanking force look very smart and are vigorously mounting motor-cycles preparatory to going on duty.

In every direction women are active: as bankers, as students of science, as broadcast announcers, as sales-women, as beauty specialists, as shop assistants, and so on.

Waitresses and wine-shop ladies were not unknown in the old days; in fact, it is reported that girls served in wine-shops and restaurants in the fifteenth century and earlier. The system was abolished with the coming of the Manchus in A.D. 1644 and has been revived, in Westernized form, only lately.

An Imperial romance centres on Love-Pheasant Li, a beautiful girl who assisted her brother in his wine-shop. One day the third ruler of the Ming Dynasty, Yung Lo, who ruled from A.D. 1402 to 1424, and who built the northern capital as it stands to-day, visited the wine-shop incognito. Love-Pheasant served him; he fell in love and made her a concubine.

This happened at Tatung, away from the capital. When the time came for the Emperor's return to Peking, Love-Pheasant sickened and, before he reached the capital, news of her death reached him. A large funeral was ordered and yellow clay was used in building her tomb.... So greatly did the Imperial lover treasure the thought of Love-Pheasant. To the amazement of all, the yellow clay turned red; miraculous protest against unsuitable use of the Imperial color. Love-Pheasant's premature death was also attributed to the fact that a lowly waitress was no fit person to enter the Imperial harem. In China even the forces of nature express themselves as outraged by undignified conduct publicly manifested on the part of rulers.

The stage, heretofore occupied exclusively by men, who played women's rôles, now permits actresses to appear. Moving pictures have opened another sphere of activity. Miss Butterfly Wu in *The Two Sisters* gained the acclamation of her countryfolk; and when Miss Juan Ling-yu, a famous film-star, committed suicide as the sequel of an unhappy love affair her funeral drew crowds from the four winds!

An incident significant of a new point of view occurred in 1935. The singing girls of Nanking were reported as indignant because the Bureau of Social Affairs had rejected their plea to change the design on badges worn to denote their profession. The badges showed a peach-flower, age-old symbol of light women and prostitutes. They argued that nowadays professional entertainers are not necessarily one or the other; that they considered peach-flower badges an insult. The Bureau of Social Affairs rejected their plea and warned them that unless they obeyed orders their business would be suspended!

Prostitution is now illegal, but how China will succeed in her attempts to remove the social evil remains for the future to reveal.

☯

The latest call to women comes from Wang Hsiao-yin, a woman, formerly Member of the Legislative Yuan. Writing in the *Eastern Miscellany* of January 1, 1937, she describes 'What Women Should Do during National Crises.' The summary reads: 'Words must be backed with deeds — Example of Spanish women — Chinese women must first secure liberty from old conventions — Wider education necessary — Ignorance not a virtue — Scope for women's active organization — Encouragement of native industries — Expenditure on cosmetics and amusements discouraged.'

In the body of the text the following paragraphs appear:

> Together with more education, there should be more well-organized activities, as organization is just as important as education. Foreigners always laugh at us for being in a state of disorganization, and they are right to a great extent. In these critical years women should organize to work for liberty in political, economic, and social standing. We require organization among the women in towns, rural districts, and in different vocations as well as in homes, so that every woman can have a part in the work of saving the nation.
>
> Training is also important for women in their work for the nation, as in either political, productive, or military work women's help is indispensable. They can take part in propaganda work, in collecting funds, in transportation, policing, nursing, air-defence work, fire-fighting, taking care of children, in espionage, food prepara-

tion, etc. Every woman should be trained as a unit in national defence operations, and she should also be trained in the spirit of sacrifice. In Soviet Russia women receive training just like men, and no less than eight hundred thousand women have intensive training in every branch of military science.

So long as there is still a desire in our hearts to survive, there is hope, and with the crises now coming to a head, the women of China should rise to the occasion and fight for the glory of the nation.

The Three Sisters:
Remarkable Women of China To-day

The Soong family was made for China, not China for the Soong family.
Remark attributed to Mrs. Sun Yat-sen

THE ladies of the Soong family, Mrs. H. H. Kung, Mrs. Sun Yat-sen, and Mrs. Chiang Kai-shih, form a noted trio. Their father, at his baptism into the Southern Methodist Church in Wilmington, North Carolina, took the name of his sponsor: Charles Jones. How he first came from China to America is not recorded, but after graduating from Vanderbilt University he returned to China as a 'Christian missionary, to spread the Gospel and to teach English. He helped found the Y.M.C.A. in China. He became a printer. He published Bibles. He built a church. He was an upright and God-fearing man. Eventually he became a revolutionist, serving Sun Yat-sen as secretary and treasurer.' My quotation is from George Sokolsky's sketch, 'The Soongs of China.'

Charles Jones Soong, who died a number of years ago, married Miss Ni, also a Southern Methodist. She was a devout woman who deeply influenced the lives of her three sons and three daughters. They regarded her with rare devotion and deeply mourned her death. It is the three daughters with whom we are now concerned; they are evidence of the important part played in modern China by her women.

☯

Soong Ai-ling — Accomplished Years — Mrs. H. H. Kung, wife of the Finance Minister of China, was educated at Macon, Georgia, and is popularly considered not only the cleverest of the three sisters, but the leader of the brilliant Soong Clan. Her husband, a Christian, traces his descent from Kung Fu Tzǔ, the great sage of China, known to foreigners as Confucius. H. H. Kung was the acting Y.M.C.A. secretary in Japan when Soong Ai-ling was secretary to Doctor Sun Yat-sen. They met, fell in love, and married.

Mrs. Kung is reputed to be an able financier and a keen observer of political trends. The children of the union, two daughters and a son, show outstanding charm and intelligence.

☯

Soong Ching-ling — Righteous Years — was also educated at Macon, Georgia, and there used the name Rosamund. On her way to China, after graduation, she stopped at Yokohama. Here Doctor Sun Yat-sen, in exile after the 'Second Revolution,' had his headquarters. As a child she had played at his knee; now, a beautiful girl of twenty-three, she married him — a man twenty-six years her senior — and devoted her life to the furtherance of his aims.

Nine years of striving lay before the couple, years during which Ching-ling was eyes, ears, and support to the idealist. To write the story of those years would be to write the history of pre-Kuomintang China and follow the course of its temporary merging with Communism. In 1925, two years before the final triumph of his party, the Kuomintang, Sun Yat-sen died.

At this moment Communist principles, learned largely from

Russia, were in the ascendant. Bolshevik advisers desired that Sun Yat-sen be given a public funeral such as had been accorded Lenin. Soong Ching-ling, however, herself a Christian, successfully insisted that a religious service be held for her husband who had lived and died in the Christian faith.

Burial was not yet. A public funeral, gay with red flags and Communist insignia, also took place. Sun Yat-sen's body was placed temporarily in Pi Yün Ssŭ, a temple in the Western Hills outside Peking.

The Revolution ran its course. In this course occurred a break between the Chinese leaders, Chiang Kai-shih, T. V. Soong — brother of Ching-ling — their comrades, and the Russian advisers, who returned, discredited, to their homeland.

The widow of Sun Yat-sen, convinced that this was betrayal of the Master's cause, cut herself loose from family, friends, from all that she had striven to accomplish, and went into voluntary exile in Moscow.

Three years later the great coffin containing the Master's body was moved from the Western Hills to Purple Mountain outside the walls of Nanking, there to be buried in a magnificent tomb, shrine of the Revolution. Ching-ling crossed the Eurasiatic continent from Switzerland to follow her husband's bier as it was borne up the countless white marble steps leading to its resting-place. All were awed as they watched her frail figure pass. Selfless devotion to a cause commands respect.

Sun Yat-sen is the Hero, the Pattern, for China to-day. Did she so wish, his widow, whom the Chinese admire immensely, could wield great power. She prefers, instead, to live a secluded life, true to principles which, so she declares, are not being fulfilled. Militantly opposed to Japanese imperialistic aspirations, she signed, in 1934, a proclamation entitled 'Basic Program of the Chinese People in a War against Japan.' The chief editor of *Nichi Nichi*, a Japanese newspaper in Shanghai, wrote at length to her asking if it be possible that she had done this. A paragraph in his letter reads:

> We are confident that such nefarious activities and propaganda as carried on by you would throw China and her people into further difficult position, and your movement would be looked upon as highly unpatriotic one.

Mrs. Sun Yat-sen replied at equal length, saying in part:

> I wish to state that not only am I one of those who participated in the publication but also share fully the views of my colleagues and fellow-members of the Organization of the Chinese People for Armed Self-Defense.
>
> We do not invite the imperialist Japanese Journal to tell us the duties of a true patriot of China....

No secret is made of Soong Ching-ling's view. She is warmly in sympathy with what she calls 'a revolution built on mass support and for the masses.' Furthermore, she recommends anti-Japanese action. At the Third Kuomintang Plenum held in February, 1937, she is reported to have presented a petition giving reasons for opposing Japan at once: (1) Japan is economically incapable of waging a prolonged war; (2) the masses of Japan are opposed to war, and (3) Japan's fighting strength is on the decline and army technical equipment is obsolete. She concludes:

> From these points it can be seen that Japan cannot really defeat China. The Chinese must free themselves from their fear of Japan and make a firm stand against its imperialism.

A general petition, said to have been drafted by her, contains the following words:

> The best way for China to check Japan's aggression is to tolerate Communism and re-examine the Three Principles of the People written by Doctor Sun Yat-sen. To do this the government and the people should be fused, a People's Congress called forthwith, and all talent and ability — whether within the Kuomintang or without, rich or poor — drafted for the task of reorganizing the present National Government and putting new life into our Revolutionary Front.

The third daughter of Soong, Mei-ling — Beauteous Years — by name, graduated from Wellesley College, Massachusetts. Upon her return to China she interested herself in social work especially for women, acting as secretary for a joint committee of the American, British, and Chinese Women's Clubs formed in 1921 for the study of factory conditions in China. Later she was a member of the Child Labor Commission; her knowledge, therefore, of industrial conditions is considerable.

Handsome, vivacious, of dominant character, she played a leading rôle among her countrywomen. On December 1, 1927, General Chiang Kai-shih, then temporarily in retirement, and the third daughter of Soong were married.

For the last ten years Soong Mei-ling has been eyes, ears, and support to Chiang Kai-shih, as Soong Ching-ling, during the last years of his life, was to Sun Yat-sen. To write the story of these years would be to write the history of Kuomintang China, a task which cannot be here undertaken.

During the extraordinary crisis of December, 1936, when

the Generalissimo was kidnapped and held prisoner in Sian, his wife played the principal part in his rescue. Her clear-sightedness prevented a devastating rescue expedition which must have rocked the country. Her courage in herself flying to Sian brought negotiations to a successful close. China should be grateful to the Soong daughter, Beauteous Years. The history of the kidnapping and rescue of Chiang Kai-shih is told in a series of nine articles, four by Mrs. Chiang and five by the Generalissimo himself, published in the *New York Times*, April 16–24, 1937. They are both fascinating and remarkably interesting.

The social work accomplished by the Chinese Government during the last decade is immense. Aviation, roads, and communications generally have been improved; the capital has been planned, educational projects have been pushed, strenuous attempts to suppress Communism have continued. Mrs. Chiang Kai-shih herself has founded a school, in which she takes immense interest, for the Orphans of the Revolution. Lately she has been appointed to the post of Secretary General of the Commission of Aeronautical Affairs, one of the most important in China. During the last few years the *New Life Movement*, aimed at the social regeneration of China, has been preached in cities, towns, villages, and hamlets.

On February 19, 1937, the third anniversary of its founding, Generalissimo Chiang Kai-shih, President of the Executive Yuan, promoter and leader of the movement, gave a short radio speech enumerating five points to be stressed. On the same day his wife broadcast a speech in English which was relayed to America. Reception was excellent. How shrinks the world!

Through the ether sounded a woman's voice uttering, in fluent English, sentences regarding the cause she has at heart:

> The New Life Movement was inaugurated three years ago to quicken and deepen the work of reconstruction. Since then the nation has progressed farther than we had dared to hope, giving us all a new faith in the future of our race.... It has not been easy to improve communications, remodel cities, and set forces in motion that will eventually improve the living conditions of farmers and workers....
>
> In a very real sense, the New Life Movement is gathering together spiritual forces that are partly indigenous and partly from abroad.... The river of new life released three years ago in Nanchang is gradually gathering into one great flood.... First and foremost let us mention the needs for unity and internal peace.... The unification of the armies is not sufficient in itself. There must go with it that oneness of purpose and broad-mindedness that enables men of all parties and of every faith to keep in step regardless of conditions.... The President of the New Life Movement has said over and over again to me and to you: 'New Life is something we live, not something we promote.'... A change of heart within each of us will soon produce the new and prosperous nation that we all long to see.

Throbbing silence of the air succeeded the words, spoken with he conviction of one who believes.

The movement is founded on ancient Chinese virtues and is expounded in a pamphlet scattered throughout the Central Flowery State. Mrs. Chiang Kai-shih sent me a copy of the excellent English translation which she has made. Unfortunately this is too long to quote. It is but one evidence of the constant help she is to the Generalissimo, whose every effort she furthers. Her knowledge of English, for instance, is invaluable to him; she serves as his interpreter, thus avoiding risk of deception. Personal courage is one of her assets. She accompanies Generalissimo Chiang Kai-shih on the most hazardous expeditions. She seems, indeed, to combine in her person the virtues of past times and of the present. It would be difficult to imagine a more devoted and united couple than are Generalissimo and Mrs. Chiang Kai-shih. Their energies are lavishly expended for the country they are privileged to serve, and which is privileged to possess them as servants.

Soong Mei-ling is a devout Christian. In a little booklet called *My Religion* she sets forth her belief in simple forceful terms. She acknowledges therein the profound influence exercised by her mother upon her life and that of the Generalissimo who, after their marriage, entered the Christian communion.

Elsewhere she records, in a beautiful paragraph, her feeling for her husband:

> On New Year's Eve, my husband and I took a walk in the surrounding mountains. We discovered a tree of white plum blossoms, flowering profusely. What an omen of good luck! In Chinese literature the five petals of the winter plum portend the five blessings of joy, good luck, longevity, prosperity, and (to us most desired of all) peace! The General carefully plucked a few branches and carried them home. When our evening candles were lighted, he presented them to me in a little bamboo basket — a New Year's gift. The plum blossoms had looked graceful and lovely on the tree, but massed in the basket by candlelight they took on an indescribable

beauty, their shadows on the wall making clean, bold strokes like those of the great Ming artist, Pah Dah Shan Run. Perhaps you can see why I am willing to share the rigors of life at the front with my husband. He has the courage of the soldier, and the sensitive soul of the poet.

Communist Women

NO BOOK dealing with contemporary China can omit mention of Communism, which during the last decade has caused the Central Government acute anxiety. The Communists, convinced believers in their cause, consider the Kuomintang Government reactionary traitors to the Revolution, who exploit the masses. Among the Communists are many women; women who shared with men the hardships entailed by the 'heroic trek,' forced by the pressure of government troops, from Fukien and Kiangsi to far-off Kansu. Many bob their hair, dress as men, and pursue active propaganda work. A number have been executed during the last decade when a bitter anti-Red policy has been pursued by Nanking.

There is the possibility to-day of rapprochement between the Kuomintang and the Communists. The latter and many others contend that brother Chinese, instead of fighting each other, should stand united against foes from without.

Agnes Smedley, an ardent American, allied with the Communist group, writes moving stories of their destinies, and during the winter of 1937 gave a series of radio talks from their headquarters in the Northwest. These talks can easily be heard in Europe, which by means of air threads is now closely bound to Asia. An English friend of mine, for instance, first heard the news of King Edward's abdication, on the air, when she was among the foothills of the Tibetan border. News, therefore, in regard to the Communists of China is gradually seeping into world ken. So far not a great deal is known. Edgar Snow, an American journalist, obtained an interesting interview with the leader Mao Tse-tung and has sent fine photographs to America.[1] These show active and intelligent women, several of whom carry prices on their heads.

Whatever individual reaction to the tenets of Communism may be, unstinted admiration must be accorded the gallant protagonists, who often pay for their convictions with their lives.

[1] The interviews appeared in the *China Weekly Review*, November 14 and 21, 1936. As they were reprinted verbatim in the Moscow papers they are probably approved in Russia. Photographs and articles about the Communists were published in *Life* and *Asia*.

The Shifting Scene

NOT only in her habits but in her appearance has the Chinese woman changed. Gone are the flowing robes of mediaeval days; gone the embroidered coat, the light gauze skirt, the square trousers and tiny shoes of Manchu times; gone, too, the little high-collared jacket worn with full, ankle-length skirt, affected in the pre-Kuomintang decade; and gone are the various types of head-dress women have worn in different eras. To-day the majority of Chinese women dress in a long straight coatlike gown fitting closely to the figure. It is fastened under the right arm and is slit up on either side to give freedom in walking. This fashion is in itself revolutionary. The figure, instead of being concealed as it has been hitherto, is completely revealed. Furthermore the leg, covered only by a modern stocking, is exposed. Hair is frequently bobbed and given a 'permanent wave.' This if it be skilfully done is charming and effective. The cheap bob and permanent wave of the factory girl is, however, hideous beyond words. The texture of Chinese hair does not lend itself cheerfully to a tight 'crinkle'; therefore the unfortunate girls often look like animated golliwogs, those fuzzy-headed toys for children popular a few years ago.

As is so often the case, remarks about China must be qualified: the word 'gone' in respect to fashions may be used in connection with large cities and treaty ports where the fashionable assemble, but does not express the situation in country

districts. In 1935 a group of Chinese newspapermen made a
tour of investigation in Hunan. One of them wrote in amazement:

> Many of the young maids in the rural areas of the
> province are still wearing the costumes considered as
> fashionable at least fifty years ago in Shanghai and other
> cities closer to Western civilization.
>
> Dainty young maids of the Hunan rural districts staged
> a fashion parade for the visitors unconsciously when they
> put on their best dresses on the occasion of the Chinese
> New Year's Day.
>
> Pink and light green are not only the favorite colors
> but also form the favorite color combination. With a
> few exceptions, young girls were seen wearing pink coats
> and green trousers, or green coats and pink trousers.
>
> Pink silk stockings and light green shoes complete the
> fashion.
>
> Unlike modern Chinese girls, they never returned the
> stare of a stranger. When they felt a pair of searching
> eyes cast on their dainty faces, they blushed and turned
> their heads away. To look upon a modern Chinese girl
> in Shanghai, if you are attractive enough, is to engage
> in an eyesight endurance battle with the fair maid.
>
> When they walk, they walk gracefully like a princess
> moving towards the throne to be granted an audience by
> a foreign king and queen. They walk like Mr. Mei
> Lan-fang when playing a female rôle on a Chinese stage.
> When they speak, their voices are hardly audible.
>
> Not all of the girls in Hunan, however, follow this
> fashion. Some of them waved their hair, rouged their
> cheeks and lips, polished their finger-nails, and put on
> their high-heeled shoes just as those 'modern girls' in
> Shanghai do.

In the same year a tragedy was reported from a village

twenty miles east of Peiping. A certain Miss Liang became engaged to a young Wang. It was a modern engagement in that the young people cared for each other; the parents, honest, conservative farmers, approved. Miss Liang, however, imbued with modern ideas, began to wear modern dress, bobbed her hair, showed her legs, behaved, moreover, in an extremely modern way, not hiding her beauty in the least. On the contrary she strolled about the village and *talked with young men*. Soon farmers from neighboring villages began to flirt with Miss Liang, and worst of all the old women began to gossip.

Old Wang and old Liang met, discussed the situation. The respectability of both families was being menaced. To them, as Miss Liang would listen to no reproofs, but one course seemed possible. The account reads:

> Miss Liang was taken to a quiet spot outside the village by the outraged parent and future father-in-law and there buried alive, bright new clothes and all.
>
> Hearing about it next morning, young Wang was frantic. His love for Miss Liang and his grief at her murder were so strong that he proceeded at once to the District Government, where he lodged a formal accusation against his father and Mr. Liang.
>
> Although according to the old laws, and according to custom, parents are entitled to do away with daughters who bring dishonor to the family name, the new laws are different. It is recalled that some months ago a man and his wife in Tientsin were sentenced to life imprisonment for a similar offence. It is not known, however, what action will be taken in the present case.

How hard the road of progress!

Dress is occasioning much agony of mind to the Chinese.

To the conservative, modern fashions seem indecent. All sorts of recommendations are made to the Government urging this reform or that. Some of these recommendations are de-lightfully quaint. Proposals, sent to the Government by a gentleman in Hankow, reveal that the Chinese passion for categories is not extinct. Since the beginnings of time the 'Five Virtues,' the 'Three Luminaries,' the 'Seven Precious Things,' and many other combinations have been discussed. The gentleman referred to would dress his fellow-country-men symbolically. His suggestions are twelve, among the most interesting being:

> *Article Two.* All men should wear school uniform, with three pockets, representing the three principles of Sanmin Doctrine, and five buttons, representing the Five Powers of the Constitution [that is, the five powers of the Executive, Judicial, Legislative, Control, and Exam-ination Yuans]. The coat should come to five inches above the knee, and the sleeves should reach the wrist. *Article Three.* The color should be blue for autumn and black for winter. *Article Four.* Men who are not yet engaged to be married should have white buttons; those engaged should have blue buttons; married men should have black buttons; widowers should wear yellow buttons, and those who have married again should again wear black buttons. Thus one can tell at a glance whether a man is married or not, in order that ignorant girls may not be seduced by men, and the immoral atmosphere may be purified.... *Article Nine.* Girls who are not en-gaged to be married should wear a queue, tied with red or white ribbons; those who are engaged should have blue ribbons. On the day of their marriage, the queue should be cut off. Widows could grow their hair again, and when they remarry, they can cut it [the queue] off again. *Article Twelve.* Prostitutes should be allowed to

dress only in green. All the other colors should be forbidden them.

Doubtless accepted styles in dress, like everything else, will gradually evolve.

The well-dressed young woman of fashion in China is extremely smart. Incredibly svelte, she seems poured into her long gown; sleeves, often short, show ivory white arms; lacquer black hair, beautifully arranged, lies smoothly in place; jewels worn are fine but discreet. In a word, the Chinese lady of fashion is one of the most exquisite products of modernity — she would, moreover, satisfy early standards of beauty as expressed in one of the odes:

Fingers   tender   shoots   of the white grass;
Forearm   viscid sap of the fir-trees;
Neck   long white larvae of the tree-grub;
Teeth a row of melon seeds;
Square-headed-cicada forehead, and moth-antennae eyebrows.[1]

The question of names in China is one most perplexing to a foreigner. The complication of nomenclature for men is not relevant to our theme. Women are given a picturesque 'milk name' such as Dragon's Jewel, or Jade Lute, and a more serious name upon marriage. Curiously enough, considering the fact that she 'goes out from the door' when she weds, a woman then retains her own surname. By courtesy she may be addressed by her husband's surname, but terms approximating to our 'Mrs. Jimmy This' or 'Mrs. Tommy That' were not used in the old days. In official documents the two surnames are given. Suppose a daughter of the Liu clan marries a son of the Pei; she is designated as Pei, Liu, Shih,

[1] *Classic of Poetry*, Part I, Book V, Ode 3, translation by Florence Ayscough.

shih being the term for clan. So used it denotes that she belongs to the Liu family by birth.

Modern usage has brought about change. Mrs. Chiang Kai-shih, Mrs. Y. Y. This, Mrs. H. H. That, are continually referred to, especially in foreign intercourse, but a Chinese of the old school would be sadly puzzled.

In the olden days elderly women often formed pilgrim bands, visiting a number of temples in turn, there to worship; such women were called 'incense guests.' Devout Buddhists, they practised vegetarianism for weeks, months, and often for life. A dear old tailor, Amah, whom I employed told me that her son proposed a feast in honor of her sixtieth birthday. She replied that she had no desire to 'kill plenty duck, chicken' and eat their flesh, that she preferred to use the money he proposed to expend on a pilgrimage. Off she went to the Nine Flowery Peaks, the Great Mountain, and who knows where! She collected joyous impressions for her remaining years.

Such pilgrimages are still popular; bands of women each with a distinctive badge, each with a yellow or orange bag for incense sticks slung over her shoulder, form picturesque processions on the hills and in the valleys of China.

Women's organizations now abound. Even the most fashionable clubwomen devote themselves to social service of one sort or another, child welfare and education being, naturally, the most important interests.

On March 8, 1935, I was a deeply interested participant in the celebration, by the Women's League of China, of International Women's Day. Its inauguration is vague, but Women's Day is supposed to have had its origin in America in 1909. In China the celebration was first held in 1914. It is now popular in the Far East. In 1937, for instance, five girls from Buriat, Mongolia, covered in one hundred and thirty-seven days, on skis, the four thousand miles to Moscow, in order to share in the celebration of Women's Day. Thirty thousand people present in the stadium cheered them vociferously when they appeared.

To return to the meeting in Shanghai: several hundred Chinese women assembled for the midday meal, acting as hostesses to women of other nationalities from the cosmopolitan society of Shanghai. Around the walls hung portraits of Florence Nightingale, Susan B. Anthony, the Russian Grandmother of the Revolution, Ellen Key, and others who in different parts of the world had opened the door of opportunity to their sisters.

To one like myself who could recollect the restricted social intercourse of pre-Revolutionary days this gathering of earnest, progressive women was nothing short of miraculous.

My mind went back to another gathering; one which I had attended thirty years earlier, one also international in composition, but in character how different! Once more I stood, in memory, within the walls of the Summer Palace at Peking. It was a glorious Autumn day; the Empress Dowager, Tzŭ Hsi, was to receive the ladies of the Legation Corps in audience, and I was among the guests.

Officials ushered the company into the Throne Hall. There sat, in the centre of a raised daïs, the remarkable woman known as Old Buddha. A throne at her left hand, lower than hers, was occupied by Kuang Hsü, the Son of Heaven. As we entered she sat quite still looking down, her eyes veiled. When the company was assembled she looked up. Her eyes were large, wide open, and piercing to a degree. 'Deceit with those eyes upon one would be difficult to practise' was the thought that flashed through my mind. One by one, we ladies mounted the daïs by steps to the west, made our courtesy, and backed down a little stairway on the east. The audience was succeeded by a feast. Chinese and European dishes followed each other, a chain of dainties. When the feast was over the Empress Dowager, who had not been present, was carried in, sitting on a platform borne on the shoulders of sixteen men.

The appointments in the Palace were beautiful, the gardens exquisitely planned and planted, but realization of isolation was forced upon the consciousness. How could individuals, living within those rose red walls, surrounded day and night by hundreds of eunuchs, know anything factual of the outer world, and especially the world beyond the seas? An amazing, a forceful woman Old Buddha undoubtedly was, her personality was remarkable; but — how could she know? How could she know?

☯

With a start I was once more conscious of the wide hall in Shanghai. Spring light poured through the windows. A woman's voice was speaking, a Chinese woman's voice. The words it uttered gave assurance of knowledge, of realization regarding international problems of the day.

How has this change been accomplished? Who is responsible? Who opened the baton-door that her sisters might stream into the world, untrammelled?

I lifted my eyes to a portrait which hung in the centre of the main wall: the portrait of Ch'iu Chin, Gem of Autumn, the martyr. She it was who, more than any other person, helped Chinese women to emerge from their seclusion.

Part Two

CH'IU CHIN AND HER ATAVIC ANCESTRY

THE ARTISTS:
Li Ch'ing-chao
Chu Shu-chên
Wei fu-jên
Kuan fu-jên
Ma Ch'üan

THE WARRIORS:
Hua Mu-lan
Women Warriors Through the Ages

THE EDUCATORS:
Pan Chao
and her great-aunt
Pan Chieh-yü

Ch'iu Chin — Gem of Autumn

ARTIST, EDUCATOR, REVOLUTIONIST, MARTYR

Her hot heart was given, a whetstone, that the country sharpen its dull sword

THE personality of Ch'iu Chin has interested me for some years, but I found data in regard to her life difficult to assemble. It was said that her daughter Wang Ts'an-chih taught in the Shanghai school which Ch'iu Chin had founded. Search failed to discover Ts'an-chih. People could tell me certain details in regard to the young woman: she had travelled to America to study; while there had learned to fly, was indeed China's first aviatrix; she had inherited her mother's literary talent and wrote a good deal; yes, she was probably in Hunan, or maybe Peking; no one knew.

I read the booklet edited by Ts'an-chih which contains selections from her mother's work, and her own. It has indeed formed the basis for my study of the Honored One, whose poems according to law are charming productions dealing with flowers, birds, and peaceful scenes. The pieces in irregular form are more revealing in a personal sense. I have, therefore, selected a few of these for translation.

A week before my departure from Shanghai in the spring of 1935, lucky chance brought me the address of Wang Ts'an-chih, or Wang Kuei-fên, as she now calls herself. She lived barely a mile from my Grass Hut. We met. She was charming, most friendly, and ready to give all the help she could.

At the time of her mother's death she was but a little child; therefore, her recollections in this regard were nil. I dined at her home, saw her tiny daughter, and enjoyed the sword dances which she performed to please me. This art she pursues with fervor, daily practising with a teacher. The names of the pieces she danced were: 'Swallow Enters Nest,' 'Yellow Bee Enters Cave,' 'Clever Dog Hunts,' and 'Dragon-Flies Dot the Water.'

Although she could tell me but little about her mother, she gave me the photograph of Ch'iu Chin which forms the frontispiece to this Part, and as we parted insisted that I accept a handsome green jade pendant.

My authorities for Ch'iu Chin's life are: *Ch'iu Chin Nü Chieh I Chi*, being her collected works, as well as sundry biographies, arranged by her daughter Wang Ts'an-chih, published in 1929; notes in English given me in 1935 by this same daughter; notes in Chinese given me in 1935 by Mr. Nung Chu, who knew Ch'iu Chin; sketches of her life in various Chinese biographical collections; a paper by Lionel Giles, M.A., D.Litt., *Ch'iu Chin: a Chinese Heroine*, read before the China Society, in London, March 29, 1917; a few extracts from the Chinese press; and *La Politique Chinoise*, by Albert Maybon, Paris, 1908.

Heavy heat hangs as a rule over the canals of Shao Hsing during the Sixth Moon, which corresponds to our July. In the year 1907, however, when at daybreak on the sixth day (July 15) a party of Imperial soldiers, accompanied by executioners, led a prisoner out to martyrdom, a chilly north

Ch'iu Chin, Gem of Autumn
Revolutionary leader executed July 15, 1907
by order of the Manchu Government

wind was blowing. Only one member of this sad cavalcade was calm: the prisoner herself, a young woman dressed in the red robes of a criminal. Onlookers, even the hardened executioners, shuddered with dread. The prisoner knelt. Attendants wearing round pointed hats of office performed their duties. One, his foot braced against the sole of hers, drew back her arms, another drew forward the glossy black hair, the executioner himself lifted in his two hands the cruel broadsword used on such occasions and steadied himself, legs well apart. In an instant with a singing sound the broadsword descended, striking the young woman's head from her frail body. Her age was thirty-three years, five moons, twenty-six days. Legend has it that above this scene clouds of five colors hung in the sky. Why did this execution take place? Who thus suffered decapitation?

To answer the first question certain historical consideration is necessary: During the years when the prisoner trod this earth China passed through a series of crises which tore the hearts and brought to birth in the breasts of its sons and daughters a militant patriotism; this patriotism, as differentiated from love of one's 'ancient village,' had been unnecessary in the old scheme of things.   The people, the officials, the Court, and the Son of Heaven himself on his Dragon Throne, had always believed that China was the world centre, that the Ruler was the world ruler, and that the countries of the Four Quarters were inhabited by people who lived more or less in a state of barbarism; by people who came to the Glorious Central State in order to gain benefit from its products and to absorb its culture. Most firmly of all were they convinced that the dwarf men of Sun's Root Country — that is, Japan — were a lesser folk, negligible from every point of view.

During the nineteenth century a series of shocks culminating in the Sino-Japanese War of 1894–95 sadly shook these convictions, and the years 1894 to 1900 were, politically, of supreme importance to China and its people.

The Dragon Throne itself was occupied by aliens. The Manchus, summoned in A.D. 1644 by a Chinese general to aid him in the suppression of a rebellion, had presumptuously mounted the throne left vacant by the suicide of Huai Tsung, last sovereign of the Ming Dynasty. Although two and a half centuries had passed since that day, although the administrators were predominantly Chinese — sons of Han, as they loved to call themselves — many anti-dynastic secret societies flourished and there was strong feeling against the 'Manchu dogs,' interlopers from an alien land, who still held Heaven's Decree to rule.

Furthermore, strong feeling was beginning to crystallize against barbarians from the West who throughout the nineteenth century had become more and more aggressive. English, Americans, Germans, French, Russians, all insisted upon intercourse with China, insisted upon the right to teach their creeds to the 'black-haired people,' and finally insisted — preposterously — that they be received by the Son of Heaven himself on a basis of equality. The situation is summed up in the following paragraph:

> In 1842, China was defeated and compelled to sign a treaty, moderate in its terms, but imposed by the victors; but she was not humiliated. In 1858 and in 1860 she again suffered defeat, and again she had to submit to terms imposed by the victors; but her ministers might console themselves with the reflection that her situation was due to the Taiping ulcer eating at her bowels, and not

to the external wound inflicted by foreign arms. In 1885 she brought a year of hostilities to a stalemate. But now, in 1895, she was not merely defeated — she was humbled. Her armies had never once scored a victory, but had fled from every field of battle, and had surrendered one strong position after another. Her fleet, on which many hopes had been based, had been driven ignominiously to the shelter of fortified ports. Her commanders had shown themselves all incompetent, and many, cowards. Her administration was as inefficient and as corrupt in the hour of the nation's peril as it notoriously was in time of peace; and her people, while they had acquired some sense of nationality, were still an inchoate mass, in which self-interest was the only motive power and blind fury replaced patriotic endeavor. . . . To all experienced observers — experienced in the ways of the West but not in those of the East — it seemed clear that dismemberment was impending and was inevitable.[1]

Among those in whom the sense of nationality had been roused was the prisoner in question who, paying with her life for the anti-dynastic plots which she had nurtured, went so quietly to her doom.

This young prisoner's surname was Ch'iu — Autumn, her given name Chin — Hard-Brilliant-Gem; one assumed name Hsüan-ch'ing — Jewel-of-Intelligence; another Ching-hsiung — Vie-With-Male. She called herself Chien-hu Nü-chieh — Mirror-Lake Woman-Champion. Springing from an official family she, the youngest child, who was considered 'the pearl,' had been educated in the Classics, and in the writing of poetry. At the age of eighteen she had been married to a youth named Wang whose family was intimate with her own. The Wang family were natives of Hunan Province, whereas

[1] Far Eastern International Relations, by H. B. Morse, and H. F. MacNair.

Ch'iu Chin's native village was Shan Yin — Hill's Shadow — not far from Shao Hsing in Chê-kiang Province.

A few years after their marriage the young people proceeded to the capital, Peking, where Wang held the position of Circuit Commissioner.

The Northern city must have seemed strange to the woman from the South. Among the crowds in the streets were many Manchus, the women dressed in long straight gowns, faces heavily powdered and brightly rouged; hair gayly decked with flowers and dressed high over a flat band which projected on either side of their heads. Their shoes also were unusual: of natural size with a sort of hoof in the centre which raised the wearer three or four inches from the ground. Camels came in trains from the desert, heavily laden mules brought fruit from the North; blue-hooded carts rumbled past on studded wheels, different indeed from the boats of the South. Life in the capital under the shadow of the Rose Red Palaces must have been a great experience for Ch'iu Chin, an experience which she and her husband regarded from opposing points of view. The excitement, too, was great. Dwarf men from the Eastern Sea had defeated China in the war which lasted from July, 1894, to April, 1895. Formosa now belonged to Japan, no longer to China. Rumor declared that the money intended for naval improvement had been used by the Empress Dowager to build the Summer Palace. Small wonder the Japanese found victory easy. The Chinese were dazed by defeat; the Western Powers, too, were amazed, and quickly entered upon that phase of activity known as the 'Battle of the Concessions' when China like a melon seemed likely to be sliced. Awakened to a realization of China's impotence the Emperor, Kwang Hsü, determined upon reform, calling a notable progressive, Kang Yu-wei, to his aid. For 'One Hundred Days' during the summer of 1898, Imperial Edicts commanding change here, improvement there, followed each other, an unbroken line. But the forces of reaction were too strong: in September the Emperor was forced into obscurity and his Imperial Aunt, the Grand Dowager Tzŭ Hsi, once more took power into her own hands. For the moment hope of change vanished.

Ch'iu Chin found these happenings almost too agonizing to bear; her ardent nature suffered intensely, nor did she find sympathy from her husband. He, an official, belonged to the Conservative Party. Public affairs were of intense interest to the young woman. Although the mother of two children, a son and a daughter, she refused to devote her life to family cares.

The year 1900 saw that strange explosion, of complex origin: the Boxer Rebellion.

One day in May a strange, heavy cloud brought darkness to the spring morning. Popular belief held that under cover of this cloud the 'Boxers,' endowed with supernatural powers, came to earth. Members of a secret society, the I Ho Chüan — Fists of Righteous Harmony — carried flags blazoned with four characters meaning 'Cherish Dynasty, Exterminate Foreigners.' They claimed to be invulnerable, fearing neither bullet nor spear.

At the end of the month the French Minister wrote his Government in Paris as follows:

> Peking, Tientsin, and Paotingfu are encircled by bands of maddened and fanatical people, whose numbers are swollen by an excited crowd of vagabonds, and who, being maintained by leaders in high position, rob, pillage,

burn, and kill as they pass. For the moment their activity is directed against Chinese converts, Catholic and
Protestant.... They do not conceal their object to get
rid of all foreigners...by means of destruction of religious missions and a general insurrection against
European and American residents... and on their flags
they now assert that they act by imperial command.

By mid-June the foreign legations were besieged; not until
August 14 did relief reach them; then the allied forces of
Japan, Russia, England, the United States, France, Austria,
and Italy marched through the towering gates of Peking.
At dawn on August 15 the Court fled; fled to the West, where
for two years it established an administration in Sianfu.
Peking, in possession of Western barbarians, was looted and
abused, many inhabitants fled, many others lost their lives.
A sad period, indeed, which made a painful impression on the
eye-witness Ch'iu Chin. A Chinese biographer writes: 'Ach-
ing urgent impulses raised by Rebellion of *Kêng Tzŭ* Year.
Thereupon she raised up, led, a girls' school, she herself
bearing responsibility. All new books, new magazines, none
were not unfolded, looked at; therefore she clearly comprehended the reasons for developments at home and abroad.
Perceiving the foreign tide of affairs her feelings surged as
water impeded gradually deepens.'

Among the quaintly phrased notes in English on her
mother's life given me by her daughter, Wang Ts'an-chih,
I read:

> During Boxer Rising of 1900 Ch'iu Chin was virtually
> irritated by the political chaos which apparently pre-
> sented. Two issues arousing the attention of every
> intelligent mind:
> 1. The corruption of the Manchu Government.

2. The intervention of the foreign powers into domestic affairs of China. The latter certainly degenerated the status of China as a sovereign Nation.

Ch'iu Chin brooded deeply on these matters and found herself utterly at variance with the husband to whom she had been married by family arrangement, a system which she abhorred. One of her poems touches on this matter; it reads:

STRIVE FOR WOMEN'S POWER

We women love our freedom,
Raise a cup of wine to our efforts for freedom;
May Heaven bestow equal power on men, women.
Is it sweet to live lower than cattle?
We would rise in flight yes! drag ourselves up.
Wash away the humiliation before us, the disgrace,
    reddening ears in shame.
If men consent to being bound in longevity as our
    comrades.
Our hands, white as pure silk, will toil to restore, to
    magnify, the rivers, hills of our land.

Former practice was deeply humiliating:
Maidens, young girls were actually mated like cows,
    mares.
New light dawns on time of illustrious culture.
Man's desire to stand alone, supreme, to enslave us
    underlings must be torn up by the roots.
As raw silk is slowly whitened by boiling thus shall we
    slowly cultivate wisdom, understanding, learning,
    study,
Sustaining weight of responsibility on our shoulders,
    our heads.
Heroic women of our land shall never see defeat.

To Ch'iu Chin, the progressive, her husband's views seemed utterly reactionary; she therefore said to him: 'Our ideas are different; it is as if we lived in the under earth prison' — a term used for hell. 'I do not desire to live in hell nor do I wish you to be there. We will part. You shall have the son, I will take the daughter.' Part they did, but the daughter, then an infant, seems to have remained with her father's people.

The various accounts available are not clear regarding the chronology of Ch'iu Chin's life at this period. It is recorded that, on her own responsibility, she established a girls' school; that she delivered a public lecture against the evils of foot-binding — this Doctor Giles translates in his pamphlet on her life; and that she helped an imprisoned member of the Reform Party to expedite his trial, by sending him, anonymously, part of the fund she was saving for her own education.

My Chinese teacher, Mr. Nung Chu — that is, Mr. Culti-vator-of-Bamboos — himself a revolutionary, knew Ch'iu Chin, and from his notes on her life I learn that 'she had a male cousin older than she. His surname Hsü, his given name Hsi-lin. A fine scholar who had passed the second degree in examination. When these two discussed matters they agreed absolutely: both were progressive. Hsi-lin said: 'Our country is in the hands of the Manchu people.' Ch'iu Chin replied: 'The glory of its return is my affair.' Hsi-lin continued: 'This cannot be accomplished by one person, by two persons, nor by farmers who till the soil. It must be done by educated people.'

It was decided that Ch'iu Chin leave for Japan, there to study political science and the modern ways which had brought power to the inhabitants of Sun's Root Land.

Once more I quote a Chinese biographer: 'One day stripped

hair ornaments, and ear-rings, in order to lavish her wealth on learning. Lone body travelled to eastern circuit of the sea, there to remain at school.' An extract from a Chinese newspaper describing her departure reads: 'She then determined to rush-as-a-dog-from-a-cave out from inner-apartments-place, to rush-as-a-dog-from-a-cave out from household halls. She straightened shoulders; to save country her responsibility.'

Women in the capital who were her friends brought wine and organized a farewell banquet at a pavilion South of Peking. In the bright clearness of an April day, 1904, Ch'iu Chin departed.

Courage was required to take this step, moral courage of high order. The official circle in which she lived found it shocking that a young woman, brought up in seclusion behind the baton-door, should leave home and children; should forfeit that joy considered the inalienable right of every Chinese woman: the joy of congenial marriage. In spite of the break which eventually occurred between Ch'iu Chin and her husband, I like to think that for a few years she did rejoice in happy marriage. The poem 'Autumn Rain' gives internal evidence of such fact. It may not be autobiographical, but, as the scene is laid by Hsiang River in Hunan, was probably written in the first years of her marriage.

SUNG TO THE AIR:
T'ANG T'O LING — AUTUMN RAIN

Autumn! sound of cutting-bowel rain.
Mist screens the waves; Hsiang waters flow.
Unhappy, silent, mount alone to dressing-room in
upper story.
Tonight loved one has gone,

Who   can bear   me   company?
I count   watches   of the night.
Cold   intense;   under coverlets,   padded quilts,   I shiver.
Mad-dog   wind   rattles   curtains,   hooks.
Lift lamp,   rise again,   crouch   in warmth   of brazier.
Inside   window   water-clock   drips;   outside   window
      rain   drops,
Incessant: drip,   drop,   drip,   drop — augments   my
      grief.

Exactly what force accounts for the mental revolution which transformed an affectionate wife into an ardent social reformer, it is difficult to say. The plunge into the boiling cauldron which was Peking during the years following the Sino-Japanese War, and which included the Boxer trouble, accomplished much. Public affairs began to absorb her, and at this time Ch'iu Chin is reported to have said, with a great sigh: 'Men who dwell in the world should assist, relieve those in difficulty, danger; should spew out personal responsibilities which, having embraced, they carry on their backs. How can rice, salt, and the petty fragments of daily life be the end for which they live?'

If the utterance of such sentiments were shocking, how much more so was her action! A young woman proposed to travel, and travel alone to a foreign land — incredible!

Her estimate of herself is expressed in the lines:

SUNG TO THE AIR:
THE OVERFLOWING RIVER RED WITH BLOOD

My body   does not   attain
In prominence   to those   of men;
My heart   verily   transcends
In ardor   those of   men.

My liver,   my gall,   throughout life
For the sake of others,   have often   burned.
The uneducated,   the learned;   among them,   who knows
    me?
At road's end   brave heroes   are often   snapped off,   ground
    to powder:
Choking   red dust of the world!   where   seek   one in tune
    with the harmony   of my thought?
Tears   drench   my pale green   sleeve.

Loneliness assailed her; it transpires in a poem she wrote en
route — a poem given to a Japanese gentleman. Consider
how far emancipation had already gone when a young woman,
brought up in the belief that men and women should have
no intercourse whatever, could speak with a fellow traveller
and cap rhymes with a stranger.

CAPPING RHYMES WITH SIR SHIH CHING
FROM SUN'S ROOT LAND

Be slow to say   this   woman   is not   brave,   heroic,
Mounting   wind,   she goes   alone,   ten thousand   *li*
    East.
Poem   describes   single   sail   on empty,   vast   sea;
Bright   moon   a carved gem;   soul   dreams   of Islands
    Three;
Sadly   gazes   homeward: bronze   camels,   symbols of
    Empire,   crumble to ruin;
Sweating   chargers   go forth   in vain,   their   courage
    has no reward.
Grieving   for home,   grieving   for Country,   heart   deeply
    pierced.
How   protect   lonely   traveller   ferried   by Spring wind?

☯

Cherry blossoms tossed against the sky when Ch'iu Chin reached Tokyo, then place of pilgrimage for reformers from China. Here assembled exiles who gloried in defying hated Manchus, men whose actions had made life at home dangerous. About them gathered ardent students like Ch'iu Chin.

The reformers were divided into two schools. One comprised followers of Kang Yu-wei, who advocated a change within the monarchical system; the other, led by Sun Yat-sen, believed that the Manchus were hopelessly degenerate, that monarchical systems were outworn, and that the founding of a republic was essential. The latter group took as name Ko Ming Tang — Alter Decree-of-Heaven Party — referring to the ancient belief that the Emperor of China, Son of Heaven, ruled by direct Decree of Heaven. This decree was only supposed to exist while the ruler behaved as a perfect ruler should. Disorder, discontent, cataclysms such as drought or flood, were interpreted as evidence that Heaven was displeased, and that the Decree should be 'altered.' In such case the Ruler, bowing to heavenly disapproval, should abdicate; did he not do so the people should organize rebellion, and force him from the Dragon Throne. In China the Divine Right of Kings, as understood in the West, has never been recognized, whereas belief in the People's Obligation to Rebel has, from early days, been a fundamental tenet. Eventually the Manchu rulers acted as their predecessors throughout Chinese history have often done: they abdicated, directing in the document which sealed such action that a republic be founded. The Western World marvelled. 'Amazing! Unprecedented!' It was neither the one nor the other. The people of China had clearly expressed, by disorder here, by revolt there, that they were no longer content; the leaders declared that a republic was what they wished — well, a republic they should have! This abdication, however, did not take place until 1912; we are now concerned with the spring of 1904, when Ch'iu Chin landed in Sun's Root Land, Japan.

Her daughter's notes read: 'Shortly after the period of storm and stress — the Boxer Rebellion — Ch'iu Chin went to Japan with the intent of launching a higher education, especially with reference to political science. At the time when Doctor Sun Yat-sen, the founder of the Republic of China, organized in Japan the Ko Ming Tang, Ch'iu Chin was the first woman member of the party.'

I have used as far as possible the Chinese idiom in quoting the various descriptions available of the young revolutionist's appearance, personality, and tastes: her face was wide and plump, her beauty striking, she was excitable, light-hearted, intelligent, and decided, impulsive, inspired, and of great personal courage. At books she was clever, comprehending, and was most able in writing essays, those compositions which the Chinese describe 'as melody resolved or colors perfectly blended.' Her urge for reform was unusual; as also her bravery and vigor. As for tastes: she liked to read *Record of Champions Who Used the Two-Edged Sword*, greatly admired such people as Chu Chia and Kuo Hsieh, fighters who sacrificed themselves for others, and looked upon the hero Yo Fei as a 'pattern.' Yo Fei, who lived in the twelfth century, and who strove to prevent the Golden Tartars from conquering that fair land which is China, lost his life through treachery of a Prime Minister, himself in league with the Tartars. The tomb of this hero, on the shores of West Lake Hangchow, was, and yet is, a shrine for the patriotic.

Such a person as Ch'iu Chin became an ardent adherent of

the Alter Decree-of-Heaven Party, soon taking her place as a leader among the students, men and women, who thronged about her. Versed in repartee, magniloquent, she often startled her audience. Profoundly opposed to the times, she frequently took refuge in wine, finding the stimulus helpful, but her head must have been strong; one record reads: 'Even when affected by wine, manner was as before.' Sad songs weakened Ch'iu Chin; she feebly beat time to their rhythm, then, rousing herself, waved her two-edged sword, and performed posturing dances: 'Strength returned in high degree!'

The Chinese student body in Japan, at this time, was tremendously active, enthusiastically forming debating clubs and patriotic societies, carefully training tender sprouts which budded from the tree of learning. Ch'iu Chin and others of like ambition, among them women students, formed the Society Kung Ai Hui — Identical Love Society — its aim: overthrow of the Manchus. Meanwhile, Ch'iu Chin trained as a speaker.

'Her talents, numerous as a heap of stones, a pile of Autumn leaves, caused fame to rise daily, as rises the magpie-of-happiness.

'The many students in the Eastern country admired the Honored One greatly and considered that if she blessed a meeting by her presence it immediately had glory. Entering the hall, Ch'iu Chin would walk quickly towards the stage, pick up her skirts, energetically ascend the steps, open her lips, and let forth a blast of words. Audiences were stirred, hearts and souls seemed to float as on water; of those who heard her there were none whose tears did not flow in lines, spotting the sleeves of their robes. Among those who followed her, swam with her, there were none who did not sigh, admire.'

Two photographs, taken at this time, are interesting: one

shows Ch'iu Chin in Western clothes, dressed as a man. She smiles deprecatingly under the preposterous cloth cap, worn well forward and slightly to one side. In the other she wears Japanese kimono, haori, and scarf; the puffed head-dress of Nippon rises above a face sternly intent; her hand grasps a naked dagger.

In spite of popularity, fame, and the interest of study, homesickness, to which Chinese are peculiarly susceptible, often crushed Ch'iu Chin, who expresses herself in a poem:

LOOKING FOR A LETTER FROM HOME WHICH DOES NOT COME

(Sung to the air: *Slave boy ugly as a demon*)

Oppressive   the breath   of Heaven!   Walk   listlessly   to,
    fro,
Too indolent   to blacken   moth   eyebrows,
Disinclined   to stick   gold pins   in hair,
A plaintain leaf,   not yet   unrolled,   is my heart.

Deep,   deep   matters, I dwell on,   treasure   in breast.
Idly   trace   patterns   on ashes   in brazier.
Lean   now here,   now there;   stroll   on outer gallery;
Look   hopefully,   *very*,   for harmonious   writing from
    home   —   wild goose   does not   come!

Perhaps homesickness was augmented by the departure for China of two fellow students to whom the following poem was written:

WATCHING SEA TIDE

(*Presented to Yen An and To Kun, sisters returning to our country*)

Think   much   on pain   of parting,
Weep   sadly   for time   of adversity.

Within borders tyranny; beyond borders outrage;
   unanimous our denunciations.
World conditions terrify.
Fearing leaders may hesitate, followers tremble.
Fellow countrymen blind-hearted dull, blind-hearted dull,
   what are you about?
Wounded, by emotion, this lonely heart is sad.
On waters, before me, desire to embark,
To part waves, mount wind,
In half a moon touch shoulders with friends.
Alas! Moment comes quickly, quickly, when hands
   must break apart.

To homeland, friends return;
Fatigued, weak, I remain.
Intelligence must bud as trees bud, sprout as plants sprout,
Control of our country is not yet restored.
Hope you, honored sisters will use your strength:
   lead, reform, degenerate age;
Cure malady, study what shall glorify;
Struggle, bring forth resplendent blossoms by power
   of lotus tongues.
To dim-sighted make all clear — exorcise dragon of
   deafness.
Calling, rouse many thousand elder sisters, younger
   sisters,
Let all hear Fifth Watch Bell.

Spring, 1905, found Ch'iu Chin herself on the way back to
China, to visit an ailing mother in Chêkiang and also to
obtain financial assistance. She had helped others in their
studies, thereby diminishing her resources.

Crossing the Yellow Sea she meets a Japanese who shows her a map. What a humiliating map! On it the results of the Russo-Japanese struggle are clearly shown. As the incident occurred in the spring, before the Treaty of Portsmouth had delimited Japanese gains, it is probable that the map which So Chü displayed was even more grievous, for a patriot to observe, than the definitive one would have been. Ch'iu Chin writes:

ON BOARD A SHIP IN THE YELLOW SEA TO SO CHÜ, A MAN FROM SUN'S ROOT LAND

(Looking at a map showing battlefields in the Russo-Japanese struggle)

Went! riding ten thousand *li* wind, now come back
    again;
On Eastern Sea is lone body; Spring thunder de-
    presses.

Can I endure to look at altered colors on face of
    pictured map?
To allow that hills, rivers be ravished, turned to
    ashes?

Unstrained wine does not quench grief-for-country
    tears;
Spears alone can bring deliverance; from ranks of
    learned I will go out.

Will regard lightly spilling blood, or taking ten times
    ten thousand skulls;
Must hold Heaven, Earth; regain, restore its strength!

After the visit South, a journey to the capital is undertaken and a poem is composed on the way. The habit of inditing thoughts on this wall or that is widespread in China, and constantly indulged in.

WRITTEN ON A WALL WHEN LEAVING SHÊN RIVER ON THE WAY TO GLORIOUS CAPITAL

Once more road from home stretches three thousand *li*.
Turn head, gaze at clouds, suffer increase of frontier-pass emotion.
In high hall have a mother hair on temples white;
No clear-eyed comrade helps harmonize my work of reform.
Heart and brain vexed, harassed, unstrained wine brings no relief,
Confused, tangled, are threads of emotion, I dread to hear oriole-song.
Spreading branches, peaceful moon; am thin, exhausted in Capital City;
Lonely pillow chilly, desolate, — dreams are not perfected.

The summer of 1905 was very busy for Chinese revolutionary leaders; people must be roused, plans must be laid, above all dead secrecy must be maintained. Ch'iu Chin enrolled in the Kuang-fu — Glorious Restoration Society — and made an extensive tour among the mountains of Southeastern Chêkiang. She had long discussions with her cousin the ardent revolutionary Hsü Hsi-lin whose intimate friend and aid she became, and decided to return to Tokyo for further study. September, month when the air of Japan is laden with moisture, when typhoons come raging from the Southern Seas, found her once more in the capital of Sun's Root Land, but studies were for the moment impossible: she fell ill. After a month of inactivity, however, she entered the Jissen Jo Gakko, Training College for Women.

The summer at home had not proved encouraging in regard to the state of public opinion. Bronze camels, symbols of Empire, which had stood outside early palaces, seemed to have fallen in the dust; Ch'iu Chin gazes West — from Japan — and calls upon her sisters to come out from within the baton-door and unite with scholars to save the land.

AFFAIRS OF THE COUNTRY STIR EMOTION

The people   chatter   like swallows   in unstable nest;
I mourn   fallen   bronze camels   of weakened   state.

From   East   invasion!   grief   is not yet   healed.
Gaze   West   —   what   are the plans?

Great   scholars   consider   throwing   down   their brushes;
Inmates   of the baton-door   long   to carry   spears.

Who   is able   to aid the land   —   to bring back   days
    of peace?
Saving us   from   raging   wind,   waves   of destruction.

Winter brought great difficulties. The Manchu Government, realizing the growth of subversive doctrine in China, realized also that the forcing house for the cultivation of revolutionary blossoms was Tokyo. Request was therefore made to Japanese authorities that restrictions be laid on Chinese students. Uproar among youths and maidens resulted. Meetings of indignation were organized. Ch'iu Chin helped to form a league, members of which pledged themselves to return to China unless the oppressive regulations were rescinded. This did not happen. The regulations requested by the Manchu Government, enforced by the Japanese Government, remained as decreed. Uproar subsided, but

Ch'iu Chin refused to be one who meekly bowed the head: shaking dust from her garments, she returned to China.

Arrived in Shanghai, another poem is written on a wall:

SHÊN RIVER

How many   moan,   weep   silent   tears,   for wounded state   of Land?

Men   strive   only   for glory,   show,   compete   in fine clothes.

Vulgarity,   decadence   fill my eyes;   grief   has no   end.

As rivers,   streams,   flow   downhill,   so, daily,   love of country   ebbs.

☯

Ch'iu Chin's object being to stir the flames, make flow the waters of revolution, she now concentrated on rousing patriotism among the people; she addressed them in the Chinese idiom, analogous to our term 'brethren,' as companions of the womb. The spoken word does not reach far. A writing-brush holds wider audience. Therefore she wrote, hotly, freely, and often.

ALTER DECREE OF HEAVEN — A DISCUSSION

I sigh! Alas! Venerable fathers, elder brothers, younger brothers, who should know the portent of the day, do they realize the portents of these days? Do they realize that in the portent of this day it is intolerable that the Decree of Heaven be not changed?

Heaving wind, drenching rain, dashing waves, roaring waters (of foreign invasion) oppress the people. Manchu thieves, Han traitors, come from every quarter, bind us in nets. I and my companions of the womb are in the fatal position of Hsiang Yü who on four sides heard the songs of Ch'u, yet people do not realize that we (of the revolutionary class), because of our great idea, may not, not diligently, sharpen our knives and exhort all, instruct all. Like fish deep in a cauldron, swallows in a burning nest, from dawn to dark they are careless of their lives, not realizing its hazard, its steep precipice of danger. Do I and my companions of the womb differ, then?

Finance Ministers, who covet cords of cowries, are never satiated. Although they bear responsibility, they exhaust taxes in kind, rents for lands or houses — to appropriate these their function — but they do not give the people report of their administration.

Discarded, cast by roads and pathways, are the people, while officials, ascending as the sun ascends, tranquilly sing songs, perform posturing dances; with extravagant words the people's representatives rule autocratically: this is the real state of affairs. It is announced that all have power, but men of Han are actually peeled, pared. Even in deep South command of soldiers is grasped by the venal Manchus who desire to collect all wealth, all taxes levied, in one corner: the Capital! They raise soldiers indeed, collect taxes indeed; always, always, seizing by force, flaying. In a word: over the Han Clan they hold, Death Decree!

In frontier's closed time we suffered that the Han should be left on the side as if dried up, withered, while neighbors to the four sides were encroaching. The Manchus treated inhabitants of the land as thieves, while flattering the foreigner's manner of behavior and bestowing as gifts our greatly loved rivers, hills! Alas!

Venerable fathers, elder brothers, younger brothers, unite to attain one purpose; hold one remembrance of our ancestors, our forebears, the foundations of our country, its difficulties, dangers. Regions for our sons and grandsons to place their feet will not exist. Ponder deeply, on way vile Manchus govern. Each group must treasure in its bosom memory of foundations laid by ancestors; must silently seek control, power, in all Below the Sky; must realize it is not easy to revolt, to alter the Decree. Unfurl our banners, prepare our drums, exterminate those, ugly-as-demons, who devastate the land. Our willing banners shall assemble! The Han shall manifest united zeal!

CLOSING A DOOR ON MY THOUGHTS OF THE GOVERNMENT

(Sung to the air: *Companions of the Womb, our Bitterness*)

Companions of the womb, — our bitterness!
Companions of the womb, — our bitter bitterness, like
    yellow wormwood   bitterness.
A thousand   pounds   is weight of oppression;   difficult
    to feel at ease!
Soul,   spirit,   groan,   weep,   verily we are   worthy   of
    pity.
hsü! chüeh-hu! on this square   earth   oppressive government
    fierce as a tiger!
What   day   will see   return   of great peace   years?
On all sides,   stand   like   forests,   extra tax stations;
Inspectors in stations,   customs officials   number   thousand
    ten thousands;
Fierce as hyenas,   wolves;   venomous   as snakes,
One   glance   at goods,   supplies,   from their   mouths
    drips   saliva.
Now We Must!
Must!
Must raise soldiers!
Sweep away,   clear away,   noisome   mists,   see   green
    heavens.
Raise in hand   white steel weapon,   seek   people's despots.
Relinquish   body;   save   people;   this is sacred   duty!

Companions of the womb, — our bitterness!
Companions of the womb, — our bitter   bitterness,   like
    yellow wormwood   bitterness.
Companions of the womb   whipped,   flogged,   like dogs,
    horses.
People's oppressors   treat   themselves   like gods,   im-
    mortals.
Opium smoked   is taxed,   wine   is taxed —
House tax,   shop tax,   nothing   not fully taxed.
Stockings,   shoes,   such trifles,   all   are taxed.
Each   plant,   each   tree — there is no clemency.
Now We Must!
Must!
Must raise soldiers!
Sweep away,   clear away,   noisome   mists,   see   green
    heavens.
Raise in hand   white steel weapon,   seek   people's despots.
Relinquish   body;   save   people;   this is sacred   duty!

Progress, satisfactory to an ardent patriot, was difficult
to make. Fellow students in Japan had shared rebellious ideals
but in China patient peasants — millions of patient peasants
— sowed rice, weeded cotton, rose with the sun, slept at nightfall, asking only that taxes be not too high, that magisterial
interference be slight. Political consciousness barely existed.
Ch'iu Chin longed for a comrade.

SUNG TO THE AIR:
RIVERS, HILLS OF OUR LAND ARE THUS

Alone   in back-room,   where influence of Heaven descends,
    a woman   chants   sad   songs;
hsiao,   hsiao   drops   water   from eaves,   flooded by rain.

A comrade,   arrow of whose knowledge finds target of my
        soul   is difficult   to meet.
Turn of an eye: light of time   flows past.
Hair   on temples   tossed by wind,   dishevelled.
Cannot   express   depth   of passionate   grief.
Count   times   sun   has set   on my   impoverished   road.
I —   in bitterness,   alone.
Land —   miserable,   pitiful;
Sad   that   it should   bring forth   a miserable   pitiful
        woman.

Exclaim: 'will return home!'   —   return home,   where?
Rouse myself,   turn   head.
Land,   of ancestors,   snores   in sleep   as of yore;
Aliens   insult,   encroach,   usurp.
Within   our borders   corruption,   defeat.
To take command   —   not one   brave   leader.
Heaven   must   have   eyes without pupils
To endure: that our land   should be thus,
To endure: the Manchu   barbarian.
A split   bean!   a sliced   melon!
Is   our loved   land.

Education obtained at so much sacrifice must at once be
put to use; furthermore, what better way exists of spreading
revolutionary doctrine than by teaching? Ch'iu Chin would
teach.

In February, 1906, she was recommended to a school in
Nanzin, North Chêkiang, but to her intense annoyance the
post was given to another woman: Hsü Tzŭ-hua from Shih
Mên — the Stone Gate. Ch'iu Chin went to see her rival,
whom she found responsive, intelligent, sympathetic, and
wholly delightful. Hsü Tzŭ-hua insisted that the Honored

One remain as her assistant. For the next six months the two women worked together in close intimacy. Ch'iu Chin had at last found a *chih i*, a comrade, the arrow of whose knowledge met the target of her soul.

Life at Nanzin proved too restricted. Revolution must spread from great centres. Ch'iu Chin moved to Shanghai, where she assisted in forming a new college, opened a branch of Kuang Fu — Great Restoration Society — and stood out more and more as a leader. Plans for an uprising were forming and active preparations were in progress. Ch'iu Chin hired a house in Hongkew, a part of Shanghai, and supervised the manufacture of bombs. An explosion which injured the Honored One and her assistants and, moreover, shook the neighborhood ended this activity. Governmental attention must be avoided.

The next effort undertaken was the stirring of feminine opinion. The need of a publication for women was urgent. Newspapers in general, though still not common, were increasing; by 1906 they were, indeed, numerous. For women nothing existed. Together Ch'iu Chin and Hsü Tzŭ-hua founded the monthly *Chung Kuo Nü Pao* — *Middle Country Women's Publication* — destined to have innumerable descendants. The Honored One wrote a prospectus setting forth aims and needs.

INSTRUCTIONS FOR CUTTING THE BLOCKS ISSUING A WOMAN'S MAGAZINE IN THE CENTRAL STATE (A.D. 1906)

> In our language are two miserable, pitiable, hazardous, dangerous words; they are: 'black darkness.' Black darkness is not comprehending reality, unreality; not having sight, hearing: without unity in man's affairs. Mankind should classify, through thought and reflection, its

methods of procedure. The frontiers of black darkness are miserable, pitiable; the ten thousand thousands fail to observe, to analyze, their hazard, their danger. To be in hazard, in danger, and not know this hazard, this danger, is doubtless real hazard, danger. To be in hazard, in danger and not know this hazard, this danger, is then great black darkness. Do those whose bodies dwell within black darkness, *yeh!* hazard, danger, *yeh!* consider how to save themselves and save others, eh? Furthermore sunk, sunk, in the dark prison, the ten thousand seem identical; although there exist those with intelligence bright as comets they cannot employ their skill. Shall I not then place myself on precipice of life's hazard and danger, use strength great as that of a Buddha; relinquish body on the frontier of Black Darkness realm, let shine great light and brilliance as from a supernatural lamp, lighting the innumerable people that all may climb the precipice? Is this not great love and compassion? Those who selfishly cherish life do not help those below. Who does not rejoice in life, hate death, pursue good fortune, shrink from disaster, thus ignoring steep places of peril, indifferent to them. Not that they are indifferent, but that they do not realize them. If I can waken women from deep drunkenness, fill their startled hearts with ten thousand terrors, then they themselves will evolve plans; is this not preferable to plans I make for others, eh? If you do not act thus, although you sprinkle everywhere ten thousand jars of Kuan Yin's all-saving willow-branch water, I know it cannot really ferry to salvation people of the world!

Thought should be given to the black darkness of our Central State: what it is like! To the hazard, danger of the road before our Central State: what *it* is like! To the black darkness of woman's realm in our Central State: still more what it is like! To the hazard, danger of the road in woman's realm of our Central State —

still more what *that* is like! Sad, downcast, I grieve, moved by affection I rise, I run forward calling loudly to elder sisters, younger sisters, companions of the womb, begging them to establish a woman's publication in the Central State. Ah! slowly, slowly a thread of light is piercing the black darkness of our woman's realm which, shut in on all sides, for four times one thousand years has existed until the present day. Ah! endless, endless, the long road, how shall we compass it? One hears of those who find the first impulse easy; those who find complete fulfilment hard. If the needle pointing to the four quarters be not correctly set, a mistake, minute as down on plants, in size the one thousandth part of an inch, will cause error, a thousand miles of error.

'The mirror of better days is not far distant'; looking back, the past ten years, condition of students' realm in this our Central State can be realized: In schools, to be established, we should hold examinations to bring prosperity to our time, our generation. Chanting aloud the Classics, head held high in air, must resolutely be discarded. As grain slowly expands, as grain slowly expands, so must we slowly practise foreign words, phrases, essays, literature. Who does not say: modern youth, modern youth, their ideals are great, but the bright sun of their understanding is obscured; their true principles are not yet evident. Those who beg instruction are, as a rule, without definite direction, without psychological perception; fruit of their planting, forsooth, is the production of many followers, with intelligence sharp as awls, who evolve into able compradors or interpreters. In the past ten years the wind of custom has slowly veered. Indeed I have known many students who consider the Eastern Circuit as it were a pathway over the high hill to success; who consider foreign halls of study to be good substitutes for the old examinations. Present-day students in foreign lands look upon each subject of study from the

viewpoint of its suitability for a graduate of the third
degree. These names and callings still clang in my ears.
From now on we shall see daily rising higher the hot
steam, the hot steam of foreign students in the Eastern
Circuit, *wu hu, alas!* Do the students who then shape
themselves advance a step? Do they go back a step? I
dare not say! My desire is that this malignant striving
shall not enter our woman's realm, confusing the issues.
On the road leading from our woman's realm we must
not climb those unworthy steps, pass those inglorious
grades. It is I who dare decide!

It sounds! We who have passed the night in drunken
stupor, who are not yet roused, hear first movement of
the sunrise bell. In Eastern quarter gleams the first clear
light of dawn. Perception after wakening will not be
long delayed. Men's hearts are weak, infirm of purpose,
cannot stand alone; what is raised to the East is overturned in the West. In our realm of women this is the
more so. If we lack whips with which to switch;
builder's lines stretched taut with which to adjust;
lack the swiftly moving compass with which to set our
course; perhaps, engulfed in their depths by mighty
waves and whirling eddies, we shall drown. Therefore
all to left, to right, should rouse the strength and power
of public opinion to examine, carefully as does a super-
visor, the country's people. What is charged with this
official duty if it be not a newspaper?

I would now bind, twice ten thousand times ten
thousand women in single indivisibility under our guidance; would at dawn and dusk penetrate women's realm
throughout the country discussing general control in
women's affairs; would provide women with dashing
waves of independence in life's course; would rouse women's essence, spirit, to rise as birds in flight over fields,
leaving swiftly earth's dust, that they may speedily cross
frontier into great world of Light and Brilliance. I

desire that they be leaders, awakened lions; advance messengers of learning and intelligence; that they may serve as rafts crossing cloudy ferries; as lamps in dark chambers. That they may let shine, from the centre of women's realm in our country, bright light resplendent, glittering rare in the beauty of its color; that, on the whole earth ball, they startle the hearts, snatch the eyes of men, causing all to applaud, rejoice. I desire my companions of the womb, uniting to encourage themselves enthusiastically, to expend their strength, to pray that this magazine be established.

I have never seen a copy of this journal. Doctor Giles describes the second issue, which is in his possession. The first three articles are entitled 'Notes on Moral Philosophy,' 'Female Education,' and a 'Happy New Year'; these are followed by the second instalment of 'Hints on Nursing,' translated from the English by Ch'iu Chin who had picked up considerable knowledge of that language. These 'Hints on Nursing' are reproduced in the booklet by her daughter and comprise chapters on ventilation, diet, bed sores, sleep, use of the clinical thermometer, and so forth. The 'Hints' are followed by stories and poetry. Doctor Giles considers the magazine to be of high literary quality and probably far too intellectual for its intended readers. Unfortunately ladies, who lived behind baton-doors, did not respond as enthusiastically as it had been hoped they would do and the publication was soon short of funds; in fact, outlay sat still, pay was obstructed. Ch'iu Chin did not allow herself to be weary nor desist from labor, but put forth the silken threads of writing and increased her efforts. Daily she went out, walking through wind and snow, begging assistance, succor, so busy that she did not realize the pitiful, the pitiful, bitterness of toil. The biographer continues: '*wu hu*, alas! We can say that her hot heart was given, a whetstone, that the country could sharpen its dull sword!'

At this time, the winter of 1906–07, her mother's death obliged the Honored One to make a short journey to Chêkiang, where she travelled back and forth among the pointed peaks studying roads and waterways in preparation for the rebellion which she, Hsü Hsi-lin, and other leaders planned. Hsü Hsi-lin, a man of wealth, had bought official rank and had been appointed to Anking, capital city of Anhui Province, where he acted as second in an academy for drilling police. Since he had had experience in Japan he soon acquired power. Ch'iu Chin and he felt that if they sowed seed in two places, she in Chêkiang, he in Anhui, flowers would bloom on both sides.

Unfortunately the flowers bloomed too quickly. In Kiangse a premature armed uprising took place. No other province moved. Many lives were sacrificed; the Government, warned, was on the alert, and the abortive movement soon subsided.

This tragic failure made Ch'iu Chin yet more fiercely determined on revolution; she encouraged those about her. Official suspicion had not yet turned in her direction; she was appointed Principal of the Ta-t'ung College of Physical Culture in Shaohsing, the Manchu Prefect himself, Kuei-fu by name, coming in person to present a complimentary address.

It is an amazing tribute to Ch'iu Chin's personality that in pre-revolutionary China a woman should be appointed to such a post. Her daughter's note reads:

> Upon returning to China she became the principal of the Ta-t'ung College of Physical Culture, consisting of

about one thousand students, who later on formed the basic unit of her army. Additionally she was also the leader of a large army made up of the people. She sometimes dressed herself as a man and nobody could consider her as a woman. She could do boxing and fencing very well. Above all she possessed both heroic mind and noble spirit. Once a man under wrong conviction was put into prison by the Governor of Chêkiang. On hearing of this Ch'iu Chin was deeply affected with grief, and redeemed the man out of jail by paying a considerable amount of ransom. After the man was released Ch'iu Chin avoided herself from seeing him.

Record exists of a visit paid on March 17, 1907, by Ch'iu Chin and her comrade Hsü Tzǔ-hua to the tomb of the Sung hero Yo Fei. The two women walked back and forth until dusk spread over West Lake and hills grew dim. Hsü Tzǔ-hua asked her friend if she would like to be buried near the shrine of her 'pattern.' Ch'iu Chin declared that such honor would be a happiness too great. Hsü Tzǔ-hua then promised to care for her friend's funeral should the need arise, but added, 'Of course I may die first, in which case will you see that I am buried here?' Ch'iu Chin laughingly promised to do so — if it did not cost too much! The friends parted in a spirit of raillery. They were to see each other but once again, and then for a short hour.

Revolutionary plans crystallized. By June posts had been allotted; each group knew what was expected of it when the moment for action came. Ch'iu Chin arranged to discuss final details with her cousin Hsü Hsi-lin in Shanghai, and on the way thither passed through Stone Gate where, in the darkness of night, she visited her comrade Hsü Tzŭ-hua. Money for the proposed uprising was needed; Hsü Tzŭ-hua immediately gave all her jewelry for the cause. The Honored One took it gratefully, then, slipping kingfisher green bracelets from her own wrists, gave them to her comrade as a memento, at the same time reminding her of the promise made at the grave of Yo Fei. They never met again.

The rising was planned for July 19, but once more flowers bloomed too quickly. Impatient insurgents in Central Chê-kiang acted on July 1, and Ch'iu Chin sent a messenger, who travelled to Anhui by sunlight and by starlight, to inform Hsü Hsi-lin of this happening.

The Governor of Anhui had issued commands that all revolutionaries be seized. Hsü Hsi-lin thought: 'Better I seize him before he seizes me.' He therefore invited the Governor on July 6 to inspect a police drill. When the dignitary arrived Hsü Hsi-lin approached, gave a military salute in the European manner, and, drawing a revolver from his boot, fired on the Governor three times, inflicting mortal wounds. Hsü Hsi-lin then cried in a loud voice, 'I glory in belonging to the Revolutionary Party!' called his pupils about him, and took refuge in the arsenal. Imperial soldiers besieged the place, and when the ammunition of the besieged was exhausted captured Hsü Hsi-lin who was trying to escape by the roof. He was led before the dying Governor and then before a tribunal, where he frankly declared revolutionary principles. The Vice-Governor pronounced the death sentence: Hsü Hsi-lin's body should be opened: his living heart removed.

The Government was aroused, repressive measures increased, officials behind the great black doors of their bureaus trembled, not knowing where revolt would next appear. In

Shaohsing a member of the local gentry, one of those whom the sharp tongue of the Honored One had wounded, went to Kuei-fu, the Manchu Prefect, and laid information against Ch'iu Chin, whom he accused of being connected with Hsü Hsi-lin. The Prefect at once ordered his official barge and started for Hangchow, seat of the Governor, to whom he made personal report.

The news of Hsü Hsi-lin's execution did not reach Ch'iu Chin until July 9. It is recorded that she wept. Did she feel that his action had been overimpetuous, ill-advised? Had he not cast away all hope of immediate success? Tears did not help, regrets did not help. Ch'iu Chin knew that she must act. On July 10 she and the students held a meeting. Some suggested immediate local rising and assassination of the Prefect. Such action would have run counter to the plans already made for the attack on Hangchow planned for the nineteenth. Ch'iu Chin decided to wait, to try to carry out the plan agreed on.

At dawn July 12 students crept in with a message from Hangchow: Imperial soldiers were moving, plans must be abandoned; what counter-stroke could Ch'iu Chin suggest? She called a mass meeting of students; this plan was discussed; that plan was analyzed; no decision was taken. Many students left the college and hurried back to their homes.

Early the next afternoon word came that a body of Manchu soldiers was actually marching on Shaohsing. Could this be true? Scouts went out to see what they could see. Returned, breathless. Soldiers were entering the city. Students urged Ch'iu Chin to escape, but she did not answer. About a dozen remained with her but when troops actually appeared in front of the college some of these slipped out at the back, swam the canal, and vanished. Soldiers searched the college, finding arms and revolvers. Meanwhile Ch'iu Chin sat quietly in her room and, with six others, was taken prisoner.

At her trial the next day she refused to answer questions — merely asked what her fault had been. The Prefect Kuei-fu, who had presented the complimentary address upon her induction as Principal of Ta-t'ung College, admired her; he and his wife had been good to the energetic young woman of whom they were fond. Hiding his face with his sleeve, he ordered that she be removed.

Ancient Chinese law required that a prisoner admit his crime, hence the use of torture, but Ch'iu Chin had refused to speak. Poems which she had written were found, two of these were considered proof of guilt. They are 'Autumn Wind' and 'Song of Precious Knife.'

AUTUMN WIND

Autumn wind rises *hsi-i-i* one hundred grasses yellow,
Autumn wind by nature violent, vindictive,
Forces myriad flowers to bend their heads awry.
Help me, Autumn chrysanthemum, to brave Autumn frost.
Autumn chrysanthemums are rooted in the Yellow Seed;
The *chung*, the *lou*, lift folded petals, reach the windy clouds.
Autumn moon, a mirror round, reflects its splendor from the stream.
One surge clear of ripples dares to heave, to move;
Last night wind, wind, rain, rain — Autumn.
Autumn frost, Autumn dew, heart suppresses Autumn grief.

Green, green, are tender leaves which, blown, fear
    to fall.
Circling tree-tops, Hu vultures ominously croak;
Chilly, soughing, Autumn wind is a jade-stone lute.
At Han frontier, T'ang passes, Autumn thoughts
    shoot forth like arrows.
Beyond frontiers, high Autumn; Hu horses fat,
    well-fed.
Brave General, enraged, summons yellow gold
    shields.
Gold shields come; extend like clouds; fight Hu
    dogs.
Brave General laughs much, calls sons of Han.
In Yellow Dragon land, they drink deep draughts
    — the wine of liberation!

SONG OF PRECIOUS KNIFE

Han household Palace pillars stand in slanting
    sunset-light;
Fifty Centuries in age — old country now is dead.
Deep, deep, sunk in sleep, several hundred years.
The folk, whose ears shame should redden, unrealizing,
    perform tasks of slaves.
I think of early ancestors who lived at Hsien Yüan,
Went forth, rose and wheeled, settled in K'un Lun
    hills;
Spread — over the earth, reached from Yellow Stream
    to Long River.
Their great knives quickly conquered Central Plain.
Grievous cries sounded from Plum-Blossom Hill —
    what could be done?
In Emperor's City, thorns, weeds, buried the bronze
    Camels.
Many times turn head gaze toward Capital's Glory;
In ruined country pitiful songs fill air, moans resound,
    silent tears flow;

In North, from   eight countries,   allied   soldiers
Seize   rivers,   take hills;   other regions,   traitors   be-
    stow   as gifts.
White Seed   comes   from West.   Ring   warning bell!
To me   our Leader   presents   a gold-washed   sword.
Possessing   this   my heart   is full of courage, pride;
To redden   its steel,   is now   the thought   which   rules
    me,
One hundred   times   ten thousand   skulls   are but so
    many   feathers.
When at leisure   on bathing day,   will gaze,   a hundred
    times,   on sword's   precious light.
Inadequate   my life,   how rise   to greater   heights?
I take   an oath: 'Desire   in death   to find   life's   road.'
Within   our frontier,   harmony,   peace,   depend   on
    armor,   weapons.
Ching K'o   guest of   Ch'in Prince,   whom he was sent to
    kill,   took his dagger,   wrapped in a map,   but the
    handle protruded.
He struck one blow,   did not succeed,   was seized,   lost
    his life.
It matters not   attempt failed,   essence   of evil   Prince
    was startled.
I would   lead   by the hand   people   of my ancestral
    realm;
In every   corner   of Yü's   country   seed   of slaves   in-
    trudes.
Fellow-countrymen,   fellow-countrymen,   your   hearts
    are dead!   What   shall be done?
I seize   in hand   hair-pencil,   write   'Song of Precious
    Knife.'

Precious   Knife,   your song   strengthens   my liver,   my
    gall,
Revives   souls   in this dead land,   calls   on the multi-
    tude   to rise.

Precious Knife,   and   my best self,   —   who joins   our
 band?
Am done with   friends,   done with   foes   *but*
Do not   regard   you,   foot of steel,   as a thing,   lacking
 courage:
To save country,   rare   achievement,   I rely   on you to
 fulfill.
Consider   Cosmos   a furnace,   Yin, Yang,   its fuel,
 hsi-i-i-i.
Will collect   steel   from   Six Islets   of world.
Fuse,   cast,   put forth   a thousand   times ten thousand
 Precious Knives *hsi-i-i-i-i*,
Make clear,   pure,   our sacred   land.
Connecting,   an unbroken thread,   with burning,   burning,
 awe-inspiring   flame   *hsi-i-i-i*   of our ancestor   the
 Yellow Emperor;
Will   wash clean   unnatural   shame   which   for a thou-
 sand,   a hundred,   years has sullied   our annals!

Once more Ch'iu Chin was brought to trial. She, fearing
that some inadvertent word might implicate a fellow revolutionary, refused to speak. She, whose lips had often let forth
a blast of words, remained silent. However, she wrote one
sentence while in the court, a sentence of seven characters
containing not only a play on her own surname Ch'iu —
Autumn — but a reference to Autumn, the time of executions,
the time of decay. The sentence reads: 'Autumn rain, Autumn
wind, Autumn-heart-grief, slay.'

Sentence of decapitation was passed. Ch'iu Chin begged
that she might be spared the humiliation of baring her torso
as she passed through the streets. This request was granted.

At daybreak on the sixth day of the Sixth Moon, *ting wei*
year, according to our calendar July 15, 1907, she was led to
execution.

None dared to claim body or skull; they lay on the execution ground near Shaohsing Pavilion until some charitable association, providing a coffin, buried Ch'iu Chin on a near-by hill. Here it remained until, sometime later, her young son escorted his mother's remains to the family burying-ground by Hsiang River.

Never was execution more impolitic. Among the people terror spread. Young girls, who had given up foot-binding, feared that they might be considered revolutionary and reverted to the practice. Children were taken from the schools, reaction against modern ways was felt.

The execution of Ch'iu Chin showed that the authorities were intent on destroying the barely hatched ideas of reform, on drying the springs of progress. The gentry of Chêkiang impeached the Prefect who had ordered execution, and public opinion in neighboring provinces was roused; so much so that an Imperial Censor brought the matter to the direct attention of the Throne, and the Empress Dowager, when she heard the tale, is reported to have wept.

Ch'iu Chin's death was fecund. Although she had not attained her object, hearts of rulers were stirred.

Four years passed. Years which brought fruition of Ch'iu Chin's hopes: the Decree of Heaven was altered, alien Manchus stepped from the Dragon Throne, Sun Yat-sen returned from exile to become first President of the Chinese Republic, declared in the autumn of 1911. Although he soon withdrew in favor of Yüan Shih-kai, Sun Yat-sen held a governmental post and exerted great influence among the people as Father of the Revolution.

He and other leaders felt that burial beside her pattern the ardent patriot Yo Fei was Ch'iu Chin's due. During the sum-

mer of 1912, therefore, the coffin was fetched from Hsiang
River and rested once more beside West Lake. Many attended
the funeral and many came later to an 'escort grief meeting':
such is the Chinese idiom for 'memorial service.' A photograph of the more prominent is included in Ts'an-chih's pamphlet, Sun Yat-sen himself being seated in the centre of the
group.

To-day an elaborate monument, in early Republican style,
covers the grave. It is approached through Wind and Rain
Pavilion, where laudatory phrases are suspended. In a near-by
building relics of the Honored One are treasured. Among the
greatly admired specimens of her handwriting are antithetical
phrases written on her mother's death at the age of sixty-two,
the text of the incriminating poem 'Autumn Wind,' and a
number of rules and regulations for the army she helped to
raise. There, too, hangs the blood-stained robe worn at her
execution, and in a little box, made in Fitchburg, Massachusetts, for an Iver Johnson revolver, lie the kingfisher green
bracelets given Hsü Tzŭ-hua as a keepsake.

Hsü Tzŭ-hua, Ch'iu Chin's comrade, the arrow of whose
knowledge found the target of her soul, composed a long
epitaph which is engraved, in the handwriting of Wu Chih-
ying, upon the Honored One's tomb. It has furnished many
details for this account of her life. The closing section
reads:

Years but thrice ten and three. *wu hu!* alas! inhuman!
Meditate upon traces of her conduct, actions: she flouted
limitation of lesser virtues, gave way to, indulged own
overbearing disposition: Liking wine, liking sword-play,
would not be bound by rites, laws; shoots of uprightness
she diligently heeded. When an audience, like grain
growing rank and close, sat widespread, words of her

discussion issued sharp as lance-points, an arrow from the bow her resolute virtue. People, unceremoniously treated, feared greatly, none dared oppose color of her speech, by even a soft hair of down.

Although loving her own path she was encircled by a law — the Way of Right Conduct. From first to last this was never overstepped. Because sharp lance of speech was not held back, by half the people she was hated, by half feared.

wu hu! alas! that Honored One should die in such manner. Had already borne son, daughter, one of each, who at this time were by Hsiang River.

Later, in Seventh Moon, Hsü Tzǔ-hua of Stone Gate, lamenting the Honored One's imprisonment through revenge, pained that she had met with tyranny, grieved that her years were not long, resentful that her ambition was not consummated, invited Wu Chih-ying, learned woman from City of the Wu-t'ung Trees, to join in purchasing a piece of ground at Hsi Ling bridge, there to bury the Honored One. Used inscriptions on grave to inform coming world that not only under Southern Sung were heroes lightly put to death; that all shall esteem, remember in their hearts her fiery heroism; that those who walk back and forth looking down in meditation, looking up with respect, shall sob aloud as their tears flow, shall not endure to leave.

She lies beside the grave of Prince Yo. May the flower-of-their-fame never fade.

☯

Ch'iu Chin is a figure unique in Chinese history. Her atavic ancestry can, however, be clearly traced. Forerunners have evinced her various characteristics. Women artists — the word includes calligraphists, poets, and painters — women warriors, women educators have been known since early days. None, however, has combined in one person the qualities which, ripening to fruition in the twentieth century, made of Ch'iu Chin a pattern for a new age.

The Artists

LI CH'ING–CHAO: POET

Red sleeve tends incense
At night studying books.

IDEAL marriage is expressed in the two lines quoted above, which are illustrated in one of his fine line drawings by the Ch'ing artist Wu Yu-ju. A Chinese realizes instantly that the woman who tends incense — a wife's duty — is young, otherwise she would not wear red. The couple are evidently scholars. What more delightful than nightly impingement of two minds?

A long simple table covered with a length of striped brocade, a candle, burning incense, cloth-covered books, picture rolls standing in a bronze container; in vases, sprigs of flowers, branches of pine; outside the round window, where hangs a light reed blind, bamboos sway in the breeze. Such is the picture.

History records a marriage which this picture may well illustrate: the union of Chao Ming-ch'êng, his style Tê-fu, to Li I-an, her style Ch'ing-chao, whom the Chinese consider their greatest poetess. A note on the bridegroom's life reads:

> Chao Ming-ch'êng's father was about to select a wife for his son. Ming-ch'êng resting quietly by day dreamt that he hummed a poem; upon awakening could recollect only three lines. His father elucidated them saying:

'They clearly indicate Ming-ch'êng will be the spouse of
a lady who can write poems and essays.'

Later the venerable Li had a daughter, a daughter
named I-an — Mutation of Peace — gifted with literary
ability. Shortly thereafter she knotted in happiness the
girdle of a bride.

The happiness of early wedded life endured — Tê-fu —
Virtuous Eminence — and Ch'ing-chao — Limpid-Light —
assimilated the joy of intellectual life in perfect accord. Each
found in the other, 'one, the arrow of whose knowledge met
the target of the soul.' They lived in what is now the Province
of Shantung, during the last days of Northern Sung, a dynasty

which occupied the Dragon Throne from A.D. 960 to 1126; a period in several ways unique. The Founder, instead of 'raising the standard of revolt' against his predecessors in the customary manner of the Sons of Han, was forced by his soldiers to assume leadership in the strife-ridden country. Seizing him, they draped his unwilling person in imperial yellow and bore him to the capital. The Empress Regent, the lawful Son of Heaven being but a child, bowed her head in abdication. The Sung Dynasty was, therefore, founded in peace and, beloved of the people, reigned in peace. Nor did downfall come from internal difficulties as is also customary among Sons of Han. Golden Tartars from the North, stern barbarian nomads, swept into a peaceful China and, in 1126, bore the artist Emperor Hui Tsung into cold captivity. This happened after Tê-fu had died and while Limpid-Light was trying to rescue the treasures her husband had assembled.

During the one hundred and seventy-six years of peace, a gift to the people of China from the Sung Emperors, artistic and cultural activity of the land reached its apogee. The brilliant virile life under the T'ang rulers never approached the exquisite introspection which came with the Sung scholars, artists, and philosophers. Furthermore block-printing, invented at the end of the T'ang Dynasty and but little used during the period of confusion which, under the Five Dynasties, then ensued, was developed under the Sung. The first printing of Classical Books, begun under the Five Dynasties, was finished A.D. 953. This had immense influence on contemporary thought. The supply of books rapidly became plentiful and cheap, yet beautiful. Sung editions bought to-day show fine technical control of the unwieldly blocks.

The Emperor Hui Tsung, a fine artist, and a devoted patron

of the arts, founded the first Academy of Painting in China and organized it on the lines of a Confucian college. He himself instructed the students, judged their works, and awarded degrees. The landscape artists of the day painted the marvellous 'portraits' of hills and water, revealing the inmost spirit of every scene. In the *Pi Fa Chi, Records of Brush-Work*, a conversation between an old sage and a young painter is recorded. Doctor Sirén's translation reads:

> 'Painting is to make beautiful things; and the important point is to obtain their true likeness; is it not?' He answered: 'It is not. Painting is to paint, to estimate the shapes of things, to really obtain them; to estimate the beauty of things, to reach it; to estimate the reality (significance) of things and to grasp it. One should not take outward beauty for reality. He who does not understand this mystery will not obtain truth, even though his pictures may contain likeness.' I asked: 'What is likeness and what is truth?' The old man said: 'Likeness can be obtained by shapes without spirit, but when truth is reached, both spirit and substance are fully expressed.'

Ceramics too were exquisite: the celadons, color of willow buds in Spring or the soft bloom of sedum; the cream and the brown *tzŭ chou* ware; the marvellous *kuan*, of an elusive color, neither green nor blue, shot with ruby-red as in fine brocade; the *ju*, rays of moulded moonlight; all were jewels of the kiln.

Bronzes from early days were collected with avidity. Inscriptions cast upon them were deciphered; replicas were made and treasured. Philosophers argued loud and long, as did social reformers. The dynamic era of Northern Sung throbbed with cultural activity.

Among the collectors none was more keen than Chao Tê-fu. On the first and fifteenth of the month he would go out, pawn his clothes, and, with the proceeds, buy bronzes, books, and rubbings of inscriptions on famous stones. He would also buy fruit. On his return home he and his wife would eat the fruit and gaze at his 'trophies of the chase.' All this and more Limpid-Light herself relates.

If Ming-ch'êng — or Tê-fu; his names are interchangeable — was a collector, his young wife was a poet. She wrote largely in a form introduced under the Sung known as the *tz'ŭ*. Far more flexible than the 'poems according to law' perfected under the T'ang, the *tz'ŭ* is composed to fit some well-known air. The lines, irregular in length, must conform to a strict rhyme and tone pattern. They require handling by a dexterous maker of verses. For this reason they are especially difficult to translate, their virtue residing largely in the brilliant technical finish which cannot be transferred from one language to another.

The *tz'ŭ* of Li Ch'ing-chao are considered perfect. Once, so the record states:

> Ming-ch'êng was obliged to 'bear-on-the-back light bamboo-boxes': to travel far-away. I-an could not endure such partings. She wrote 'The Severed Plum Blossom,' a *tz'ŭ*, and sent it, on an embroidered handkerchief, to Ming-ch'êng.'

THE SEVERED PLUM BLOSSOM: RESENTFUL
GRIEF AT PARTING

Fragrance   of rose-red   lily root   has left   jade sleeping-
    mat   this Autumn.
Slowly   loosen   my silk-gauze   skirt.
Alone   he embarked   on spear-orchid   boat.
Who   sends   embroidered   letters   from   among   the
    clouds?

Southering time   wild geese   form characters on sky;   moon-
        radiance   wells through   Western Pavilion.
Faded   flowers   toss in wind;   streams   flow   freely.
Of   one type   thinking-of-each-other   thoughts,
In   two places   Autumn-heart-grief.
No way   to melt,   remove   this passion;
Its essence,   falling   from   locked eyebrows,
Lights   on heart's   tip.

On the festival of Chung Yang — in Autumn when nights
are chilly — she wrote for her husband:

INSPIRED BY WINE IN SHADE OF FLOWERS

Thin   mist,   thick   clouds,   sadness   throughout   the day.
Happy-omen   incense   in gold   brazier   has burned out,
Once more   glorious   Chung   Yang   season;
Jade   pillow   is placed   within   silk-gauze   tent,
At turn   of night   chill   first   penetrates.

After   yellow   dusk,   beside   Eastern   bamboo-fence,
        raise   wine-cup;
Scent   of darkness   overflows   my sleeve;
Say   not   the soul   faints   not   in ecstasy;
Roll up   the blind.   Wind   from the West.
Faded   this person   as are   these   yellow   chrysanthemum
        blooms.

Ming-ch'êng, it is recorded: 'sighed and expressed admiration, but, fearing he could not match it, felt the demon of shame
in his heart. Bending his mind to the subject, he made great
efforts attempting to surpass her poem. In his determination
he withdrew from receiving guests and for three days and
nights forgot food, forgot sleep. Having composed five
times ten *tz'ŭ* he slipped among them the one I-an had written,

then showed them all to his friend Lu Tê-fu (Lu, Virtuous Scholar). Once and again — thrice — Lu Tê-fu tested the poems, said: "Only three lines are extremely beautiful." Ming-ch'êng enquired which. Pressed, Lu Tê-fu replied, quoting the last three lines of I-an's *tz'ŭ*.'

Ming-ch'êng did not suffer seriously from jealousy. He rejoiced in his wife's talents, as is clearly shown in the account which I shall presently quote of their life together. All too short it was. Nomad invaders swept from the North, the people fled before them. Treasures collected were dispersed. Li Ch'ing-chao lived on, south of the Great River, a lonely widow. Of her lyrics collected in the booklet *Sou Yü Tz'ŭ* — *Scoured Jade Tz'u* — less than a score remain; nor can they be precisely dated. Born in the fourth year of *yüan fên*, corresponding to A.D. 1081, the date of her death is unknown. She is supposed to have lived her latter years near Hai Ning, in Chêkiang, where the great bore of the Ch'ien T'ang River rushes upstream against the tide. At certain times of the year it forms a boiling wall of water twenty feet and more in height. Did Ch'ing-chao ever describe this stirring sight with her magic writing-brush? We do not know.

I have translated a group of the poems. They deal with love and longing, with the life a Chinese woman led behind the baton-door. The great bird P'êng referred to in the dream poem, a *tz'ŭ* which conveys the inconsequential aura of events in the realm of sleep, is a supernatural creature capable of moving an infinite distance in one flight. It is a symbol of a successful poet.

REMEMBER A DREAM

(Sung to the air: *Yü Chia Ao*)

Interlocked cloud billows of the sky melt into mists
of dawn;
On point of setting is Star River; a thousand sails
dance.
As in a dream, my soul returns to Lord of Heaven's
Palace;
Hear words of Heavenly Lord:
'Whither do you return home?' is asked with deep
regard.

I reply: 'Road is long. Sigh daily as sun sinks
at horizon edge.
Study writing of poems. Deceived, think I have found
lines that startle men.'
On wind from nine times ten thousand *li* distant Great
bird, P'êng, flies straight.
Wind ceases, — drops.
Thistledown boat blown, reaches Island Hills of
the Immortals.

SUNSET OF SPRING

(Sung to the air: *Yüan Wang Sun*)

Dreams cut short; water-clock run dry;
Sorrow deep; wine-fumes annoy;
Pillow of happiness emanates only cold.
Kingfisher screen faces dawn.
Without the door who swept withered red petals?
Night wind came.

Cut short notes from jade *hsiao*; in what place my man?
Spring also is gone.
How could he endure to fail return-home tryst?

This passion, this desire,
This moment I entrust to passing clouds,
To seek a clue from Spirit of the East.

JOY AFTER WINE

(Sung to the air: *Ju Mêng Chin*)

Remember river pavilion as sun went down;
Deep in wine did not perceive return-home road.
Joy ended. In twilight, boat turned back,
Erred, entered deep pool of lotus blooms.
Wrangled at the ferry; wrangled at the ferry;
Gulls, egrets rose startled, a rapid flight.

PASSION WITHIN THE BATON–DOOR

(Sung to the air: *Yü Chung Hua*)

White silk cords her slender waist.
She cannot endure nostalgia of Spring.
On fresh evening make-up fall shadows of sparse
     plum-blossoms.
Willowy, willowy, graceful, graceful, what does
     she resemble?
A drift of floating clouds.

Vermilion lips move: song is lovely.
Indulged, she suffers, suffers from vexation.
Bye-path hidden in peach-flowers
Leads straight to ferry.
Hopes disappointed she gazes toward Green Jasper
     Terrace: Clear night moon
Should shine on wheel of return-home chariot.

TREASURED EMOTIONS

Window, with rattling lattice, torn paper; broken
     book-stand, no writings, no books.
Official rest-house! indignant, regret it should be thus.

First   Secretary   of Ch'ing Prefecture,   miserly Lord   of
        square-holed   cash,
Flutters,   flutters,   day   by   day   among   joy-producing
    affairs.

To   write   poems   must withdraw;   close   door;   drop
    intercourse   with friends.
Cease   work,   rest   in quiet   fragrance;   think   lovely
    thoughts.
In   struggle   of world   I long   to find   a friend   to depend
        on,
Do not   desire   a teacher   like   Tzǔ Hsü-tzǔ.

PASSION OF THOSE PARTED

(Sung to the air: *A Butterfly Loves a Flower*)

Clear,   after warm rain;   soft   breeze   now   breaks up   ice;
Willow's   eye,   plum-tree's   cheek,   realize   stirring   in
        Spring's heart.
With whom   can I   enjoy   thoughts   inspired by wine,
    poems   sprung   from passion?
Tears   melt   remains   of face-powder;   flowered filigree
    head-dress,   heavy.
Try   to embroider,   with   gold   silk thread,   a lined
    robe;
Hill-high   pillow   is pulled   awry,
Bends   gold   love-pheasant   on   hairpin.
Alone —   heart   wrapped in grief —   have   no   good
    dreams.
In depth   of night   snip   off,   toy with,   soot lamp-flower.

THOUGHTS IN THE WOMEN'S ENCLOSURE

(Sung to the air: *Dotted Red Lips*)

Silence,   solitude,   deep   in women's   enclosure,
A single   inch   of soft   intestine   holds   a thousand
    threads   of grief.

Regret Spring; Spring goes;
How few   the drops of rain-flowers-rain.

Lean, now there, now here, on low-railed screen
But passion is not assuaged.
My man! is where?
Fragrant grasses merge with Heaven,
But his return-home road cuts short my vision.

SPRING PASSION

Desolate, lonely the courtyard;
Fine rain, needle-point wind persist;
Door sequence must be closed;
Loved willows, gay flowers will bud in Cold Food
    Season,
Ever, ever, breath of Heaven vexes men.
Wakening after wine, I rub my head;
Gone is rich flavor of writing poems at leisure.
He left for wide spaces, crossed over their bounds;
Ten thousand, a thousand heart's thoughts are difficult
    to send him.

Is the *tz'ŭ*, 'Parting,' autobiographical? It may be so.
Perhaps it was written when Li Ch'ing-chao and Tê-fu separated by the bank of the stream; he to fulfil official business,
she to convey their treasures to the South. They never met
again. The 'Song of White Poplar Pass' alluded to in the
tz'ŭ was written by Wang Wei and time and again was recited
by friends on parting. It was often repeated on the same occasion, not merely once, but many times. It reads:

SONG OF YANG KUAN, WHITE POPLAR PASS
By Wang Wei

Wei City at dawn, rain lays light dust;
At traveller's inn green, green, willows in new leaf.

Exhort companion yet again to empty wine-cup.
With no old friend he will go west beyond White
    Poplar Pass.

PARTING

A *tz'ŭ* sung to the air: *Fêng Huang T'ai Shang I Ch'ui Hsiao*

Fragrance cold in gold lion-incense-burner,
Quilt thrown back lies in red waves.
Rise, listless, comb own hair,
Indifferent to dust thick on rich dressing-case.
Sun touches height of reed-blind hook:
In breast springs dread of separation, of cut-apart
    bitterness.
Would speak of affairs, many, few; still desist.
Am newly thin; not from wine-sickness,
Not from Autumn grief.

Release him, release him, he will turn, go-away!
Recite one thousand, ten thousand times 'White Poplar
    Pass.'
Realize: impossible to keep him.
Think of friends in Wu Ling, far away;
Of Ch'in Pavilion enveloped in mist.
Stand alone; before me, only flowing water.
He should think of me, the whole day; pupils of eyes
    staring, congealed.
Pupils of my eyes, stare, congealed.
Now is added new grief.

Time of Twilight and the famous *Shêng Shêng Man* seem to
have been written during Ch'ing-chao's widowhood.

TIME OF TWILIGHT — SPRING

(Sung to the air: *Spring in Wuling*)

Wind drops, faded flowers scent the dust.
Weary; after sunset comb my hair.

Chattels   remain;   husband   has gone;   my charge,   my
        charge,   is ended.
Would   speak,   but   tears   flow.
Hear   that by Shuang Ch'i — The Paired Stream — Spring
        is glorious;
Propose   to float   there   in small   boat,
Perhaps   a little   Shuang   Ch'i   pinnace.
Laden,   it   might not   move
Bearing   an excess   of grief.

SUNG TO THE AIR: *SHÊNG SHÊNG MAN*

I

Search,   search,   seek,   seek,   lone,   lone,
Drear,   drear,   sad,   sad: to the uttermost,   the uttermost.
Sudden   warmth   comes   although   it is cold-time   season.
Now   very   difficult   to rest.
Three   tiny cups,   two flat saucers,   of weakest wine,
How   can they help   withstand   sharpness   of dawn-rising
        wind?
Wild geese   fly   over,
Verily   heart   is wounded.
Think   of friends   whom   in   old   days   I knew.

II

Yellow   blossoms   piled,   heaped,   overflow   the court.
Pining,   haggard,   weak   as   now,
Who   is there   able   to gather?
Stand   beside   the   window
Alone,   by myself;   how   live   until   the dark?
wu t'ung trees   are   wrapped   in misting   rain.
Drop,   drop,   drip,   drip;   until   yellow   dusk.
This   goes on,   —   a sequence.
Can   the   one   word   ' grief' express   all?

In addition to the poems, Limpid-Light's writing-brush has bequeathed to us a record of her life with Tê-fu, and of her adventures on a Southward journey. It forms what the Chinese call a *hou hsü* — an 'afterwards preface' — to the famous 'Chin Shih Lu' or 'Golden Stones Record,' being the catalogue, of over two thousand inscriptions from his collection, left by her husband Chao Ming-ch'êng. With what care must Ch'ing-chao have preserved the precious manuscript from the depredations of bandits who ravaged the land and destroyed the treasures Ming-ch'êng had collected. The *hou hsü* I quote below.

A little 'short stop' was written when Limpid-Light, then poor and old, refused, as did the early warrior Hsiang Yü of whom she writes, to pass 'East of the River' and return to the homeland. She and he both cringed at the thought of appearing in poverty and despair among their 'old fathers.'

SUMMER DAY: A SHORT STOP

At birth should become a Valiant person;
At death, should make an heroic ghost.
Until this day think of Hsiang Yü
Who was not willing to pass East of the River.

Further details of her life I leave to be told by Li I-an — Mutation-of-Peace, her style Ch'ing-chao — Limpid-Light — in:

PREFACE TO THE *CHIN SHIH LU* — *RECORD OF GOLDEN STONES*

I married into the Chao Clan during *hsin i* year of the Chien Chung period (A.D. 1101)....
The household, plain as pure white silk, was poor and frugal. (My husband) Tê-fu — Virtuous and Eminent —

had great learning. Each dark-of-the-moon, each full-of-the-moon, he took leave, went out, pledged his clothes, and, taking one half one thousand coins, walked to Hsiang Kuo Monastery, where he offered prices for rubbings of famous inscriptions on stones; then buying ripe fruit he returned home. Sitting opposite each other we inspected (what he had bought) amused ourselves while sucking and eating (the fruit).

Two years later he became an official and had opportunity to collect and collate, to exhaust completely, old writings, and rare characters in all-below-the sky; had copies made of unprocurable books; bought writings and paintings by famous men as well as rare and ancient vessels.

We once had in our hands a peony flower scroll by Hsü Hsi, keeping it overnight, unrolling, gazing at it; the price demanded, twenty times ten thousand coins, we had no plan to meet. For several days husband, wife, sat facing each other in resentful disappointment. Tê-fu became prefectural official of two departments, draining his Imperial Pay in the matters of metal and wood: books of the ancients. Whenever he bagged a book — as a hunter bags his quarry — we investigated, collated, and the very same day read it critically. Whenever he obtained famous paintings, cup-shaped vases, or other vessels we toyed with them, unrolled, rolled the paintings, smoothed the vessels with our hands; pointed out imperfections and defects. When one candle had burned, it was our rule to stop. For this reason our treasures were good, finely worked. Writings, paintings all arranged were higher in quality than those of other households. After each meal we sat in Return-Home Hall, brewed tea, and pointing to the piled, heaped-up books and histories, said: 'A certain matter is referred to: in a certain book, in a certain roll; now on which page, in which line is it found?' Our object: the one who hit the target and the one who did not, the one who conquered, the one who lost, should drink tea in order of precedence. The one who hit the target then raised the tea-cup, the one who had failed laughed heartily so that the tea was overturned and spilt on his bosom; the one unable to drink would then rise defeated. In the books and histories of one hundred households, if no characters were faulty, lacking (Tê-fu) instantly offered a price, storing them and making alternative editions.

During the *ping wu* year of Ching K'ang period (A.D. 1126) Tê-fu being Prefect of Tzŭ Ch'uan, hearing that the Lo, a Mongol tribe, were invading Kaifêng, the capital city, filled square bamboo boxes and flat oblong boxes to overflowing with those things we doted on, doted on; how sorrowful, how sorrowful! We knew that we could not protect these things.

During *ting wei* year of Chien Yen period (A.D. 1127) suddenly the elder lady — my mother-in-law — died. We came South. The larger articles could not all be taken — therefore we first omitted the books printed from large and heavy boards; paintings in sets of many scrolls; vessels without inscriptions for recognition; we also omitted books with volumes already examined, paintings of the level and ordinary class; and vessels too large or too heavy. The articles taken filled ten and five carts, which were placed in stout cargo boats to ferry across Huai River. At our old home in Ch'ing Chou we locked these articles in ten rooms, expecting during the next bright year to make ready boats and fetch them. They were transformed — burnt to embers, ashes.

During the Sixth Moon, *i yu* year (A.D. 1129), Tê-fu dwelt awhile in a house at Ch'ih Yang, proceeded then, alone, to the Travelling Palace (while I continued Southward journey). Gazing down from the bank upon our boat he said parting words. My heart echoed with dread. I questioned him: 'When news from the city comes, be it of safety or of danger, how shall I act?' He answered from afar: 'All, you cannot attain to keeping. First relinquish heavy storage wagons, next the clothing and quilts, then follow written documents, next rolled maps and pictures, finally the old vessels. Only the Sung jars are to be preserved: what you yourself can carry upon your person. Never allow the stored, the lost, to pass from your mind.'

On narrow pathway the galloping horse departed.

During the Eighth Moon Tê-fu lay ill — not again did he rise from his bed.

The Six Palaces — that is, members of the Imperial Family — at this time travelled South. I deputed Tê-fu's assistant officer to store books, twice ten thousand rolls, and twice ten thousand volumes of inscriptions from golden stones of fame. I then left for Hung Chou. When Winter came Lo Tribesmen sacked the place. Finally all was relinquished. One may say that our treasures, ferried across the river in stout barges, were now scattered as clouds, mist.

A small surplus remained, a few rolled rolls; a few written volumes; poems by Li, by Tu, by Wei and by Liu and collections of essays: the *Shih Shuo* and the *Yen Tieh Lun;* inscriptions from stones, several tens of volumes, and a few rolls; also *ting* — tripod vessels — *nai* — incense braziers — and several low flat bamboo boxes of Southern T'ang books. I, the lonely mate, stored these in my solitary bedroom.

Northern rivers were not open to travel, therefore passing T'ai and Wên, I paused at Ch'ü in Yüeh, finally arriving in Hang and sending treasures to Ch'êng-hsien.

In Spring, *kêng hsü* year (A.D. 1130), Imperial soldiers succeeded in causing the death of many rebels. Taking my entire possessions I entered the household of the late General Li. Of ten articles but five or six remained. I still had five or seven bamboo boxes and arranged a house in

Yüeh City (present day Shao Hsing). One evening a robber dug a hole in the wall and bearing five boxes fled away. In the end, the Official Shui of Wu Province obtained them at a cheap price. There remained not one complete set; wrappers were destroyed, series of books and writings were mixed, confused. Suddenly seeing these books, it was as if I saw my loved man; my heart recalled Tê-fu at Tung Lai in Ching Chih — Hall of Quiet and Peace — arranging slips on books; laying fragrant herbs between the leaves; adding the hanging tags; laying together ten volumes to fill a wrapper — as he did in the beginning. Each day he examined two volumes, wrote an addendum to one volume, thus twice a thousand volumes had addenda; only five times one hundred remained. The handwriting was still fresh as new, yet on his grave trees already arched their boughs. Then I realized: To have the have one must suffer the not have; those who rejoice in union must endure separation. This universal law is the Rule of Life.

My slight record, from end to opening, is a warning to the learned, the accomplished, to all in this floating world who love ancient things. I close.

CHU SHU–CHÊN: POET

Wind blows flame of red candle her tears make a pool,
An inch of fragrant heart is dead, sunk in despair.

UNDER the Southern Sung Dynasty (A.D. 1126–1278), a few tens of years later than did Li Ch'ing-chao, there lived a lady who is famous for her exquisite *tz'ŭ* and also for her sad life. The sadness lay in the fact that she and her husband were not congenial. She was refinement personified, he was a *ts'u jên*, a coarse untutored person. Few details in regard to her life are known. The exact date is undetermined; her father's given name, her mother's Clan name, her husband's surname are unknown; she appears to have had no children. Her life was spent sadly writing poems, which are collected under the title *Tuan Ch'ang Tz'ŭ — Cutting Bowels Verses* — a name recalling the Chinese belief that emotion is seated in the five viscera.

There is no suggestion that the husband ill-treated Shu-chên from a physical point of view, nor, as he was an official, did she suffer poverty. No, they were out of sympathy, and the exigencies of a woman's life, within the baton-door, prevented her from developing outer interests. Hence, for the last six centuries, her name has been a universally recognized synonym for misery. Realization of how widespread this recognition still is, was brought to me one day in Shanghai, when collecting the material for this book. I directed Er-fa, a minor member of the staff, to go and purchase for me the *Cutting Bowels Verses*. Now Er-fa is a youth of about seventeen to whom the benefits of formal education have been denied. He has taste and has cultivated his talents with unusual zeal, but, at the time of which I speak, could not be described as in any way a learned person. He exclaimed at once, however: 'Oh! *Tuan Ch'ang Tz'ŭ*, by Chu Shu-chên, she was very unhappy. Her husband was a *ts'u jên*; not clever. Yes, very sad. The father thought only of money. He should not have chosen a stupid son-in-law.'

Er-fa's remark was, to me, revealing. It threw a shaft of light on woman's life in ancient China. Everything turned on marriage. Denied happiness of wifehood and honor of motherhood, a Chinese woman was isolated in her lovely courtyards.

Internal evidence of the *tz'ŭ* shows that, in her youth at all events, Chu Shu-chên lived in beautiful surroundings. She writes of her home as a place with an East Garden, a West Garden, a Western Two-storied Building, and a Sweet Cassia Hall. She leans on the rail in a summer-house surrounded by trees. As a little girl she showed cleverness and loved to read books, she also wrote *tz'ŭ*, practising assiduously. My teacher Mr. Nung chu — Cultivator-of-Bamboos — finds her work exquisite. The evanescent charm of *tz'ŭ* which depends on sound, on choice of character, on rhyme, and on rhythm is lost when brought into a strange language. The content often seems slight to a Western reader. To Mr. Nung the following verse suggested a world of loneliness which he described in passionate terms: 'The character in the first line should be "together," not "alone"; a young woman must have companionship, otherwise she sickens. Morning and evening she should put on fresh make-up. What use if there be no one to see? How can she sleep alone, how can her dreams form?' He continued at length in such vein, bemoaning the lot of a lonely wife.

SUNG TO THE AIR: MU LAN HUA

Walk   alone,   sit   alone.
Sing   alone,   drink a toast   alone;   then   sleep alone.
Stand   by myself,   spirit   wounded.
Nothing   to be done;   slight   cold   envelops   my person.
My passion,   who   is aware   of it?
Tears   wash away   remains   of morning   make-up,   not
      half   is left.
Autumn-heart-grief,   illness,   are   bound together;
I snuff the wick,   lamp is cold,   dreams   do not form.

Mid-Autumn Night the household unites in a feast; it is the season of full moon, the circle suggests happy marriage, union of husband and wife. Shu-chên writes a dainty *tz'ŭ*, full of allusions, in which she expresses her longing to be united with a man whom she can love, but finds herself tied to one whom she cannot care for.

The poems give a picture of the lady who called herself Yu Lou Chü Shih — Scholar who Lives in the Retired Two-storied Pavilion — but are not of special interest to Western readers. She and Ch'iu Chin were alike in that each was fated to uncongenial marriage. The lady of the twelfth century had no outlet for her energy other than in writing sad poems, whereas she of the twentieth century did much to change the course of history.

WEI FU–JÊN: CALLIGRAPHIST [1]

Iron strokes, silver hooks: describe the writing of Wang Hsi-chih

IN THE writing-brush the Chinese possess an aesthetic instrument of supreme vitality. Its tip filled with ink, rubbed liquid on the ink-stone, is capable of conveying thought, emotion, all rhythms of nature. As our musicians improvise, harmonizing one exquisite theme with the next, so Chinese artists improvise, blending one supple stroke with its peer. To them a 'writing' is more important, more revealing, than is a picture. A picture has certain bounds of objectivity. A writing, apart from its matter, is purely subjective. The curves and lines, the perfection of balance, of tone gradation, the swift momentum of the brush, and a hundred other details are what the Chinese so greatly admire. Through the ages calligraphists have been honored. Of the leaders, among the most honored, is a woman.

The Lady Wei — Wei *fu-jên*, her name Shuo — Lustrous,

[1] A delightful chapter on calligraphy appears in *My Country and My People*, by Lin Yu-tang.

her style Mao-i — Beautiful Curves — lived for seventy-eight years during the confusion which beset the Chin Dynasty, and died A.D. 350. Her husband, Li Chü, Governor of Ju Yin, the present-day Ying in Anhui, from his youth showed military skill as well as great intelligence. He was therefore a leader when the Chin Dynasty fled to the South and made Nanking its capital. He died as the result of a fall from his horse, being buried at Hsiang Yang.

The dignified Lady Wei lived on, a highly honored widow, and practised her art. Her nephew Wang Hsi-chih, who is considered the greatest calligraphist of all time, reverenced her as his teacher.

In the genealogy of calligraphy the Lady Wei is given as

the link between the great Chung Yu, who died A.D. 230, and the still greater Wang Hsi-chih, whose life spanned the years A.D. 321-379.

The writing of Chung Yu is described as being reminiscent of flying wild geese fluttering above the sea and posturing cranes floating in the sky, while the writing of Wang Hsi-chih is said to be light as drifting clouds, vigorous as a startled dragon.

The Lady Wei and her predecessors excelled in the *li shu*, a style of character rather square and blunt. Wang Hsi-chih evolved the freer forms, the running hand and 'grass' characters untrammelled by convention. He it was who lived to meet his friends on the third day of the Third Moon, at Spear Orchid Pavilion near Shaohsing. There, far from the turmoil of battle, brought to the North by fierce Nomads, the scholars drank wine, and wrote poems in artistic competition.

In 1922 I visited Spear Orchid Pavilion, then newly restored, and found it one of the most exquisite spots imaginable. An extraordinary air of refinement enveloped the grounds and the simple white buildings. It formed a perfect shrine in honor of a calligraphist. What it may have suffered since, in a decade and more of revolution, I do not know.

The Chin period was one of disaster and despair. Art suffered. Of what was created much perished. Creative spirit, however, like the blossom of a crocus hidden deep in earth throughout dark winter, waited but to bloom.

Comprehension of calligraphy presupposes apprehension of the animistic principles underlying Far Eastern art. A perception most difficult for Occidentals to capture. The manifestations of nature in their living rhythms are dynamic, not static — so it is with calligraphy: life's movement is its most treasured characteristic.

Furthermore, it reveals the soul of the writer. Kuo Jo-hsü, an artist of the Sung period, wrote a treatise: *T'u Hua Chien Wên Chih, The Record of Seeing and Hearing in regard to Scrolls and Paintings*. He makes the following statement (the translation is my own):

> Therefore he of the Yang Clan did not receive *ch'i yün* — the resonance of the spirit — from his teacher, nor did Lan Pien transmit it to his son; *ch'i yün* descends from the loom of Heaven, issues from the storehouse of the soul. Hence looking at the style of signatures — that is, proofs of identity — may be called seeing the heart's seal. This style originates in the heart. A man must think earnestly to perfect its form and rendering. The rendering will then be in harmony with his heart. This is called 'the seal'....
>
> Furthermore calligraphy and painting spring from ardent thought. They are its record on silk or paper. If this record be not a 'seal,' a proof of identity, what is it?
>
> If even these signatures betray all nobility and meanness, disaster and good fortune, how could calligraphy and painting fail to reveal the height, the depth, of man's *ch'i yün?*
>
> Now calligraphy and painting are the same! Philosopher Yang said: 'Words are the "voice" of the heart, calligraphy is the "portrait" of the heart.' Voice, form, manner — the high-minded, the despicable, each can be recognized.

In this great art the Lady Wei excelled. In the *Chin Shu — Records of the Chin Dynasty* — her writing is enthusiastically described: 'Her true characters are like the crystals of a shattered jade vase; splendid as the moon on a terrace of jasper; pliant as branches of a sweet-scented tree waving in light wind '

The *Book of One Hundred Beauties* contains the following verse:

THE LADY WEI

White wrist lightly brushes, fills, fair paper,
Lovely her new style: characters correctly placed like flowers
    worn in hair.
She rests; discusses writing-brush arrangements of Chung, of
    Wang, but writes as she wills.
Once again appear the beauties of slender Flying Swallow
    and robust Jade Ring.

The allusions in the last line are to the famous beauties Chao Fei-yen, the Flying Swallow, who was so tiny that she is said to have danced on the uplifted palm of a courtier, and Yang Kuei-fei, famous beauty who nearly caused the downfall of the T'ang Dynasty. She was unusually large — not to say fat! The heavy lines and light lines of Lady Wei's calligraphy suggest to the writer these two famous persons.

Of the life of Lady Wei few details are known. The dignity of her personality, the ripeness of her years have, however, impressed the ages. For sixteen centuries, and more, the aura of her genius has enveloped womanhood.

Her gift, calligraphy, was manifested by Ch'iu Chin.

KUAN *FU-JÊN:* PAINTER

PICTURE OF PLUM BLOSSOMS AGAINST THE MOON

(Painted by Kuan fu-jên)

After snow, white quartz branches weighted, are still;
In time of frost jade stamens are cold.
Blossoms in village before house cannot be reached;
Display them across moon's centre to admire.
From Book of One Hundred Beauties.

THE Golden Tartars, whose incursions caused Li Ch'ing-chao's Southward flight, were, in the thirteenth century, themselves

engulfed by the Mongols, whose leader Genghiz Khan terrorized not only Asia but Europe. In A.D. 1263 his successor
Kublai Khan established the capital in Peking, and by 1279
had driven the last of the Sungs literally into the sea, the
boy-sovereign of the day flinging himself into the waters
which wash the coast of Southern China.

At this time Chao Mêng-fu, a lineal descendant of the soldier
who founded the Sung Dynasty, retired from official into
private life. He was a man of twenty-five, an artist of note,
being both painter and calligraphist. The young wife, whom
he adored, was equally gifted. Her name Kuan *fu-jên* — the
Lady Kuan — is listed among the great artists of the Central

Flowery State, she being also both painter and calligraphist. The instincts of the young couple were conservative, which is perhaps natural in a time of iconoclasm. The Mongols, whose service to the world is that they opened communications throughout Asia, habitually left destruction in their path. In the case of China, however, they were induced by Yelu Ch'u-ts'ai, an extremely intelligent Kitan, to preserve the population and profit by its skilled workers. Once established in Peking, the Mongol emperors themselves began to appreciate the art and scholarship of the vanquished, but many works of creative genius had perished before this occurred.

Chao Mêng-fu in revulsion turned his eyes to the past and praised the 'spirit of antiquity.' Doctor Sirén translates one of his colophons on a painting which reads:

> The most important quality in painting is the spirit of antiquity. If this is not present, the work is not worth much, even though it is skilfully executed. Men of to-day who know how to paint with a fine brush in a delicate manner and to lay on strong and brilliant colors consider themselves able painters. They are extremely ignorant, because if the spirit of antiquity is wanted, their works are faulty all through and not worth looking at. My pictures seem to be quite simple and carelessly done, but true connoisseurs will realize that they are very close to the old models and may therefore be considered good. I record this for the benefit of real connoisseurs and not for the ignorant.

Chao Mêng-fu formed his style on that of T'ang Dynasty artists, painted horses as did Han Kan and landscapes in the style of Wang Wei. His young wife, however, devoted herself to the themes dear to members of Hui Tsung's academy under the Sung Dynasty: bamboos, and plum-blossoms painted in monochrome. She also executed flowers and birds with great skill.

After the Lady Kuan died her husband wrote a famous grave-piece in which details of her life and parentage are given. Her paternal grandfather fled from the troubles in Ch'i, present-day Shantung, and settled at Wu Hsing in the fertile province of Chêkiang in modern Hu Hsien. The people respected him deeply and named his estate Perch of the Virtuous. The Lady Kuan's father was by nature unusually kind and courteous. His public spirit and fidelity were renowned in village and hamlet. The Lady — her name Tao Shêng — Way of Righteousness Rising as the Sun, her style Chung Chi — Second Beauty among three Sisters — is described by Chao Mêng-fu as follows:

> *fu-jên* from birth brilliant, intelligent, surpassed others. Her father regarding her as exceptional, desired to obtain remarkable son-in-law. I, the person who writes, came from within the same village gates as did her father. He regarded me also as exceptional, believed I must attain wealth and rank. Therefore *fu-jên* returned home in marriage to me.

After living several years in retirement Chao Mêng-fu in 1286 responded to the Imperial call and consented to take office under the Yüan, or Mongol, Dynasty. He and his wife left their green mid-China home, left the bamboo clumps, the rice-fields, the waterways, and journeyed to the capital. Peking, a small Northern frontier town, was very different to the city it became under the burgeoning imagination of the Mings, who, more than a century later, built the palaces we know. Remains of Kublai's earthen wall can still be traced, but even the site of the city differed in part from that

of the Ming capital. Here Chao Mêng-fu entered the Board
of War as secretary. The grave-piece is largely concerned
with the rapid steps which carried Chao Mêng-fu to favor,
to the ranks of high officialdom. He served in the capital
and in the provinces, holding various posts. At each step
the Lady Kuan accompanied him. This procedure was somewhat unusual. Chinese ladies were apt to remain at home
and arrange that concubines accompany their husband on
official journeys. Not so the Lady Kuan. She travelled back
and forth, ignoring weariness.

By the year 1311 Chao Mêng-fu had become a Han Lin, he
had attained the rank of Academician in the Writing-Brush
Forest. This was a high honor. Members were allowed to
place a tablet over their doors bearing the words: *t'ai shih ti*,
Younger Brother of Great Historians. If brethren of the same
family attained the honor they were designated Elder and
Younger Brothers of Writing-Brush Forest. The scholar who
passed with highest honors was called 'the leader'; the second
was designated 'eye of the list'; the third, 'he who has
picked the apricot flower'; and the fourth, 'he who makes
known the series.' When her husband became a member of
this august assemblage the Lady Kuan, also, was given a
title; Wu Hsing Chün *fu-jên*, the Lady of Wu Hsing Region.

A year later the couple took leave of absence from Court.
Chao Mêng-fu wished to erect a tablet to his ancestors, while
the Lady Kuan not only had family business to attend to,
but wished to erect a pavilion in honor of her dead father and
to offer sacrifice to his soul and her mother's soul. They left
for Wu Hsing.

Another year revolved. Imperial envoys came with summons and once more Chao Mêng-fu and Kuan *fu-jên* travelled

to the capital. He to return to his post in the Writing-Brush Forest. On the fourth day, Eleventh Moon, of this year, 1313, the Lady Kuan painted a hand scroll showing groups of bamboo leaves, lengths of stalk, curved branches, and blown twigs. It appeared in London, at the 1936 Exhibition of Chinese Art held at Burlington House, among the National Treasures lent by the Chinese Government.

In 1318 the Lady Kuan was given a yet higher title: Wei Kuo *fu-jên*, Lady of the Wei Principality. This gave her a position approximating that of a feudal lord. It will be remembered that the sisters of the lovely Yang Kuei-fei, who nearly wrecked the T'ang Dynasty, bore similar titles. The grave-piece gives details of life in the capital. Lady Kuan was welcomed at Court and loaded with favors. The Mongol ladies found her a delightful companion. Later ages stress her refinement and charm. Her husband's writing-brush gives a vivid picture of the beautifully dressed artist, of her charity, her religious devotion, her talent, her capability in directing the household, her reverence in the ancestral rites, and above all her devotion to him whom she accompanied so devotedly. Their nine children are dismissed with a word, but doubtless the Lady Kuan cared for them to perfection.

Wei Kuo *fu-jên*, as she should now be styled, was not to enjoy her honors for long. A year later, 1319, she had a return of bitter illness from which she had already suffered. The Chinese call it 'foot-anger illness.' To-day we use the Sinhalese word *beriberi* to describe the same complaint, one of a most distressing nature. The Emperor and ladies of the Court were disturbed; Imperial doctors hurried to and fro, took the Lady Kuan's pulse, looked at her, but their remedies were of no avail. The Lady Kuan was very ill. Bamboos and plum-blossoms, birds and flowers, lovely characters full of life's movement would no longer spring from her magic brush.

In the spring, 1320, Imperial 'command' was obtained for the journey home. The Lady Kuan longed for the soft beauties of the South. The misery of travel did not daunt her. In a boat she would suffer the burning pains, the gastric irritation, the swelling of feet and legs, the disturbance of her heart's action, she would proceed on the Grand Canal, the highway for tribute, to the mid-China home.

On the twenty-fifth day of the Fourth Moon, which corresponds to our May, she, her husband, their son Yung, and attendants went out from the Great Capital. Fifteen days later, on the tenth day of the Fifth Moon, the cortège reached Lin Ch'ung in Shantung. Here, in her boat, the Lady of Wei Principality entered the dream of death, her age five tens and eight. The character used to describe her passing is the one used to announce the death of a prince or feudal lord. The latter portion of the grave-piece, written in her honor by Chao Mêng-fu, concludes this record of a great lady who reflects glory to the ranks of womanhood:

> *wu hu* alas! desolate indeed. I with son Yung, guarding coffin, returned to Wu Hsing, buried it in Tê Ch'ing Hsien. Her sons three persons, her daughters six persons. *fu-jên's* manner was winning, her intelligence clear as moonlight.
>
> The four virtues of women: Right Behavior—chastity, docility; Proper Speech; Proper Demeanor — to be pleasing, submissive; Proper Employment — embroidery, the use of silk and thread; not one was not evidenced. Beating wings of her writing-brush flew high, spread ink on essays. Although she had not studied, she was naturally

gifted. With judgment she arranged household affairs within, without. When the year revolved bringing season for oblations, for sacrifices to early ancestors, if she were not ill, fittingly dressed in rich and exquisite clothes, she bent her body in reverence.

Her father's Clan were accustomed to spending themselves for others; she redeemed girls sold to houses of prostitution; people who had not enough, she supplied, giving ungrudgingly. Her behavior to guests and travellers, her actions in all worldly affairs, never varied from the centre of propriety. In harmony she observed all regulations.

Her heart believed in Buddha's Way. With her own hand she wrote *Chin Kang Ching*, the Diamond Sutra; it filled several tens of scrolls. She also subscribed to temples on famous hills; to famous priests.

The Emperor commanded that *fu-jên* write a thousand essays, ordered Imperial jade-workers to turn jade rollers for these. The inspired writings were presented for the sovereign 'to look down upon' — to inspect. He had them wrapped in brocaded covers, thus preserved and stored. He commanded also that I write the six styles of characters in six rolls, and that Yung write one roll. In addition said: 'I have thus decreed that later generations may know that my dynasty possesses a woman person who writes beautifully, as well as one household in which members can all write. This is a rare happening.'

fu-jên often painted ink bamboos, bamboos in color, to present to Inner Palace, and was grateful for favors Enlightened One let drop. He bestowed jars of Imperial wine as used in private apartments. *fu-jên* often visited Hsing Shêng, Palace of Prosperous Enlightenment; Emperor's Great Empress commanded her to sit, bestowed food, thought, and consideration; Imperial favors were abundant as rains. Honors received from the Two Palaces were glorious.

Because of *fu-jên's* death, Clan within, without the household, relatives on her mother's side, were all deeply moved, grieved. Of friends who came to me was none whose tears did not flow. Thus may virtue of *fu-jên* be realized.

MA CH'ÜAN: PAINTER

Open out the scroll, know only fragrance from ink scars.
Written on a painting by Ma Ch'üan

THE Lady Kuan was not the only woman who gained renown in the 'Clan of Vermilion and Green,' as the Chinese designate painters. A little lady of later date is Ma Ch'üan — Fragrant Flower — whose works are of rare refinement. Mr. Cultivator-of-Bamboos — my teacher, Nung Chu *hsien shêng* — gave me an exquisite example. He told me the following concerning the painter, who lived at the end of the seventeenth and beginning of the eighteenth centuries, which reveals an attitude of mind much admired by the Chinese.

Ma Ch'üan's grandfather, Ma Tsung-lien, was a *chin shih*, a scholar of high rank, during the reign of the Emperor K'ang Hsi. His son, Ch'üan's father, had a palsied hand; could do nothing; is therefore not noted. When Ch'üan was a tiny child she asked her grandfather why he had so much ink — several of his rooms being filled with cases of ink-stick. She said: 'You have no shop. Why so much?' He replied: 'This is a precious thing. To ordinary people it looks to be all of the same color. I, who have spent much silver upon it, see eight colors.'

The Chinese often refer to people who have 'a craving for ink,' a phrase difficult for Occidentals to understand. Such people have a passion for monochrome works, written or painted, and collect ink-sticks with enthusiasm. The black substance is made from a mixture of (1) oil of sesamum, rape, or *wu t'ung* seed; (2) varnish; (3) pork fat. These are burned together to make a lampblack. To the paste made from this, glue is added, and the mass is beaten lustily on wooden anvils with steel hammers. Musk, or Baroos Camphor, is added for fragrance and gold leaf to give a metallic lustre. The mixture varies in fineness and careful preparation. It is finally pressed into elaborately carved wooden moulds where, in about twenty days, it dries. The ink-stick, a facsimile of the mould, is then lifted out and gilded. Many poetic names are given to the different kinds of ink. Poets refer to it as *hsüan shuang*, 'black frost,' a name also used for the Taoist elixir of life. It is indeed an elixir of life for artists of the writing-brush, be they poets, painters, or calligraphists. By its aid they attain immortality.

Little Fragrant Flower at times accompanied her grandfather to Peking. Their home being in Chêng Tu, capital of the far Western province Szechwan, on the borders of Tibet. Ch'üan noticed that their friends burned incense sticks in an incense-burner. 'She, who was accustomed to rubbing sweet-scented ink-sticks on smooth ink slabs in order that her grandfather might paint or write characters, found the incense sticks overpowering and coarse.

Mr. Nung described the exquisite scent of old ink — 'fine, so fine — like a thread from a silk-worm.' I may remark, parenthetically, that to visit a shop where Chinese ink is sold is a delightful experience. The beautifully moulded cakes are stored with great care; old pieces are fitted into brocaded boxes for safe-keeping. Their evanescent fragrance is indescribable.

Ch'üan's grandfather taught her to write. She did not like

it. He asked: 'Why is this?' She replied: 'You tell me that ink has eight colors. I write. I see but one.' Tsung-lien nodded his old head wisely and said: 'So, seven colors are invisible? A pity. If you do not care to write, then paint.' This she did, learning unaided to manage the brush and developing what the Chinese call 'craving for ink' — works in monochrome. Her work is powerful, unusual. Her favorite themes flowers: the spear-orchid; the plum-blossom; the 'water immortal,' which we call narcissus; and a blossom called 'tea-flower.' This last is not the flower of the tea bush but is larger. In form it is not unlike dogwood. My own example of her work is a picture of the tea-flower.

The child grew up and returned to Szechwan. Her paintings were admired by relatives and friends. Some she executed with the speed of fire, others took more than a year to complete.

The fame of Ch'üan was such that houses in the province which lacked a painting by the young woman were said to be without light. The tale is told of a man, very rich, but uncultivated — ts'u, as the Chinese call it. The word is difficult to translate. The character shows three galloping deer and suggests a person who is untamed, untutored, unpolished as wild deer would be. Not bad, merely an ignoramus, a ts'u jên; the word jên means 'person.' The man I speak of built himself a new house and hung therein a pair o. antithetical phrases by a noted woman calligraphist. Friends came to admire. One said: 'Alas! you lack one thing.' 'What can it be?' the owner cried. 'I have all these treasures.' 'You have no picture by Ma Ch'üan,' was the reply. The rich man grieved. How remedy this lack? He asked friends here, there, on every side: 'Do you know Ma Ch'üan?'

Finally one said that not only did she know the painter but that she was willing to undertake a commission to obtain a picture. The rich man, wrapping fifty ounces of silver in red paper, gave it to her joyfully, saying: 'Let her paint what she likes, big or small. I will take anything.'

The friend bought a sheet of fine paper, as was customary to do if one desired an example of an artist's work, and, the money in her pocket, went to see the girl. It is usual to take a gift for a painter when one asks him 'to wave his brush.' This is euphemistically described by the Chinese as carrying 'something to moisten the writing-brush.'

Ch'üan welcomed the guest cordially, begged her, 'Pray sit.' They chatted cheerily and when Fragrant Flower seemed happy the guest asked her to paint: to paint something large or something small.

Pleased, Ch'üan painted. The picture was of a 'water immortal' rising from its leafy bulb. *Then* the guest suggested that the name of the rich man be placed upon the picture. At the same time she offered the fifty ounces of silver.

'Ah,' said Mr. Nung, 'Ch'üan was furious. She tore the picture into tiny pieces; she pushed the money away; she hurried her friend from the room; she said: "You also are a *ts'u jên*. You would have *my* painting hung in the house of a *ts'u jên!*"'

Ma Ch'üan died young before she had knotted the girdle of a bride. She never wore bright colors as did women of her age. Her dresses were always ash-grey, or black, one of the tones she loved to paint. When death approached she begged her relatives to fill her coffin with ink — only ink.

The Warriors

HUA MU–LAN: WARRIOR

Resolve of a hero, may meet an evil fate, can yet be vindicated.

HISTORIANS notwithstanding, there are individuals in regard to whom the actuality of existence is relatively unimportant. Whether or not they ever trod this globe, they have become a vital force in national tradition. In their company is found the heroine of this sketch. In China everyone, everyone, knows of Mu-lan.

Artists paint her portrait, poets refer to her in poems, actors interpret her character on a thousand stages, young revolutionaries take her as a model, the people of the one hundred surnames recite the 'Poem of Mu-lan.' She probably lived during the fifth century of our era. Some authorities state that it was under the Liang, a dynasty which ruled in the South, its capital Nanking; others claim that during her lifetime Wei emperors, in the far North, sat on the Dragon Throne. *Jên Ming Tzŭ Tien — Dictionary of Famous People —* gives cryptic information regarding her life in but twenty-seven characters: 'Mu-lan ancient days filial daughter, donned man's dress. As substitute for father joined army on frontier for ten and two years. Then returned home. People, none knew her as woman.' Then follows an indeterminate discussion in regard to probabilities in connection with the time she lived and the town she inhabited.

Internal evidence points to her being a subject of the Wei, who ruled from A.D. 386 to 557. They were Toba Tartars who under their Ko Hans — rulers — galloped out of the North, organized North China into a state, intermarried with natives of the soil, and rapidly assimilated Chinese civilization. It was a period rich in Buddhistic sculpture, a time of active adherence to the religion which had come to China from across the roof of the world. Many monuments remain in the cave temples of Yün-kang and the amazing grottoes at Lung Mên, where the earliest carvings date from late Wei times.

Art and religion have, however, nothing to do with the history of Mu-lan. For her the Confucian virtue, filial piety, was sufficient. Her story in outline is simple: As substitute for her conscripted father, who was ill, she, a girl of the people, left home and for twelve years fought in the army. Of her companions at arms, none suspected her sex, her chastity was preserved. The fighting ended, her only desires: to return home, to throw off the linked 'iron clothing,' to wear once more a skirt.

The introduction to the Mu-lan Play, which is one of the most popular, given by the noted actor Mei Lan-fang, gives a few further details. It reads:

> At the frontier, trouble. Not a day was there no fight-ing. Spears, swords, did not rest. Half the people con-scripted as soldiers. Only when not fighting were allowed to till fields. Were then conscripted once more. At night Emperor called troops. They must hurry. All whose names were 'dotted' must go. A man named Hua Hu found his name dotted. Old; ill; could not again use strength for country. At this important juncture ten thousand men could not push aside this duty. Those who

had sons could send them; those whose sons were small must go themselves. Generals in command urged as fire.

Mu-lan, regarding her person as unimportant, went instead of father to fight. Dressing as a man, she paid respect to father — left. Went straight to camp, said: 'I have come.' Proceeded to battle front, lived among the ten thousand. A *little* did not let people see she was not a man. Her care for herself was greater than of any other. She had much fighting ability, could act as leader. Body passed through one hundred battles, always at the front. Compared to fierce soldiers, she was still better. All men in camp looked on her as a 'love country youth.' For ten and two years was away. Then took off soldiers' clothes and wore her own.

As Mei Lan-fang in glittering garments waves a long lance and performs, with his peculiar, incomparable grace, the actions of battle, audiences sway with excitement, hoarse cries of 'hao hao' — Good, good! — break from their throats, and all are happy.

Another Mu-lan play appears in an anonymous book called *Ssŭ Shêng Yüan — Four Cries of the Gibbon*. The style is charming, although involved; the author uses many unusual ideographs. The play itself is too long to include in this sketch. The opening scenes give an idea of Chinese life on a farm. Mu-lan enters and, in the Chinese manner, describes her 'unworthy person,' her ancestry, and her family which consists of father, mother, herself, a younger sister Mu-nan, and a little brother. Then, chanting in the 'red-lipped' manner which Mr. Wang, with whom I read the play, described as being very difficult, she states:

A woman's fate is fore-ordained. Even those who wear skirt and hairpin can stand on earth, support Heaven (this phrase describes man's work). From army come ten rolls of writing. Each writing, each writing, each roll, each roll, bears honored father's name. His years are already in full flower: is old, weak, has many ills. Formerly, fixed arrows in bow, pursued great sea-eagle, bored through white wings.

Now, leaning on staff, gazes at wild geese flying in blue sky; calls hens; feeds dog; repairs earth walls for defence; tends fields; tames falcon, his hands too weak to hold the stricken hare. Leads older daughter, younger daughter by the hand. Watches them sitting before mirror while maids comb their hair — opens mouth and laughs for joy.

Hears now he should draw knife, kill! Frowns, brings his brows together, sighs.

The audience realizes that her father being so weak and old Mu-lan must sacrifice herself for the family. One great difficulty, however, is that her feet are bound. She must quickly change her shoes. Minute directions are given to the actor. He shall show pain in the pantomime of removing from the foot, curved like a bow, the tiny slippers women wore. Mu-lan sings once more:

> Years to perfect the pointed love-pheasant head (her little feet) now must quickly make them broad: broad as boats that float. How can I fill great boots as tho' with wooden trees? If I want on my return to marry?

A dreadful prospect! How can a big-footed woman obtain a spouse? She comforts herself. It appears that the family has a prescription which will shrink any foot to the dimension of three-inch golden lilies. Meanwhile the problem is how to make them seven or eight inches long so that she may stand steadily. This is mysteriously accomplished. Mu-lan puts on soldier's clothes. Sitting on a saddle which she describes as 'inlaid with coral,' waving her whip in farewell, she departs.

The remaining scenes of the play depict frontier fighting and her final return home.

The poem earlier referred to as being so widely known is in stark ballad form. It gives the story of Mu-lan's life without embellishment. The title Ko Han, or Khan, is the Tartar term for Emperor or King. The curious expression *huo pan*, 'fire companions,' means soldiers of the same squad. A *huo*, 'fire,' consisted of ten men.

THE MU-LAN POEM

chih chih, once more *chih chih*.
Mu-lan at doorway weaves.

Do not hear sound of shuttle loom,
Hear only maiden's sighs, moans.

Ask maiden: 'Of what do you think?'
Ask maiden: 'What do you now recall?'

Maiden does not dare to think.
Says: 'Nothing do I now recall.

'Saw last night army list,
The Ko Han widely conscripts men.

'Army list ten and two rolls,
Each roll, each roll, bears father's name.

'Honored father has no grown son,
Mu-lan has no elder brother.

'Am willing to prepare, offer price, for saddle-horse,
Will, in place of honored father, march.'

East   market   bought   swift   horse,
West   market   bought   trappings,   saddle.

South   market   bought   bridle,   head-stall,
North   market   bought   long   whip.

Dawn,   set   forth;   from   honored   father,   loved   mother,
    went   away.
Dusk,   passed   night   at   Yellow   River   edge.

No   longer   hear   honored   father,   loved   mother,   calling-
    daughter   sound;
Hear   only   Yellow   River   flowing   waters   plash:
    swash,   swash.

Sunrise   leave   Yellow   River,   start;
Sunset   reach   Black   Mountains   Peak.

No   longer   hear   honored   father,   loved   mother   calling-
    daughter   sound;
Hear   only,   on   Swallow   Hills   Barbarian   horsemen
    ride: thud,   thud.

Pace   ten   thousand   *li*   with   weapons-of-war   machine,
Cross   hill   of   Frontier   Pass   as   if   on   wings.

Breath   of   Dark   North   clings   to   gold   broadaxe,
Light   of   Han   Country   reflects   from   linked-iron
    clothes.

Great   generals   in   one   hundred   battles   die,
Strong   soldiers   in   ten   years   return   home.

Returned-home   come   before   Heaven's   Son,
In   Audience   Hall   sits   Heaven's   Son.

For ten   and two years   stratagems,   loyal efforts,   have
    continued,
Above One   bestows   one hundred,   one thousand   fiefs.

Ko Han   asks   what   I   desire?

'Mu-lan   cannot   use   official   rank,
Would borrow   bright   courser   to go   one thousand   *li*.

'They   send   me,   "a youth,"   home   to old village.

'Honored   father,   loved   mother,   hear   daughter   has
    come:
Go out from   walled village   to meet   and   escort.

'Younger   sister   hears   elder sister   has come:
Within   door   rearranges   make-up   and rouge.

'Little   brother   hears   elder sister   has come:
Grinds   knife   *rhr, rhr,*   hurries toward   pig   and sheep.

'Open   my   door   in Eastern   Pavilion
Sit on   my   bed   in Western   Room.

'Take off   my   fighting   days   clothes,
Put on   my   olden   days   skirt.

'Within   door   arrange   a cloud   head-dress,
Before   mirror   stick   yellow flowers   in hair.

'Go outdoors,   meet   my   "fire   companions";
Fire   companions   hesitate,   startled.

'Together   we marched   for ten   and two   years,
Never   knew   Mu-lan   was a woman   young person.'

Foot   of male   hare   pads   to Dark North,
Eyes   of female   hare   dart   hither, thither.

Two   hares   run   in near-by   field,
How   know   which   is male,   which   is female?

WOMEN WARRIORS THROUGH THE AGES

ALTHOUGH by far the most famous, Mu-lan is not the only woman warrior in the annals of China. A number of her sisters, doffing their skirts, have joined the fighting ranks.

In A.D. 590, a century or more after Mu-lan marched with men, a lady of the Hsi Clan, widow of Fêng Pao of Kwangtung Province, equipped a force. This force was organized to co-operate with the Imperial army in reducing the prefectural

city then in the hands of aboriginal tribes. She was no longer young. Her grandson Fêng Ang commanded the troops, but she, dressed as a soldier, accompanied the men, inspiriting them by her presence. As a reward of her service Fêng Pao was posthumously ennobled, while she was created the 'Lady of Ch'iao State.'

Ch'iu Chin, of the twentieth century, never actually led troops, but was fully prepared to do so had her revolutionary plans not miscarried. Her courage would not have flinched.

In the contemporary era many women 'help the Revolution.' Among those who joined the ranks of the Kuomintang in 1926 when they marched against the Northern War-Lords was Hsieh Ping-ying, an ardent little creature. Doctor Lin Yutang has translated some of her letters.[1] In his introduction to the book he states:

> The writer of these 'Letters,' Miss Hsieh Ping-ying, was one of the girl cadets in the Wuchang Military Academy who joined in the expedition against H —— last month. Her 'War Diary' and her 'Letters' have attracted wide attention on account of their literary interest.... Some of her admirers go so far as to acclaim her a rising star in the revolutionary literary world. The letter from Kiayü, which is here reproduced, has been translated both for its intrinsic merits and for the intimate glimpses it gives of the life of our fighting comrades.

A few extracts from the letter 'At Kiayü' read:

> That morning we started at six. Oh, the serene beauty of that calm starlit sky, the waning moon, and the wafts

[1] *Letters of a Chinese Amazon and Wartime Essays*, by Lin Yutang, A.M., Ph.D. Shanghai, 1933.

of morning air, mingled with the sound of the babbling brook — how all slept in that quiet beautiful dawn!... I know I can no longer write elegant essays and sentimental poems. I have already told you that, if I expect to resume my old literary life, I must wait until the revolution is over.

The singing birds and the blooming flowers on the way are indeed a delight to me, for I have not seen them for half a year. But I must not digress. I will tell you some important news. I actually rode on horseback for over twenty *li*. Moreover, I rode on the major's horse, one which was known to be pranky. At a village about six *li* from Kiayü, my horse and those of a cavalry officer got into a conflict. And taking a fancy to her, they came, launching a general attack on me. One of my comrades got so frightened that she fell with all her equipment. It scared all the wits — and even the mother's milk — out of me. Many fellow cadets turned their heads to look at me and smiled. Of course, I could only tell them, 'What, ho! I am not a bit afraid! Not a bit!' And really I was not afraid of death. But if I should fall and lose a leg or otherwise get disabled, wouldn't that be frightful? Well, F——, again I have talked too much.

I arrived at Kiayü first and alone. In order to look for our living quarters, I had to go about the streets again and again. 'Ah, here comes the Amazon.' — 'The Amazon has arrived!' — 'A girl officer on horseback!' Such cries turned whole crowds of womenfolk out to see me. As I was surrounded by the crowd, I could only whip the horse and hurry on. I was truly afraid of a fall, as I had never ridden before in my life. You can imagine the embarrassment I was in.

Some addressed me as 'old general,' some as 'lady teacher,' some as 'lady officer,' and one boy called me the 'lady generalissimo.' I was sweating all over and my face was burning hot, and I did not know what to do. I realized that I had become an old curio — or rather, a new monstrosity. Both the men and women stared at me from head to foot, and I believe they even counted the number of my hairs. An old woman said to me: 'I have lived eighty years without seeing such a short-haired, big-footed, uniformed female devil like you.' Ha! ha! ha! what a laugh she had, and what a laugh we all joined in!

Another woman of over forty came and offered me tea, for which I was truly thankful. Besides, she said something which was painful — but really not painful — to me. She said: 'If such a blithe young girl should die on the battlefield, what will happen to her parents at home?' I said calmly to her, 'Madam, I am ready to die, to die on behalf of the revolution and the people. As for the parents, of course we are sorry to leave them; but...'

This is my hardest, and at the same time my happiest, day since our start on the expedition. Although we sleep on the ground, although we sleep over straw like those little pigs in the sty, although our clothing is soiled with ill-smelling animal excretions, although we smell what we never smelled before and see what we never saw before in our lives, we are happy, yes, we are supremely happy, from having such joyous talks with the farmers! All the six girl cadets wish very much to talk with them, but the farmers understand only the Hupeh and Hunan dialects. Four of them were so disappointed and angry with themselves that they have gone to bed.

Dear F——, the bound feet here are insufferable. The small ones measure only two inches, but even the big ones are only four inches at their best. Once I was sitting in a meadow writing letters. A company of women came and talked with me. So I laid down my pen and began to talk to them on the evils of foot-binding. One well-to-do middle-aged woman, who had a three-inch 'golden lily,' said to me: 'Your feet are so big. Won't your husband get into your shoes sometimes by mistake?' Ha, ha, ha, ha!! All the soldiers, captains, and peasants who were standing by broke out into a big laughter; they laughed so that even a brave little girl like myself began to blush.

Brave maidens these girl cadets! So are the Communist women who, having accompanied their men on the 'heroic trek' from Kiangsi across Southern and Western China, are now helping to spread their doctrine in the far Northwest.

A photograph taken in the summer of 1936 lies before me. Cheery young women are dressed in the 'love country' cotton cloth which Chinese troops wear. The legend beneath the picture tells that they are 'Amazons.' 'A feminine battalion of death marches in Kwangsi Province, South China, in an anti-Nanking and anti-Japanese demonstration.'

Since that day Kwangsi has reunited with the Nanking Government. Let us hope that the Amazons are free to return to their homes.

In addition to the ladies who fight for a righteous cause women bandit leaders have been notorious and are even now reported. Pai *ku-niang* Pai, the young lady, kidnapped many people in the vicinity of Tientsin during the years 1934 and 1935. Whether or not she has been caught I do not know. Her counterpart, Widow Chang, terrorized Western Honan for many years before she was captured in 1931 and executed.

Chinese women assuredly do not lack courage. Liu Tsui distinguished herself in December, 1935. Leader in Peiping of the student demonstration against yielding to Japanese dictation, she rolled her diminutive person under the great

Hsunchih Gate, which was closed against the student body, and tried to raise the heavy bar. Police beat her with the stocks of their rifles and finally arrested her but did not break her spirit. She continued to agitate. 'On February 29, 1936, General Sung Cheh-yuan called out a full regiment of the Twenty-Ninth Army to effect a raid on Tsinghua University, in Peiping, when they especially wanted Miss Liu Tsui....' So reads a sentence from an account of the student movement.[1] Her photograph shows a girl of determination, eyes wide apart, expression of one inspired. It is not difficult to imagine Liu Tsui leading soldiers into action.

The cold North and the warm South; the Eastern seaboard, the Western hills, all contribute a quota of brave women. To-day their horizon is enlarged. They are ready to protect, not only their families, but their land.

[1] See 'Students in Rebellion,' by Nym Wales, *Asia*, July, 1936.

The Educators

PAN CHAO: EDUCATOR, MORALIST, WOMAN OF LETTERS
AND HER GREAT-AUNT
PAN *CHIEH-YÜ:* IDEAL IMPERIAL FAVORITE

CH'IU CHIN opened the baton-door for her twentieth-century sisters. She urged that they unbind their feet, that they choose men as friends, above all that they be educated. As an advocate of women's education she was far removed from the first protagonist. Nineteen hundred years before her day, in the first century of our era, lived Pan Chao, the greatest woman scholar in Chinese history. She not only urged that women be educated, she wrote the *Nü Chieh —* *Precepts for Women —* which, until modern days, has formed the basis of women's higher education. It is a remarkable ethical document written in classical style. According to the *Great Han Shu,* or history of the Han Dynasty, she also wrote 'Narrative Poems, Commemorative Writings, Inscriptions, Eulogies, Argumentations, Commentaries, Elegies, Essays, Treatises, Expositions, Memorials, and Final Instructions, in all (enough to fill) sixteen books. Her daughter-in-law, of the Ting family, collected and edited her works.' [1]

[1] The quotation is from *Pan Chao: Foremost Woman Scholar of China,* by Nancy Lee Swann, Ph.D., a scholarly, completely documented and detailed life. Doctor Swann has consulted all available authorities and has collated texts in Chinese, English, and French. I acknowledge gratefully the help her work has given me. Were it not that no book on Chinese women is conceivable without mention of Pan Chao, I should not, in view of her exhaustive work on the lady, have attempted this sketch.

Pan Chao came of a family who traced their descent from an ancestor born some six centuries before Christ, of 'union in the wilds,' as Chinese describe illegitimate connection. This ancestor was left to die in a swamp, but a tigress gave him suck and eventually his grandparents rescued him. The Pan family lived in what is modern Shansi. They were distinguished, not only for their learning, but for high moral qualities as well. Pan Chao's great-aunt Pan *chieh-yü* has been celebrated throughout history for her fine feeling. A member of the harem at the court of Chêng Ti, she bore, in appreciation of her literary talents, the title *chieh-yü*, and was for some time first favorite. The Emperor, in his infatuation, once requested her to drive with him in his 'chariot.'

With sensitive regard for what rulers should and should not do, she refused, saying that it was the place of courtiers, not ladies, to accompany the Son of Heaven in public. This incident is depicted on the famous scroll by Ku K'ai-chih in the

British Museum. The lady, with flowing scarlet streamers, her lacquer black hair dressed high in an elaborate head-dress, gently reproves the monarch for his suggestion. He is seated in a litter borne on the shoulders of men precisely as rulers were borne about the Palace until the fall of the Manchu Dynasty. It is regrettable to notice that a young girl is seated beside him. Unless one may make the charitable suggestion that the said young person refrained from later mounting a more public vehicle, one must surmise that Pan *chieh-yü's* remonstrance came too late.

Her subsequent history is sad. Other less worthy favorites permanently caught the Imperial eye. One of these, Chao Fei-yen — Flying Swallow — informed the Emperor that Lady Pan had denounced him to the *kuei* and *shên*, the 'demons below' and the 'spirits above.' He, furious, sent for Pan *chieh-yü* and asked her what she meant. Kneeling before the most unheavenly Son of Heaven, she replied:

> Unworthy One has heard [that he who] cultivates virtue still does not attain happiness, favor.
> For him who does evil what help?
> Supposing demons below, and spirits above, are aware [of affairs in this world], they could not endure that one, betraying fidelity to Emperor, should utter secret thoughts hidden in darkness of the heart.
> If demons and spirits be without consciousness, of what use the utterance of secret thoughts?

Rising, Pan *chieh-yü* begged leave to retire to the Palace of the High Gate, where she lived in life-long friendship with the Empress Dowager who honored her for her attempt to correct the Son of Heaven. Her farewell letter to the Emperor is a poem widely quoted. She likens herself to a fan laid by when its days of use are over. The term 'Autumn fan,' used to describe a deserted wife, is still in current use.

A SONG OF GRIEF

Newly cut, stretched, argent, white,
Pure white as frost, as snow.
A fan: perfectly formed — the circle of happiness.
Round, round, a bright moon.

Treasured in sleeve,   taken out,   put back,
Moved,   waved,   it wafts   a gentle   breeze.
Often   fear,   when Autumn   Season   comes,
When   cold wind,   whirling,   dispels   fiery   heat,
Discarded,   laid by,   it will be left   in bamboo   box.
Favor,   passion,   midway   through life   are severed.

This dramatic incident must have made a deep impression
on the great-niece of the principal figure, whose fame has
glowed throughout history.   Ladies who put aside personal
ambition to uphold a monarch in his responsibilities have
ever been rare.

Pan *chieh-yü's* nephew Pan Piao — the Tiger-Striped —had
great ability, and after the chaos of Wang Mang's usurpation
was summoned to court.   He held various posts but, as he preferred a studious life, soon retired and began to compile the
historical material which his son and daughter were to weave
into the *Great Han Shu*, the history of the Han Dynasty.   Pan
Piao died in middle life, aged but fifty-two.   His two sons,
twins, were born A.D. 32 when he was twenty-nine years old.
The first-born, Ku — Constant — became the historian, while
the second, Ch'ao — Excellent — distinguished himself ex-
ceedingly as a military officer in the wilds of Central Asia.
There for thirty-one years he subdued tribes, guarded frontiers, and protected much frequented highways of trade which
led to the Western World.   Their sister Chao — Luminous
— was not born until between A.D. 45 and 51 — the precise
date is unknown.   She was probably a gaily dressed little girl
when her father descended to the Yellow Springs below.   She
must, however, have been more than an infant.   Later she
affectionately acknowledges her debt to him: 'Grateful to
deceased father for superabundance of kindness.'

At the age of fourteen Pan Chao married Ts'ao Shih-shu of Fu-fêng in Shensi. He died early. Her subsequent conduct inspired the Chinese to coin a phrase which since that day has been used to describe the ideal widow: 'the chastity [of viduity] exercised to its limit.'

Mist of uncertainty obscures the movements of Pan Chao, her son, and 'daughters' for a number of years. One surmises, from the character of the woman, that she bent every effort to train both son and 'daughters.' No facts in regard to this span of her life have been preserved. Did she and her children live on with the Ts'ao family or did she return to the house of Pan? The Jesuits, who wrote a charming but, alas, undocumented life of Pan Chao, assert that she joined brother Ku. Did she do so she had access to a fine library, an Imperial gift to her great-uncle. In the light of future events it seems probable that she did join brother Ku. He, a noted scholar, in a day of noted scholars, was honored by the Emperor Chang, who loved literature, gathered men of letters about his Court, and discussed with avidity erudite points. He died in 88. The Emperor Ho came to the throne. There were difficulties of sorts. In the year 92 Pan Ku, the man of letters, became involved in a military plot. He was thrown into prison by a revengeful local magistrate, and there speedily died.

The *Eight Tables* and the *Treatise on Astronomy*, two divisions of the *Han History*, were incomplete. Who should succeed Pan Ku as Court Historian and bring his work to fruition? A few years seem to have passed. It is recorded that Pan Chao accompanied her son to a post in Chên-liu and while on the way composed a poem: *Travelling Eastward, a Fu*. Shortly thereafter the Emperor Ho decreed that she, a woman, come to the Tung Kuan Ts'ang Shu Ko — Eastern Gallery, Store

Books Pavilion — where favored scholars studied, and that she complete the work begun by her father and her brother. Although not called Court Historian, Pan Chao fulfilled the functions of that officer.

Her years were near the half-century mark. Her middle age must have been passed in concentrated study, otherwise she would have been in no wise fitted for this exacting task. Furthermore, the Emperor decreed that Pan Chao should enter the ladies' apartments and become teacher of the Empress Têng, then about fifteen years of age, and of the inmates of the harem. She also acted as poet laureate, composing verses to celebrate presentation of tribute or any unusual occasion. From this time she was addressed by a term of respect used in conjunction with her husband's surname: Ts'ao Ta Ku, or 'Aunt' Ts'ao.

The revelations of modern archaeology enable one to realize very clearly the surroundings of the Han Court. Did Pan Chao herself use a gilt bronze *lien*, or toilet box, love-pheasants perched on the lid and within the lid a love-pheasant painted in black and blue against a red background? Did she use a large flat wash-basin made of bronze inlaid with coiling golden dragons? Did she eat from bronze dishes beautifully decorated with scroll work, with animal motives, with likenesses of the Western Empress Mother, who rules in the Taoist Paradise? Did she wear a gold buckle chiselled in intricate design and set with stones? I fancy not; a widow in China wears ashy tones and simple dark robes. Did she use an exquisite bronze mirror kept in a lacquered case? Whether or not Pan Chao herself used them she must often have seen such things, as well as exquisite silks, painted pottery jars, rhythmic jade carvings, and bronzes in wonderful shapes. Art of the Han period has peculiar virility, and a rhythm of line which differentiates it from any existing before or since.

Life must have been full of interest. Great literary works were undertaken, and in A.D. 105 the invention of paper was announced. Ts'ai Lun, a court official, 'thought of using tree bark, hemp, rags, and fish nets' [1] to make the commodity which, ever since, has been called 'the paper of Marquis Ts'ai.' It supplanted the heavy bamboo strips and the expensive silk used to write upon until that time. The invention of paper greatly facilitated the production of literary works, although its concomitant, printing, was not invented until several centuries later.

While Pan Chao had studied and had become a scholar, while Brother Ku had written historical works, Brother Ch'ao had been leading a life of vigorous action among the tribes of Central Asia. The extent of the Han Empire can best be realized when one reflects that fine lacquer and other objects of Chinese origin have been excavated at Lou Lan to the far West, in the Lop Nor region of Turkestan, and at Lo Lang, on the eastern edge of the Empire, where Korea drops to the sea. Brother Ch'ao kept in touch with his sister. When in A.D. 100 he forwarded a memorial to the Dragon Throne asking that, on account of age and illness, he be allowed to retire from his dangerous post, she seconded it by a memorial of her own, setting forth in detail the record of his service. Emperor Ho was moved. The general, aged seventy-one, returned, reaching the Capital in A.D. 102, during the Eighth Moon, which corresponds roughly to our September. The period of White Dew had passed, leaves were falling, wild geese, follow-the-sun-birds, were winging South. In

[1] *The Invention of Printing in China*, by T. F. Carter.

the Ninth Moon the old man died. Posthumous honors were lavishly decreed, and funeral gifts were generous. Was the spirit of General Ch'ao rewarded for what his body had suffered in hardship?

During the weeks before his death he and his sister probably discussed many things. The documents, written on strips of bamboo and of wood, on scraps of silk, and one or two precious atoms of paper — the earliest paper so far discovered — tell the world to-day of many things. Of homesick soldiers, of border raids. They give prescriptions for soldiers and for their precious mounts. There are calendars, letters, and lists of clothing. In fact life at the edge of Empire is reconstructed.[1]

Three years later, the Emperor Ho died, being succeeded by an infant son who lived but a year. He, in turn, was succeeded by his cousin the Emperor An a boy of thirteen. The Empress Têng acted as regent for both these youthful Sons of Heaven. Pan Chao's influence at Court naturally increased. The Empress Têng, who when her husband died was a woman of but twenty-five, looked up to Ts'ao Ta Ku, then about sixty, with whom she had studied for ten years. Ts'ao Ta Ku proved herself a woman of decision in political affairs, as well as a scholar. It is said, in regard to some advice which she gave, 'at a word from Mother Pan the whole family resigned.' Her son was honored, being elevated to the position of Marquis with permission to wear the Gold Seal and Purple Cord of a high official.

Facts about people have their interest. Works from the pens reveal personality. It is from the writings of Pan Chao that her character and philosophy shine forth. Many have

[1] *Les Documents Chinois, etc.*, découverts par Aurel Stein. Publiés et traduits par Edouard Chavannes.

been lost, and her share in the compilation of *Han Shu* is undetermined. There remain, however, two persuasive Memorials, three short poems, the long narrative poem *Travelling Eastward*, and the seven chapters which comprise *Nü Chieh — Precepts for Women*. These reveal that Pan Chao held Confucian tenets. She believed that Heaven decreed all things; that while man was born good, unless he were educated, his nature deteriorated. To her clear, logical mind it followed that woman, too, should receive enlightenment. The Four Books of Confucian fame: *The Great Learning, Doctrine of the Mean, Discussions of Confucius,* and the *Sayings of Mencius,* formed the basis of man's study. For woman, whose need was, in her eyes, different, nothing existed. She would urge that girls be taught to read and she would provide for their use suitable *Precepts*. Internal evidence proves that the work did not appear before A.D. 106. It comprises an autobiographical introduction and seven chapters. Since Pan Chao's day the *Precepts* have been published, together with three works from other pens. The collection forms the *Nü Ssŭ Shu — Four Books for Women*. In pre-Republican days it was a popular manual for instruction within the baton-door.

A translation of the *Precepts* reads as follows:

NÜ CHIEH: PRECEPTS FOR WOMEN

INTRODUCTION

I, the writer, am a lowly person with but a monkey's wit, the sun of my intelligence is obscured by clouds. The nature given me at birth is neither quick nor intelligent. Am grateful to my lord father for his abundant love; depended on my lady mother for her flowing words of instruction in the canons of behavior.

When my years were ten and four, grasping winnowing basket and broom, I married into the Ts'ao Clan. Now more than four tens of years have revolved. Alarmed, alarmed, anxious, anxious, often feared I should be dismissed in disgrace, thus heaping shame on father, on mother, involving husband's relatives within the household, and my own kin without the household. At day-dawn, at nightfall, heart suffered bitter apprehension. Diligent in duties, did not mention weariness, but now and hereafter I realize how to avoid solicitude.

By nature unreflecting, I taught, pointed out the Way, without regularity, hence my constant dread that my son Ku might bring disgrace to the Pure Dynasty. Unexpectedly Grace of the Enlightened One is added to. He has bestowed on my lowly son Gold Seal and Purple Ribbon, for which honor I, the humble one, was really far from hoping.

My son can plan for himself. I need no more be anxious. But I am distressed that you, my daughters, who should now marry, have not been soaked in the waters of instruction; have no knowledge of the decorum required of wives. I fear that you may deviate from decorum in other houses, thus humiliate your ancestors, your Clan.

Am now ill, hindered, as a sunken stone, as water congealed. Limit of life, decreed by Heaven, is not a settled quantity. I think of you all, thus, untrained and feel dissatisfied, uneasy. I therefore make the *Women's Precepts* — seven sections — and desire you, my daughters, each to write one complete copy. You may possibly thus increasingly repair your faults. Avail yourselves of the *Precepts* to strengthen your characters. You will leave me, will 'return home'[1] to

---

[1] An interesting psychological point to be noted is that the character *kuei*, here

your husband's household. Force yourselves, then, to put forth every effort.

PRECEPT ONE
Humility and Adaptability

In ancient times those who bore a daughter, on the third day, firstly: laid her below the bed; secondly: gave her a tile to play with; and thirdly: with sacrifice, preceded by fasting, reported her birth in the ancestral temple.

To lay her below the bed, exemplified her humility and adaptability, her subservience to others.

To give her a tile to play with, exemplified the continued flight of her labor, her exertion for others, her subordination to, and absorption in, diligent toil.

To report her birth in the ancestral temple with sacrifice, preceded by fasting, exemplified her obedience to the necessity of continuing, an unbroken thread, the oblations to dead forefathers.

These three actions symbolize the ordinary life-road of a woman, as well as the teaching of the Rites and Regulations.

To be unassuming, to yield; to be respectful, to revere; to think first of other people, afterwards of herself; if she perform a kind action, to make no mention thereof; if she commit a fault, to make no denial; to endure reproach, treasure reproof; to behave with veneration and right fear; such

used by Pan Chao in connection with unmarried daughters, means: to return, to go or send back; to revert to the original place or state; to marry out; gathered to one's husband; etc. A daughter's real home is in the home of her potential husband. — F. A.

demeanor is described as exemplifying humility and adaptability.

To lie down to sleep when it is late, to be at work, early; from dawn till dark not to shirk putting forth strength; to bend the mind to domestic affairs, nor to evade such, be they troublesome or easy; to accomplish that which must be done, to be orderly, to systematize the way of conduct; such behavior is said to be absorption in diligent toil.

To be sedate in manner, of upright purpose, to serve her lord her husband; to keep herself pure, composed, not being given to misplaced jest or laughter; free from pollution, reverently to arrange the wine and food to be placed before tablets of progenitors, ancestors; such proceeding is said to be continuing an unbroken thread, the oblations to dead forefathers.

If these three categories of conduct be thoroughly inculcated, her reputation will never be tarnished, nor will degradation, insult, befall her.

If these three categories of conduct be not observed, how can reputation be far-famed, how can degradation, insult to the person, be avoided?

PRECEPT TWO

Husband and Wife

Way of husband and wife is the blending, the fusion of Yin and Yang. It reaches to, establishes communication with, the bright spirits. It verily gives full development to the cosmic forces of Heaven, of Earth. It is the great influence which maintains dignity in human relationship.

Therefore *Li Chi* — the *Record of Rites* — honors the act whereby men and women blend, as, at the horizon edge, sky and earth blend; the *Shih Ching* — *Classic of Poetry* — sets forth in its first poem 'The Faithful Birds of Love,' rightness of the act. From these it may be said the act is not, not-important.

If the husband behave not according to the canon of morality, he is without the means of controlling the chariot of his wife's conduct.

If the wife behave not according to the canon of morality, she is without the means of carrying to completion management of her husband's affairs.

If the husband control not chariot of his wife's conduct, the solemn rule of human behavior falls, a house in ruins, a broken vessel.

If the wife carry not to completion management of her husband's affairs, the rule of rightness, polished jewel of correct action, crumbles, is lost.

In consequence the functions of each, of husband, of wife, serve a like purpose.

Consider 'superior men' — so-called — of to-day. They think, merely, that it is not possible not to control their wives, that the solemn rule of human behavior cannot be correctly ordered. For their sons, therefore, they let flow in a stream words of instruction, they transmit history, gather and arrange faggots of learning. But, verily, they do not comprehend that husbands, heads of families, cannot, not have the management of their affairs carried to completion; that the rule of rightness, the sacrifice, must not, not be preserved. To teach sons and not to teach daughters, is this not to be blinded, to discriminate against the latter in favor of the former?

The *Record of Rites* decrees: At eight years of age, instruction

in the writings should begin; at ten years and five, boys should
be ready to absorb learning.

Does it not follow, then, that girls, also, should be educated?

PRECEPT THREE
Respect, Yieldingness

Yin and Yang are fundamentally dissimilar.
Men and women differ in their behavior.
Yang, through resolution, attains moral excellence;
Yin, through the pliability of a willow, attains to perfection.
Man, through strength, becomes illustrious;
Woman, through flexibility, becomes worthy of admiration.

Hence the rustic proverb: 'Bear a boy, he is like a wolf; fear,
only, he may become a lamb. Bear a girl, she is like a mouse,
fear, only, she may become a tigress.'

To cultivate the person, nothing equals respect.
To avoid contumacy, nothing equals yieldingness.

Hence it is said: The Way of respect and yieldingness is the
first principle of wifehood. It may also be said: Respect is
not other than holding to that which is enduring. And
again: Yieldingness is not other than being gentle to others,
forbearing.

Those who hold to what is enduring are moderate, content.
(They do not demand perfection in a husband.) Being gentle
to others, forbearing, is to value respect, humility.

Husband and wife desire that their love, throughout life,
be not cut in two, but if in rooms and inner chambers they
follow each other everywhere, moving in an orbit, coming
back to the same point, result will be disrespect for wife;

lust will come to birth, she will be soiled, dishonored. If lust, dishonor, already have come to birth, words, arguments, will violate propriety; venery, passion unloosed, must result. If venery, license, already have occurred, then contempt for heart of husband will come to birth. This springs from not realizing moderation, contentment.

Furthermore, in affairs of life there is indirectness, there is overdirectness; there are words which should be said, words which should not be said. Overdirectness cannot, not lead to strife; indirectness cannot, not lead to contention. If contention, strife, already are manifest, resentment, anger on both sides, will be experienced. This arises from not appreciating the virtues of respect, humility.

If boundless contempt for husband be felt, his wrath will follow. If complaints, anger, do not cease, slaps, lashes with a whip will follow. Hence rule of rightness of husband and wife results from harmonious intimacy; mutual adoration perfects the union. If slaps, lashes with the whip, already have been given, what rule of rightness remains? If complaints, anger, have been expressed, how can mutual adoration exist?

Mutual adoration, rule of rightness, would be a house fallen in ruins! Husband, wife would proceed — cut apart!

Precept Four

Qualities of Woman

Woman has four qualities:
> The first is called moral excellence of woman.
> The second is called speech of woman.
> The third is called appearance of woman.
> The fourth is called handiwork of woman.

Now concerning:

Firstly, the moral excellence of woman: it is not necessary that her intelligence be brilliant or extremely unusual;

Secondly, the speech of woman: it is not necessary that she be able in argument, nor that her words be keen and fluent;

Thirdly, the appearance of woman: it is not necessary that her face and color be beautiful, bewitching;

Fourthly, the handiwork of woman: it is not necessary that it be skilled and ingenious beyond that of others.

To be pure and reverential; to have leisure as of moonlight through an open door; to be true and constant; to be quiet, retiring; to treasure chastity and control habit until it is regular as a field of grain; to recognize that light conduct may cause the ears to redden with shame; that energetic action and calm behavior have each their law; such is described as the moral excellence of woman.

To select phrases, then speak; not to utter evil words; to choose the right moment for utterance; not to satiate others with chatter; such is described as the speech of woman.

To lave, wash away dust and dirt; to wear bright, fresh, neat, clean clothing; to bathe at appropriate times in order that the body be not reproached by dirt; such is described as the appearance of woman.

With fixed purpose in her heart, to coil and twist, splice and spin, silken threads; not to like jest or laughter; correctly to arrange the wine and food to be laid before guests and visitors; such is described as the handiwork of woman.

These four qualities represent the great credentials of

woman, in not one of which may she be defective. They are indeed most easy to attain if she but treasure them in her heart.

People of old had a saying: 'Is perfect virtue far away? I seek ardently for perfect virtue;... it descends, a bird, to earth.' This saying may be applied to the qualities of Woman.

PRECEPT FIVE

Fixed Purpose in the Heart

The Rites affirm: A husband may, within the limits of *i* — that is, dignity and self-respect — take a wife for the second time. There is no manifestation of the Way, by which a wife may make second marriage.

It is said: 'A husband, he is Heaven.' Heaven is unalterable; it cannot be set aside. For that reason a woman's union with her husband is indissoluble. If she behave in opposition to the veneration due divinity extended — which is the human spirit — then Heaven will impose penalty. If she transgress the rites and rules of dignity and self-respect, her husband will esteem her lightly.

For this reason the book *Nü Hsien* — *Patterns for Women* — states: 'To obtain the heart's purpose of one man is called eternal fulfilment. To lose the heart's purpose of one man is called eternal ending.'

In accordance with this saying how can a woman not desire her husband's heart? She who thus desires, however, need not utter flattering, specious words, nor indulge in passionate glances, and lustful intimacy. Assuredly such would not be in accordance with fixed purpose in the heart, with calm and self-control, with the Rites and the rule of dignity and self-respect, nor with living in pure restraint.

If her ears do not hear obscene words, if her eyes do not see depraved sights; if outside the house she appear not bedizened with false glitter, and inside the house she discard not correct adornment; if she mix not with crowds, if she gaze not out from doors and gates, then may it be said she acts in accordance with fixed purpose in the heart and with calm self-control.

If, however, her conduct be frivolous, her speech light, if she allow herself to be spoiled by adulation; if, inside the house, her head-dress be dishevelled, her appearance neglected; if, outside the house, her manner be seductive, enticing; if she utter words which should not be said, look at that which should not be seen, then it may be said she acts not in accordance with fixed purpose in the heart, nor with calm self-control.

Precept Six

Bending the Will to Obedience

Remember, 'to obtain the heart's purpose of one man is called eternal fulfilment, to lose the heart's purpose of one man is called eternal ending'; these words recommend fixed purpose in the heart of woman and settled resolve. Is it possible, then, that she gain not hearts of father-in-law and mother-in-law?

At times people must separate themselves from their desires, also at times duty causes destruction of self. Even if a husband say he loves his wife deeply, while father-in-law and mother-in-law say they do not like her, husband and wife must part. This is called obedience to duty which causes destruction of self.

Then how safely to gain the hearts of father-in-law and mother-in-law? Nothing equals in importance the imperative

duty of obedience! If the mother-in-law say 'it is not so' and
it be so, assuredly, it is right to obey her order. If the mother-
in-law say 'it is so' even if it be not so, nevertheless, act in
accordance with the command. Do not think of opposing, or
of discussing what is, what is not; do not struggle to divide
the crooked from the straight. This is what is called the
imperative duty of obedience. The ancient book, *Nü Hsien —
Patterns for Woman* — states: 'A wife is like the shadow from
high sunlight, the echo following sound.' How can she not
be praised, rewarded?

PRECEPT SEVEN
Harmony with Husband's Younger Brothers and Sisters

For a wife to obtain heart's purpose of her lord she must
secure love of father-in-law and mother-in-law. To secure
love of father-in-law and mother-in-law she must have approval of husband's younger brothers, sisters.

Hence the appreciation of a wife's virtues and faults, her
fame or defamation, depends directly on the hearts of husband's younger brothers, sisters. These hearts she may not
fail to gain.

All people do not realize that affection of husband's younger
brothers, sisters, must not be neglected. If the wife seek not
harmony with them she cannot obtain their affection. Not
many are enlightened. Few are without fault. The nobility
of Yen Tzŭ lay in his power to correct himself. Chung Ni
(Confucius) praised him for not repeating a fault. How much
more is this the case with woman! Although a woman act
in a virtuous manner, although her understanding be penetrating, perspicacious, is she able to be perfect? Hence, if people
of the household live in harmony, then slander is obviated.

If those within, and those without, disagree, then faults are lifted up and exposed. This must result from such influences. *Classic of Changes* states:

> Two   people of like   heart-thought
> With   united effort   can   sever   gold.
> Two people of like words:
> Fragrance of their achievement rivals that
>   of the spear-orchid.

This quotation makes clear the sense of harmony.

Concerning husband's younger brothers, sisters: They equal wife in station, but are more intimate in family relationship. Of husband's blood, they are related to wife by marriage only.

Her virtue clear as water, a modest yielding person, she can establish peace in fostering love for kinsfolk of the husband, to whom she is bound by silken cord of union. Such behavior will result in setting forth her goodness, making manifest her beauty, and veiling any flaw or crack in the gem of her behavior. Father-in-law, mother-in-law, will extol her excellence; husband will praise beauty of her character; her fame will illumine village and neighborhood. Light will extend: its rays will irradiate her own father, mother.

If a frivolous-hearted person, with but a monkey's wit, presume on her position to exalt herself in her relations with husband's younger brothers and because of her husband's infatuation permit herself to overflow with arrogance in her relations with husband's younger sisters, how can she live in harmony? Love of husband, and rule of dignity and self-respect, will run at cross-purposes. How can her repute be high?

Such behavior would cloud her virtues, manifest her faults.

Mother-in-law would be irritated, husband indignant. Vilification and detraction would exist within and without the house; her ears would redden with shame, and insult would collect on her person. Humiliation would reach to, be heaped on, her own father and mother, and she would create difficulties for her lord.

These are the respective roots of glory and disgrace, the frontiers of fame and evil reputation. Must not a woman act carefully!

To gain the affection of husband's younger brothers, sisters, assuredly nothing equals modesty and yielding. Modesty, then, is the axe-handle of virtue; yielding, then, is the way-of-action for a wife.

Realize fully, cultivate, these two qualities, they provide sufficient ground for mutual forbearance. *Classic of Poetry* states: 'Here is no evil. There is no dislike.' This expresses the Way of Woman.

A famous ballad, the tale of Chiao Chung-ch'ing's wife, written about a century after Pan Chao's death, points the moral to Precept Six. It exemplifies the inexorable working of the social law which decreed that a mother-in-law, be she right or wrong, cruel or kind, must be placated by her son's wife. The old-style Chinese would consider the ballad as warning to a wife. They would, in reading the tale of Chung-ch'ing, feel deep sympathy for him and his bride, but would realize that the young woman, in failing to gain the affection of The Mother, had broken the mould of correct behavior. For such a person, there is no place in the structure of society. Repudiated by her husband's Clan, not yet admitted to another, a transient in her own, she is a piece of floating duck-weed which, lacking roots, follows every wave. For her no one of the 'three dependencies' exists. Neither father, husband, nor son supports a repudiated wife. In death her widowed ghost is uncertain where to go.

The ballad is invariably quoted by Chinese when women are referred to, as giving a vivid picture of their life in early days. I therefore include the following translation.

THE WIFE OF CHIAO CHUNG–CH'ING:
AN ANCIENT BALLAD

Prefatory Note

At the end of the Han Dynasty, in the middle of the *chien an* period, about A.D. 208, Chiao Chung-ch'ing of Lu Chiang hamlet, a petty clerk in the Prefecture, had a wife of the Liu Clan. On account of Chung-ch'ing's mother she was repudiated. She swore an oath not to remarry. Forced to betrothal by members of her clan, she sank in the waters and died. Chung-ch'ing, hearing this, strangled himself by hanging from a tree in the courtyard. People of the time, pitying them, told their story in this verse.

A peacock flies East of South,
Flies five li, flutters back and forth.
  (*The young wife speaks to her husband:*)
'Ten and three could weave silk threads;
Ten and four learned to cut out clothes;
Ten and five swept strings of *k'ung hou* lyre;
Ten and six hummed lines of Classics: *Poems, Writings*;
·Ten and seven became wife of my Lord.
Now, in heart's centre, is often bitter grief.
My Lord has become Prefect's Clerk,

Preserving chastity, my passion never alters,
Lowly wife remains in empty bridal chamber.
We see each other, indeed, but rarely,
You come, can never bear to go, bear to go.
At cock-crow I enter loom to weave,
Nightly, nightly, do not attain to rest,
In three days cut off five rolls of silk.
Not because my weaving is slow, but
Because they dislike me, Husband's Honored Parents
    reprimand.
In my Lord's household 'tis difficult to be a wife.
Unworthy One cannot endure being ordered, driven like
    a beast;
'Tis vain to stay; — useless!
Pray tell Honored Father, Venerable Mother,
Time has come, I should be sent away, returned to father's
    household.'

Prefect's Clerk, on hearing this,
Ascends Guest Hall to tell The Mother:

'Son assists with salary that is but poor,
Yet has good fortune in possessing such a wife.
She knotted hair, came to my pillow, sleeping-mat;
Until descent to Yellow Springs, we shall join hands in
    companionship.
Three or two years has she lived with, served us,
From life's beginning, to its end, is a long time.
Wife has acted without deceit, disloyalty.
What are your wishes? Why is affection not thick?'

The Mother answers Prefect's Clerk:
'Why so much chatter, chatter?
This wife has no knowledge of Rites, or honorable behavior,
Herself takes initiative, assumes to discriminate.
My ideas have long been treasured in my bosom, heart is
    divided in hate.

You! do you have your own way?
In household to East is a virtuous maiden
Calls herself Lo-fu from Land of Ch'in.
Her body is admired, unequalled!

I, The Mother, will beg her for you.
Then can quickly send away this one;
Send her away, let her go, be cautious, do not keep her.'

Prefect's Clerk kneels a long time; speaks:
'I lie prostrate in order to inform my mother:
If this wife be sent away,
To end of old age, will not take another.'

The Mother, hearing these words,
In rage, pounds bed with her fist:
'Is miserable son without veneration?
How dare he utter aid-wife words?
Already, toward me, you fail in gratitude, rule of right
    conduct.
You will not follow me!... indeed?'

Prefect's Clerk maintains dark silence, without sound.
Once more lifts two hands in reverence, returns, enters bed-
    room door.
Begins to utter words, to converse with young wife,
Grief grips throat, he gulps, cannot speak.

(*Commanding himself says:*)

'I, myself, do not drive away Loved One,
Compelling, insisting, there is... The Mother.
For a short time, only, shall my Loved One, to father's
    house retire.
I must now serve in Prefect's office,
Ere long should come back, return home.
When I come back will go out to meet, will take you.

This thought treasure deep in your heart,
Act carefully, do not oppose my words.'

(*Young wife says to Prefect's Clerk:*)

'I cannot come a second time; perplexity, confusion would
   result from repetition.
Formerly, in sunlight time of year's revolution, I first
Left father's house, came to your honorable gateway.
Began work, complied with wishes of Honorable Father,
   Venerable Mother.
Careful of every thought, could I dare make my own de-
   cisions?
By day, by night, exerted myself to the utmost; — then
   rested.
Am lonely, depressed; bitterness, evil fortune, are knotted
   in my heart.
Words I have spoken are without guilt or fault.
To the end, have sustained, nourished, the parents; fulfilled
   all obligations.
Now suffer being driven like a beast, sent away.
How say, come a second time, return?...
Unworthy One has embroidered short coat; it reaches the
   hips.
Leaves and hill-flowers shine thereon, are brilliant.
Has red openwork silk gauze, bed-curtain,
At four corners hang fragrant bags of perfume.
Has bamboo boxes, six or seven tens,
Leaf-green jade beads strung on bright silk cords.
Each thing, each thing, in itself is different,
Of its class, of its class, at centre of perfection.
If my person be unworthy, the things also are poor,
Not good enough to present to my successor.
Nevertheless retain, keep them; I leave them to be used.
From now on, no reason for our meeting;
Forever, forever, may you be peaceful, tranquil,
Long, long, may we not die in each other's hearts.'

Cock crows, in sky is light of sun about to rise,
Young wife leaves bed, dresses with care, puts on make-up,
Dons long embroidered skirt.
For own use, for own use, takes four, five of all her posses-
sions.
Below, on her feet, treads on gleaming silk shoes;
Above, on her head, wears shining shell combs.
Her waist is supple as lustrous white silk;
In ears are bright moons, ear-pendants of pearls linked to
jade.
Fingers like pared roots of the leek,
Lips like vermilion of cinnabar.
Dainty, dainty, she takes tiny footsteps,
The essence of beauty! World holds not her pair.
Ascending Guest Hall to The Mother she raises hands in
reverence.
Anger of The Mother has not ceased.

　　(Young wife speaks:)
'Formerly, in childhood, girlhood, time,
At birth, when small, came out from hamlet in the wilds;
Had, originally, no teaching, nor did I hear flowing words
of instruction.
Felt, therefore, demon of shame in my heart at marrying
son of high household.
Received from Mother many gifts of silk and of gold,
Cannot endure Mother should drive me away as a beast to
the battue.
This day I go, returned to father's house,
I think of you, Mother, bearing toil and trouble of all
within the home.'

She then takes leave of husband's little sister;
Tears drop, a string of pearls:
'When first I came, a new wife,
Husband's little sister was protected in her pen.

This day, when I suffer being driven forth, sent away,
Husband's little sister is as tall as am I.
Exert your strength, with all heart sustain Honorable
    Father, Venerable Mother,
Lovingly care for the parents.
In first half of moon — seventh day, in second half of moon
    — ninth day,
When playing games, do not forget me.'

She goes out from door, steps into hooded cart — departs.
Tears fall one hundred and more lines.
In front, Prefect's Clerk rides his horse;
Behind, young wife drives in hooded cart.
Now he hears, now he hears not, iron-bound wheels,
    rumble, rumble.
Together they meet at mouth of Great Road.
He dismounts from horse, steps within covered cart,
Lowers head to her ear, whispers:
'Take an oath! we shall not remain in separate lands,
For a brief day you must return, must, to father's house, go,
While I to Prefectural office repair.
Not long, should come back, return home.
Take this oath! Heaven will not requite us with evil.'

Young wife says to Prefect's Clerk:
'My Lord stirs passion, his love, his love, is treasured in
    bosom;
As he sees the records, my Lord already knows
It is not long till I may hope he comes.
My Lord is a rooted rock,
Unworthy One is sweet flag, is grass growing in the river
    bed.
Soft as floss silk is sweet flag, is grass growing in the river
    bed;
Not turning, not stirring, is the rooted rock.
I have an elder brother, son of my own father,

In nature, and behavior, scorching heat of his cruelty is
    fierce as thunder.
Perhaps he will not like thoughts treasured in my bosom,
To harass my affections, he may oppose.'
She raises hands in reverence to say farewell, long he con-
    soles, he consoles.
Two lovers unable to part, unable to part!

Young wife passes through Great Gate, ascends Guest Hall
    in father's house,
Enters, draws back; is without 'face,' lacks right behavior.
The Mother strikes hands together in great annoyance,
Did not expect daughter thus repudiated.
'Ten and three taught you to weave,
Ten and four you could cut-out clothes,
Ten and five swept strings of *k'ung hou* lyre,
Ten and six knew Rites, correct behavior.
Ten and seven bequeathed you in marriage,
Words were spoken, an oath cannot be broken.
Now what is your fault, your crime,
That you are not kept, a wife; are thus returned home?'

Lan Chih — Fragrant Spear-Orchid — mortified, says to
    The Mother:
'Daughter is truly without fault, without crime.'
Greatly grieved, scornful is The Mother.

Ten and more days after young wife's return to father's
    house,
District Magistrate calls go-between to come,
Says: 'Have number three young son,
Elegant, refined, the world has not his pair;
His years, ten and eight or nine,
His words, many — his talents quick.'

The Mother speaks to The Daughter:

'Daughter may go, accede to this proposal.'
The Daughter restrains tears, replies:
'At time when Lan Chih — Fragrant Spear-Orchid — first
    returned,
Saw Prefect's Clerk who repeated three times
An oath that we knotted: never to separate, to part.
Would you, to-day, oppose love's right action?
Fear this affair is utterly shameless.
You, yourself can cut short the letter received,
Quietly, quietly, you can say thus...'

The Mother tells Go-between Person:
'Poor, unworthy, is this daughter.
Was married, was returned to door of father's house.
If unable to be wife of Prefect's Clerk
How could she, with District Magistrate's young Lord,
    unite?
Luckily you can ask, widely, for another bride,
It will not do for me to make a promise.'

Go-between Person leaves. Several days later
Comes an Assistant Magistrate, as messenger, seeking.
Says: 'In household of Lan — Spear-Orchid — there is a
    young woman,
Her forebears on register are statesmen, are statesmen.'
Says: 'There is number five young gentleman,
Proud, refined, not yet has he taken bride at dusk.
Assistant Magistrate is commanded to act as go-between,
To speak words with her father, the Deputy Official.
In truth I refer to great Prefect's family
Which has this young Lord, worthy of regard.
They already desire the Knot of Great Rightness
Have ordered me to enter your honorable gate.'

The Mother thanks Go-between Person; speaks, saying:
'My daughter has sworn an oath,
How can an old woman reply?'

The Elder Brother hears of this,
Perplexed, in heart's centre burns fire of rage.
Lifting up words speaks to The Younger-Sister:
'Why should you not discuss this plan?
In first marriage obtained Prefect's Clerk;
In second marriage obtain High Officer;
Unimportance of one, importance of other are wide apart as
    Earth and Heaven.
Proposal is sufficient to glorify your person.
If you do not act rightly, marry, how is it becoming?
What is your desire? Where will you dwell? Speak!'

Lan Chih — Fragrant Spear-Orchid — lifts head, replies:
'Custom is truly as Elder Brother says:
Withdrew from father's household, served The Son-in-Law.
Midway on Life's Road, return to Brother's gate.
He may judge, decide; will satisfy my Brother's thoughts,
How should I assume responsibility of decision?
Although the Prefect's Clerk and I agreed
To unite forever, we have no affinity.'

Now, The Brother and The Go-between make harmonious
    accord,
Promise to arrange marriage at dusk relationship.
Go-between Person steps down from seat of honor, with-
    draws;
Nods assent, nods assent, again agrees, agrees.
Enters Official Residence, tells Lord Prefect:
'Lower Officer has fulfilled your orders, your commands.
Words, fires of discussion, had real affinity.'

When Lord Prefect hears this report
In heart's centre greatly he rejoices. Happily
Looks at Calendar, consults Books:
'Convenient, profitable, within this very moon,
Cyclical signs are correct, are in mutual accord.

Good fortune comes on three tens day,
It is already two tens and seven.
My staff may go, complete wedding plans.

The words spoken, quick the preparations,
Incessant like silk threads joined, like silk drawn out,
    speedy as driven clouds
Black water-bird, red-headed crane boats lashed in squares;
At the four corners hornless dragon banners
Flitter, flutter, curl, follow the wind.
Gold chariot with wheels of jade,
Dancing, prancing, dark-dappled horses,
Saddles flower decorated, gold engraved.
The square-hole cash despatched, three times one hundred
    times, ten thousand,
All strung on bright green cords.
Varied silks, three times one hundred rolls.
In the markets buy rare meats for many guests.
Serving people four hundred or five
In crowds, in crowds, come to Prefectural Gate.

The Mother speaks to The Daughter, says:
'Lord Prefect's writing, this moment, is received.
Bright morrow comes to lead you out.
Why are upper garments, lower garments, not yet made?
You cannot, not accomplish affairs which are arranged.'

The Daughter, silent, without sound,
Covers mouth with kerchief, gulps down sobs;
Her tears flow, like water running in channels.
Moves her couch, inlaid with strass figures,
Takes it out, places it, beneath front window.
Left hand seizes scissors, measure,
Right hand grasps damask, openwork silk gauze.
At daybreak makes long embroidered skirt,
At nightfall makes unlined gauze robe.

Dusk, dusk, sun will soon be hidden
Thoughts sunk in grief, goes out from door, weeps.

Prefect's Clerk hears the news, alters his plans,
Begs leave of absence to go home a short time.
Has not traversed two or three *li*
When saddled horse piteously neighs.
Young wife recognizes sound of horse
Treads on her shoes, sees him, whom she did not expect.
Unhappy, very, from afar gaze at each other,
She knows it is her beloved who has come.
Lifts hand, strikes horse's saddle,
Sighs, moans, Clerk's heart is wounded.

   (*She says:*)
'Since my Lord parted from me, and after,
Affairs of men cannot be computed.
It is, really, not as we first intended,
Nor that which my Lord understands.
I have kinsmen, father, mother,
Who urge me, force me, as do my brothers.
They make me promise to another person.
How could I hope, for my Lord's return?'

Prefect's Clerk says to young wife:
'Congratulate my Loved One, she has high promotion.
Rooted rock in its place is firm,
Can there remain one thousand years and more;
Sweet flag, grass growing in the river bed, are soft as floss
   silk,
What they will do at day-dawn, at nightfall, is undeter-
   mined.
Loved One has this day, triumph, riches;
I, alone, face Yellow Springs.'

Young wife says to Prefect's Clerk:
'What is the meaning coming from these words?

Both of us have suffered urging, forcing,
As my Lord acts, so Unworthy One will act.
At Yellow Springs, below, we will see each other.
Do not, not fulfill this day's words.'
They clasp hands, then take divided roads,
Each, each, returns to household door.

When living people undertake 'until death parting,'
The misery, the misery, who can describe?
Of those who consider, within this world parting,
A thousand, ten thousand, do not carry it out.

Prefect's Clerk returns to his home,
Goes up to Guest Hall, raises two hands in reverence to
    The Mother, says:
'This day great wind is cold,
Wind harms trees, plants.
Fear frost may kill "spear-orchid" in the court.
Son goes, this day, to Shadow World, Shadow World,
Hereafter will mother be alone.
The reason? She made a plan; it was not good.
Cease to annoy my spirit, my soul.
May your life be long as Southern Mountain rocks,
May your four limbs, in death, lie straight.'

The Mother, hearing this,
Scatters tears, makes moaning sounds; says:
'You are son of a great house,
Of scholars, officials, at Palace pavilion.
Verily, you should not die for a wife!
Passion of the high, the low, can fade.
In house to East, there is a virtuous maiden,
Exquisite, refined, she captivates all in city, in suburbs.
I, The Mother, will beg her for you,
Between dawn and dusk, it shall be done.'

Prefect's Clerk raises hands, in reverence, goes;
Long he sighs, in empty bridal room;
Makes his plans as he stands there,
Turns head, moves toward door,
Grief in heart urges, drives him.

This day oxen low, horses neigh.
Soon after yellow dusk, young wife enters bright green tent
At margin of stream, at margin of stream.
Silent, silent, all people are at rest.
'My life is this day cut short,
Soul goes, body long remains.'
Grasps skirt, slips off silk shoes,
Raising body walks into clear green pool.

Prefect's Clerk hears of this happening;
Heart knows separation, division has come.
Turns his head, walks back and forth beneath a tree;
Hangs himself from the Southeast branch.

Two households beg they be buried together,
Buried together on Flower Mountain slope.
East, West, plant pine and cypress trees,
Left, right, sow seed of *wu tung* trees.
Branches, branches, join in canopy,
Leaves, leaves, interlock each other.
In the centre, fly a pair of birds,
Their names *yüan yang* — birds of love —
Lifting its head, each to the other calls.
Nightly, nightly, when Fifth Watch is reached,
Passers-by halt their tread, listen...
Widowed wife rises, walks, is irresolute, doubts where to
    go.

After world people we tell of these happenings,
That they be warned, this tale do not forget.

Between A.D. 114 and 120 Pan Chao died, her years in the vicinity of seventy. The Empress decreed a mourning period and, herself, wore half-mourning for the great lady Ts'ao Ta Ku. All recognized that a bright luminary had faded from the literary Heavens.

How different the fate of Pan Chao to that of her spiritual descendant Ch'iu Chin. For the one: peace, a life of study and intellectual attainments, honor, respect, appreciation and length of years. Although her desire that women be educated was not fulfilled, her example has shone, a light, to succeeding ages. For the other: strife, a life of struggle to break down customs in her eyes wrong, final frustration, and an early death of violence at the hands of men. Yet what Ch'iu Chin desired is already being fulfilled. Her courage and self-abnegation, qualities not demanded of Pan Chao, illumine the path her sisters tread.

Part Three

Postlude

THE KUEI FAN: WITHIN BATON-DOOR STANDARDS

T HE principal book for the instruction of women has been, for centuries, the *Lieh Nü Chuan — Series of Women's Biographies*. The *Kuei Fan* is composed of a selection from these tales, made during the eighteenth year of the *wan li* period of the Ming Dynasty — A.D. 1591 — by Lü Hsin-wu. The author sets forth the regulation of his book, saying that he is preparing a road of propriety which women may travel; that, as they are not educated, he is altering the deep classical style of writing in order that the matter be comprehensible: 'My words are shallow as skin.'

In addition to the selected biographies, he gives, from the Classical Books, long quotations dealing with the social relations of women. The biographies are classified and carefully annotated by Lü Hsin-wu.

The edition which I use is a reprint ordered in 1927 by Li Hsi-shan in memory of his dead wife. He writes a *po*, an addenda, giving his reasons for doing this and expresses the hope that he may give his dead wife joy.

I here summarize the work and retell a number of the tales. Actual translation is placed in quotation marks; the remainder is paraphrase.

I

THE WAY OF MAIDENS

'The Way of Wives, the Rule of Mothers, spring from the Virtue of Maidens. It is not possible that a maiden lacking virtue should become a pure, an incorruptible wife. All origins are found in the Paths of Maidens. These paths are six: The Filial, the Daring, the Chaste, the Incorruptible, the Moral, the Literary.

THE FILIAL PATH. When women have not yet taken the road to a husband's home, their filial piety should liken that of sons. To be a filial son is difficult; to be a filial daughter still more difficult. According to the custom of our country, a maiden in her home is a guest, even her mother treats her as a guest. If sons of the house be not considerate, they do not care to provide her with food and clothing nor to serve her. While she, having no real responsibilities, may wish only to nourish her vanity, and cultivate her appearance. She may easily bear resentment and lightly grieve, bursting into tears on all occasions. Furthermore she may not listen to Rules of Right Behavior.'

Having expressed his doubts regarding the filial devotion of daughters, the author now enumerates fourteen persons. They, he considers, have earned such appellation. From these fourteen tales I have selected one typical of the filial piety practised by daughters.

CHÜAN — THE COMELY ONE — AT THE FERRY OF CHAO

Chien Tzŭ of Chao, a High Official, neared the ferry wishing to cross. The ferryman, alas, was drunk, sunk-as-a-stone drunk, incapable of movement. Chien Tzŭ was about to order summary execution when the ferryman's daughter — the Comely One — intervened saying: 'Unworthy One's father heard that my Lord would come to the ferry; he had not yet sounded the waters, and therefore made offering to

the Spirits of Nine Rivers and the Three Huai Streams. He sacrificed and was overcome by the cup of happiness, which he swallowed to the last drop. His drunkenness springs from this cause. Unworthy One is willing, for her father's person, to substitute in death her own lowly body.' Chien Tzŭ naturally refused to accept such filial sacrifice declaring that no fault was hers. The Comely One argued further: 'Unworthy One's father is drunk, his body does not realize distress, his heart does not comprehend evil done, allow him to waken and be aware of his crime.'

The force of this argument appealed to Chien Tzŭ; after all, it does seem futile to punish an individual unconscious of punishment! He therefore prepared to select one of his suite as oarsman and to make arrangements for the crossing. The Comely One, however, stretched out her hand, pulled his sleeve, and begged that *she* be allowed to act as ferryman. The Official was horrified, declared that it would not be correct behavior for him to 'sit in a boat with a woman-person.' The Comely One retorted: 'Of old when King T'ang chastised Hsia Dynasty, his left horse-harnessed-outside-the-chariot-thills was a black mare, the right a yellow mare. T'ang successfully cast off Chieh, last monarch of Hsia. When King Wu chastised Yin Dynasty his left-horse-harnessed-outside-the-chariot-thills was a dappled mare, the right a red mare with black mane. Wu was adequate. He overthrew infamous King Chou. You, lordly gentleman, desire merely to cross the river; if you *are* in a boat together with Unworthy One what injury is there, eh?' Chien Tzŭ was obliged to grant that the danger did not seem overwhelming, and they set out: young girl, High Official, attendants, banners streaming in the wind.

The Comely One bent her slim body to the oar and in excitement vented her thoughts in a song which rang above
the rushing waters. Chien Tzŭ was enchanted and exclaimed:
'I dreamt that I should take a wife. Verily, is this not the
woman?' He forthwith directed that an Officer of Prayer
should arrange the marriage. The Comely One, however,
lifting her hands in reverence, declined, saying: 'Correct way
for women, if there be no go-between, is not to marry a
husband. Unworthy One is surrounded by unrelenting kinsfolk, she dare not listen to the suggestion.' Turning, she
departed, walked swiftly away.

Chien Tzŭ, the High Official, returned humbly to his
official residence, prepared betrothal presents, despatching
them to the lowly home of the Comely One, and when all
had taken place according to the rites, he welcomed as his
wife the ferryman's daughter.

Lü and other commentators consider The Comely One, in
her offer to die for her father and in her refusal to relax
ceremony as being well versed in the Filial Way and in that
of Right Behavior.

THE PATH OF DARING. The author next describes the Way
of *lieh nü*, Daring Women who are both chaste and brave.
The ladies in this category all have died rather than yield
themselves to dishonor. Sometimes their idea of dishonor
seems to twentieth-century readers strange. The famous case
of the 'Washing Silk Woman' — a popular tale still drama-
tized on a hundred stages — is one of them.

The lady's name is unknown. Aged thirty, she lived with
her old mother and had never spoken with a man. One day
when washing silk at the river edge, she was suddenly

accosted by a soldier of high rank, who was evidently in flight from an enemy. He was, indeed, the famous Wu Yüan, better known as Wu Tzŭ-hsü, of the Ch'u state who lived in the fifth and sixth centuries before our era. Seeing a jug and a bowl by her side, he begged for food and drink. This she gave him. They spoke together. He explained his plight, and asked his way. She directed him, he then continued his journey.

The Washing Silk Woman returned to her task with who knows what unwonted turmoil in her breast? Presently Tzŭ-hsü appeared once more riding quickly. He came to her and said: 'You must tell no one that you have seen me; tell no one where I have gone.' The woman rose to her feet. She looked at him. She spoke quietly but asked him how he imagined that she, who in all her life had never spoken to a man, who by so doing had lost her chastity, and this for his sake, how he dared imagine that she would now 'let words leak,' in fact, betray him? Not waiting for an answer she turned, clasped a stone to her bosom, and threw herself into the stream, where she was quickly drowned.

Various commentators discuss this story of the *Washing Silk Woman*. It is included in the *Lieh Nü Chuan*. Lü Hsin-wu, a Ming scholar, whose notes accompany the *Kuei Fan*, has modern ideas on the subject of her sacrifice. He considers her action — excessive. After all, he argues, she was not married to Tzŭ-hsü, she had no responsibility toward him, and if she did speak to him, if she did risk her reputation to save his life, surely that was no reason for her to lose her own.

In the opinion of Lü Hsin-wu only three cases in history show maidens worthy of the title *lieh*. Such must be ready to use a white and shining knife if the red blush of shame be brought to their cheeks.

One of the ladies he cites, and the only one whose story I shall tell, was a beautiful daughter of the Chan Clan. Her father and elder brother were taken by bandits and bound. She approached the bandits and by offering herself to their leader as wife, induced them to set free father and brother. Saying that she had now 'gone out from the clan' and must stay where she belonged, she urged her relatives to leave her. They did so. When assured of their safety, she cast herself from a bridge into swiftly swirling water, which speedily engulfed her fair form.

Commentators admire, not only her courage, but her quick wit which saved the leaders of her Clan.

THE PATH OF CHASTITY. The *chên* — chaste — maidens are also three. They are described as those who protect their

bodies as if they were caring for a jade goblet, or holding in both hands a brimming bowl of water. As those whose ears and eyes see only what is right and straight, whose hearts desire nothing crooked. The Commentators remark that, among women who live a protected life of ease, nine out of ten are *chên*, but among those who have difficulties, among those who are exposed to the dangers of the world, *chên* women resemble fair lotus rising from the mud. They are better than pure gold-long-fused, but, alas, are few. Among women who suffer difficulties, out of ten, nine lose virtue.

First of the *chên* is the warrior, Hua Mu-lan. Her history has already been told in the pages of this book. The second is a lady of the Han Clan who, also without detriment to her person, served among soldiers; third is the maid of Kao Yu who rather than take refuge under the mosquito net of an elderly gentleman, remained outdoors among the reeds and rushes, allowing herself to be stung to death by mosquitoes. The pests sucked her blood until she was like a skeleton! Her sister-in-law, who was with her, accepted meanwhile the gentleman's offer.

The Commentator points out that people as pure as the maid of Kao Yu are rare. He, however, considers her behavior extreme!

THE PATH OF INCORRUPTIBILITY. Maids who are economical and in no way avaricious. The author describes such maidens in a phrase: 'Those who regard profit as dust'! Of this type he cites but one: a young daughter of the Ts'ao Clan. Her father, an incorruptible official, died while leading soldiers far from home. So poor was the family that the expense of moving his coffin home for burial, a most important step in

Chinese eyes, was beyond their means. Friends offered money, fifty times ten thousand cash, a not uncommon procedure in China. The widow was about to accept the gift when the young daughter, weeping, pled with her not to do so, saying: 'My father, when alive, was unusually averse to accepting gifts, even gifts of food. If we take this money, it is as if the responsibility were on his person.' The mother yielded, and refused the strings of cash.

Commentator Lü is deeply impressed. He points out that the incorruptibility of the father had been inherited by the daughter. She, although she loves him, urges that his coffin be buried in a strange land. Even the sages took money for burial, but not the daughter of Ts'ao. This is rare indeed!

THE PATH OF INTELLIGENT MORALITY. Maidens who tread this path examine carefully their reputation, their chastity. They also understand the Way of Behavior. Five are mentioned, each in her relation to a King whom she successfully influences, giving advice in affairs of State.

The maiden with the old goitre, her name unknown, was picking mulberry leaves when the King in his chariot passed by. She did not even turn her head to look at him. Amazed at such unusual behavior the King sent for the maid, talked with her, found her so careful of her reputation and so intelligent that he made her his Queen. When he listened to her advice the country flourished. When he ignored it, as he finally did, enemy neighbors swallowed up his lands.

Lü has a good opportunity for moralizing. He points out that beauty is not all-important, that in fact beautiful women far too often 'overturn the state.' He pooh-poohs the idea that a goitre is a real disadvantage.

The story of Chên Mei, a lady at the Court of King Chêng of Ch'u, is typical of Chinese manners. The Ruler walked one day on a high terrace. Below him spread a lotus pool, spanned by a bridge, where Palace Ladies walked. The King called. All, except Chên Mei, looked up.

At this point Mr. Wang, with whom I was reading the story, exclaimed: 'How correct! People should never, with raised heads, look boldly at a King.' He then cited stage procedure and reminded me that courtiers and Palace Ladies make their entry eyes on the ground; they never look up without permission. 'I myself,' he continued, 'cannot look boldly at a high person; *mei yu fa tzǔ* — there is nothing to be done — I must bend my head and look from the corners of my eyes.'

In this case the King commanded the lady to look up. She continued to gaze at the ground. He offered her gold. She did not turn. He said she should be his wife. Her eyes remained where they were. Finally he offered to enoble her father and brothers. She turned and looked at him, sacrificing *kuei chü* — the circle of right conduct and the square of right action — on behalf of her family.

Chên Mei became Queen and tried to help her Lord with good advice. He would not listen. In protest she killed herself. The disaster, which she had foreseen, speedily evinced itself: an overindulged son rebelled, surrounding the Palace. The distracted Ruler took his own life.

Lü admires the girl's behavior up to a point, but considers that suicide was unnecessary.

THE LITERARY PATH. The path of maidens who write poems. The editor states that maids are not versed in the rites, neither have they learning, how should they write good poems? He reminds his readers that from olden times to the present day, nevertheless, many have written verses. Why does he choose but two examples? Not because of the poems, nor yet because of the maids who wrote them; but because of the love they evince. Love between men and women, who are the greatest of the ten thousand creations, is something which only sages can comprehend. In each of the cases cited, Palace Women sewed poems into the garments which were being made for soldiers on the frontier. When the soldiers found them not one but shed tears. They were moved and comforted by thoughts of the light hands which had made the garments, by the warm hearts of women left at home.

One of the ladies is of the Shih Clan. A superfluous member, among the thousand and more, of the harem during the reign of the great T'ang Emperor, Li Shih-min, known to history as T'ai Tsung — A.D. 627–650. As she sewed the wadded garment, destined for the front, she wept thinking that by rights she, a useless virgin, should be making a garment for a husband, not for an unknown foot-soldier. The poem which she slipped into the pocket of the coat, for all the world as women slipped messages into garments sent to France during the Great War, read:

To sandy   wastes   frontier   guard   marches,
Cold,   bitter-misery,   how   will   he sleep?
Wadded   battle-coat   is made   by my   light   hands.
How   do I know   at whose side   it will   fall,   as Autumn
          leaves fall?
Thoughts   revolve;   I make   the stitches   stronger;
Love   surges;   I press   in   the wadded   cotton.
Joy   of this life   has already   passed,
I long,   in a future   life,   to be   united   to my affinity.

The lady was wrong. 'Joy of life' had not passed. The soldier who found the poem showed it to his Commander, the Commander sent it to the capital where it was brought to the notice of the Emperor. The warm-hearted impetuous Son of Heaven entered the seraglio and asked who had written the verses. The lady stammered out her confession, realizing that she should die ten thousand deaths. To her joy and amazement, Li Shih-min directed that she leave the harem — the inmates were often dispersed — and that she become the wife of the foot-soldier.

So ends the section containing directions for Maidens who prepare the Way of Wives and the Rule of Mothers.

II

THE WAY OF HUSBAND AND WIFE

This is differentiated from and precedes the Way of Wives. It is said: 'Husbands, husbands, wives, wives, if the way of the home is to be correct, the husband must be righteous, the wife yielding. Then the home will be happy. Therefore, husbands and wives should be selected for their virtue, direction for their behavior should be given. A wife should recognize faults and try to transform them, responsibility is not on husband alone. Two hearts should be united in virtue, then all within will have strength.' Nine couples have, in the author's opinion, distinguished themselves.

One pair had their official residence under a willow tree. The husband — Hui — was a high-minded, much beloved magistrate. Three times was he degraded without resigning from office. His wife, impatient, asked why he endured such shame. He replied that the state was in disorder, that by remaining at his post he could help the people, and ended by asking: 'Why should I mind if my ears redden in shame?' She humbly bowed her head in acquiescence. Hui died. Pupils cried aloud his virtues, but the wife said: 'I, Unworthy One, know him far better than do his pupils.' She thereupon wrote a eulogy:

Husband was not arrogant, *hsi* ...
Husband did not cause suffering, *hsi* ...
Truthful, sincere, injured no one, *hsi* ...
Bore degradation, yielded, followed usage of the day;
Did not torture prisoners in examination, *hsi* ...
Allowed ears to redden in shame that he might save
      the people,
His virtue, great, overpowering, *hsi* ...

Although   thrice   he met   dismissal
To the end   did not   bear   grain-of-mustard-seed resentment,
    hsi . . .
Was   he   not   a Pattern   Man,   to eternity   inspiring?
    hsi . . .
He has   gone down   in death,   *hsi* . . .
Soul,   spirit,   scattered,   *hsi* . . .   *ai tsai* alas!

Commentator Lü remarks that, although it is easy for a wife
to understand inner matters, to find a married pair who comprehend both inner and outer, from the same point of view, is
truly rare.

Another couple mentioned are Liang Hung and Mêng
Kuang, who are very famous indeed. Poets constantly allude
to their ideal married life, which ran its course in the first
century of our era.

Liang Hung, a poverty-stricken scholar, supported himself
by keeping pigs. Upon one occasion he accidentally set fire
to a neighbor's house and at once offered to pay the debt in
pigs, a litter at a time. Such model behavior gained him a
great reputation; he was much desired as a son-in-law but
refused to marry.

Mêng Kuang, the daughter of well-to-do parents, was fat,
possessed by the demon of ugliness, and so dark that her com-
plexion is described as being 'black.' Her virtuous actions,
coupled with great physical strength, made up for her appearance and many suitors crowded about her door. She, in an
unusually independent manner, would not accept any one of
them. Father and mother, puzzled, asked what she *did* want.
Her years were thirty, would she never wed? Kuang replied,
'Desire husband of principle, like Liang Hung.'

Liang Hung, hearing of Kuang's words, immediately

wooed her, was accepted, and 'took her by the ear' — the
Chinese term for man's marriage. The bride, arrayed in
beautiful garments, much painted and adorned, entered his
door.

Seven days passed. The marriage had not been consummated. Bride and groom had not lain on the cool grass mat
ready spread on the bridal bed.

Kuang knelt before Liang Hung and said: 'Unworthy One
has heard that her husband is a model of rightness, she is
willing to "hold the towel and comb," now she finds herself
rejected. Pray tell her the reason.'

Hung said: 'I desired a "thorn hairpin, cotton-skirted
wife" with whom I could live in retirement from the world.
Now comes one in embroidered robes, bedizened with false
glitter. Not what Hung is willing to have.'

Mêng Kuang replied: 'Unworthy One will in seclusion
make preparation.' She laid off the exquisite robes and head-
dress and appeared in a coarse cotton cloth garment. Hung,
enchanted, exclaimed: 'This is my wife!'

They retired to a hut in the hills. There they passed their
days. He, tilling the soil, she, weaving cloth. Their evenings
were passed in playing the *ch'in* and humming poetry together. When Kuang served the meals she never looked at
Hung directly, but, when offering it, lifted the rice-bowl to
the level of her eyes.

The names Liang Hung and Mêng Kuang, to designate a
Pattern Pair, have for two millennia run through the Central
Flowery State.

III

THE WAY OF WIVES

Way of Wives, carefully subdivided into eight classes, follows: These classes are: (1) Wives Who Possess all Virtues; (2) the Filial; (3) those Who Meet Death Willingly in an Emergency; (4) those Who Protect their Chastity; (5) the Virtuous; (6) those Who Uphold the Rites; (7) the Intelligent or Penetrating; (8) the Learned.

A General Preface reads: 'The wife leans on the man. Gentle, yielding, she early listens to the words of others. She has the nature and emotions of those who serve others. She is unspotted as white silk, unwavering, the essence of truth, controls her person in the way of chastity.'

There are the Four Virtues, these she should study:

Woman's Behavior: to be chaste and yielding, yet calm and upright;

Woman's speech: not talkative, yet agreeable;

Woman's occupations: handiwork, embroidery carefully completed;

Woman's carriage and appearance: restrained and exquisite.

If the Four Virtues are present, it matters not that a woman's talents be mediocre, that she have but a monkey's wit, that her family be poor, her face plain. These disabilities do not minimize her worth.

If the Four Virtues are lacking, it matters not that a woman be unusually capable, that she be extraordinarily intelligent, that she be rich, beautiful as a flower, and fascinating; these advantages cannot hide her want of principle.

The *Kuei Fan* now classifies virtuous wives of old in eight divisions: in all sixty-three persons.

Ladies who possess all the virtues, who cannot be put in one class alone, are but five in number. First among them is the virtuous Ma Hou — Ma, the Empress — wife of the energetic founder of the Ming Dynasty, who married her when they were both poor and unknown. Power did not disturb her judgment; she ruled the harem justly, condemned nepotism, encouraged learning, and, most difficult of all, influenced her impetuous Lord, to whom she was devotedly tender.

On her death-bed he asked what her last wishes might be. Ma Hou replied that she desired he accept reproof, exercise self-control, and be as careful at the end as at the beginning.

The Second Class is concerned with Filial wives. Naturally a wife having gone out from her own Clan, this virtue, Filial Piety, is evinced towards the husband's people, especially his mother. The biographies describe how filial wives sacrifice themselves. One mixed her own blood with medicine to cure her mother-in-law, another — a widow — sold a child to buy a coffin for her husband's parent whom she had sworn to care for, while a third, with remarkable sweetness, bore wrongful blame.

Thirteen ladies, who in divers Emergencies Willingly met Death, are next mentioned. In a Foreword the author states that often in times of danger, she who desires to save the life of another must do so at the cost of her own body. The adventures of these ladies are varied; all demonstrate womanly heroism. Perhaps the most curious is the tale of Chou Ti's wife.

Dim twilight succeeded to the glorious noonday of the

T'ang Dynasty, and during this twilight disorder raged.
Clash of fighting resounded throughout the Empire; cities
were besieged; many fell. Yang Chou — where lived, with
his mother and his wife, a certain Chou Ti — suffered such
fate. It was completely looted. Conquering soldiers consumed
all food. On the four sides, men, women, and children were
put to death, their flesh being sold in the open markets. The
wife of Ti said: 'Poverty drives, resources are insufficient for
two. My Lord has old mother, he must not not-return-home.
Please sell wife, to be slaughtered, in order to procure neces-
sities of life.' Thereupon they repaired to the butchery and
a hundred pieces of money were paid to Chou Ti who, putting
them in his sleeve, departed.

The historian does not find it necessary to embellish his
terse account with a description of the despair which settled
upon husband and wife as they parted. He assumes his readers
will comprehend their agony.

Chou Ti upon his return to the village was questioned by
the neighbors. They could scarcely believe his gruesome
story; nevertheless, feeling that truth lurked in his words,
they hurried to the butcher's shop hoping to save the lady.
Alas, they were too late. There on the counter lay her lovely
head. All were filled with grief and sympathy: they collected
money to assist Chou Ti in the care of his mother, and, buying
the bones of his wife, brought them home for burial.

A significant point in this extract from the *Way of Wives* is
that no breath of blame touches Chou Ti. The neighbors
feel that he and his wife, in sacrificing themselves for his
old mother, are behaving in a correct manner.

Lü in his commentary eulogizes a lady who could rejoice
in enabling her husband to nourish his mother, who could give

her body to provide him with the needs of life. Lü exclaims, 'Honorable, right-minded the wife of Ti! Honorable, right-minded the wife of Ti!' and then admonishes all those who think of war and fighting, before treading the road of destruction to reflect upon the misery they bring about.

For his list of immortals the author chooses ten widows who have Protected their Chastity, often at the cost of their personal appearance.

The lovely young widow of Ts'ao Wên-shu was urged to re-marry. She refused, disfiguring herself by cutting off her long black hair. Shortly thereafter disorder broke out in the Empire; again her relatives urged that she take a husband. This time, in order to settle the matter, she cut off nose and ears, 'blood soaked grass-mat on her bed.' Lü, the Commentator, is shocked. He thinks that she might have used other methods and enquires how will her husband feel when she meets him, earless and noseless, in the Yin World, the World of Shade?

Eight Virtuous Wives are discussed. Each loves her husband devotedly; perfects his virtues, regulates his profession, pities his difficulties and misfortunes. They are completely sympathetic — although sometimes in a salutary manner.

The Prime Minister of Ch'i had a tall, well-made groom who was extremely conceited, dressed himself up, and strutted about in an absurd fashion. His wife says: 'You are lowly, cheap, content with being a horse-groom, yet dress yourself in fine clothes. The Prime Minister, who is not three feet high, is yet a great man, and polite. You brag and are con-

ceited.' Her husband in surprisingly humble manner thanks his wife and says: 'How alter?'

At this point Mr. Wang laughed heartily and exclaimed, 'The man must be good! Many would be enraged; he only thanks her.'

The wife gives good advice, which is so faithfully followed that the Prime Minister himself notices the change in his groom and asks how it has come about. Much impressed by the tale he hears, he reports the matter to the Emperor, who at once makes the groom a high official and gives the wife an honored title: *ming fu*.

The Commentator is delighted, and remarks that many women should perspire with shame before the wife of the horse-groom!

The wife of a General, Ch'iu Tzŭ, of the Kai State, sixth century B.C., demanded of her husband high performance of his duty. Defeat attended the arms of Kai. The King was killed. The victors announced that if the defeated officials committed suicide in the accepted manner, their wives would all be slain. This brings up an interesting point in Chinese history. Invading tribes have frequently insisted that the officials of China continue their duties under new overlordship. Thus the invaders have profited by the higher organization and civilization of the conquered state. This accounts for the frequent absorption of Nomad tribes by the cultivated Chinese.

An official who did not escape, by suicide or flight, realized that he must humbly serve the enemy. Ch'iu Tzŭ attempted, perhaps half-heartedly, to perform his task and die, but submitted to rescue and went home. His wife said in amazement: 'A few days ago you were rescued. Now what will you do?' Ch'iu Tzŭ replied with hesitation: 'I did not desire to save my person. Orders of the victors were, that the wives of all who committed suicide would be considered as involved in crime and would be slain.'

His wife answered:

'I have heard the following: If the Ruler be sad, officials who bow before him are put to shame; if the Ruler be put to shame, his officials must die. Now the Lord has died and you live. Can this be called rightness, I ask? Of the learned and the lowly many have suffered death; this did not avail in saving the State, but you are alive. Can this be called love of your fellows, I ask? In anxiety for wife, you forget love of others and rightness, are false to your old Lord, and serve the unscrupulous oppressors; can this be called the heart centred in loyalty?

'A man who has not the heart of loyalty and love, who does not behave with righteousness and benevolence, can he be called worthy?

'The *Book of Chou Ritual* states: "First the Ruler and then his official. First father and mother, then elder brother, younger brother. First elder and younger brothers, then friends locked in intimacy. First intimate friends and then the wife."

'Love for a wife is a private, a personal affair. Service to the Ruler is public duty. Now you, because of wife, have failed others, have failed in the honor of an official. Not having performed the rite of serving the Ruler, you have stolen life — you have no right to exist. I, Unworthy One, feel my ears redden with shame that I am still with you. I cannot endure that ears redden with shame on your account and yet live.'

Thereupon the wife kills herself.

The victorious Ruler, much impressed by her courage and clear-sightedness, decrees that a large building become her shrine and that she be buried with the honors due a General. On her younger brother he bestows a large sum of money and puts him in charge of Kai.

What happened to the husband is not recorded. The Commentator infers that Ch'iu Tzǔ followed his wife to the Yellow Springs, and concludes with a wondering reflection on how people who discard rightness in order to preserve their bodies will feel when they read this writing.

The Ladies in class six, those who Uphold the Rites, all behave according to the letter of conventional conduct although in so doing the five cited nearly all lose their lives. One is engulfed by floods. She will not leave the gaze-at-the-moon-terrace where her Imperial Lord left her when he started on a hunting expedition. The messenger with a counter-order arrives too late.

Another tried to hang herself because her travelling chariot broke down and she seemed fated to spend a night out-of-doors. Horrid thought: Where would her reputation be? She was rescued. The Ming Dynasty Commentator admires her conduct and exclaims, 'How different from the people to-day who paint their faces and like to attract notice!' Strange how we all look back to times more correct than our own.

Intelligent and Penetrating Women constitute class seven. They are described as seeing clearly the way of right behavior, as being true, earnest, meticulous in discussion, self-reliant, and as having great presence of mind. Characteristics hard to acquire.

The ten stories cited deal largely with quick-witted women

who are able to circumvent the wicked plans of bandits; or with those who recognize divided duty yet choose the correct path.

The eighth and last division of the Way of Wives deals with the Learned. The author chooses five persons. These five ladies are distinguished not only for learning but for other virtues as well. Nor does he choose those who are virtuous but not truly literary. The two first to be named are Pan Chieh-yü and her great-niece the talented Pan Chao. Their biographies appear in the body of this book. The others are Hsüan, the Literary and Superior, who in the fourth century A.D. opened a school and lectured from behind a red curtain in order to prevent, in those turbulent days, the disappearance of classical learning; also an Imperial concubine who wrote a very beautiful remonstrance to her Lord, which is too long to quote. The last is the concubine of the great statesman Kuan Chung, reputed to be even more talented than was her husband.

IV

THE WAY OF MOTHERS

Mothers are divided into nine classes: (1) those who teach sons according to the Rites; (2) the Upright; (3) the Benevolent; (4) the Just; (5) the Unavaricious; (6) the Stern; (7) the Comprehending; (8) Tender Stepmothers; (9) Tender Foster-Mothers — wet-nurses.

There is probably no country in the world where mothers play so responsible a part as they do in China. The social structure required a *yin* or female head to deal with matters within the household walls, to balance the *yang* or male head which dealt with affairs beyond the walls. Many men, especially officials — debarred from holding posts in their native provinces—travelled widely; the senior lady, therefore, managed the household in all its ramifications and directed the upbringing of children. Chinese men turn to their mothers with reverent adoration rarely equalled in the West. Nor must it be forgotten that the wife of the family head was the official mother of all children borne by concubines. Her immense responsibility was never relinquished; as long as she lived she directed the actions of her sons and required instant obedience.

A striking example is the case of Hsü Shu's mother. Her name appears in the *Lieh Nü Chuan*. The *Kuei Fan* does not include it. I find the story which exemplifies the 'cursing' of a son by his mother peculiarly interesting. Such cursing, for failure of duty, is characteristically, and I think purely, Chinese. A tragic example came within my own experience. But this is not the place to recount that tale.

During the wars of the Three Kingdoms, at the end of the second century A.D., Hsü Shu remained with his Commander Liu Pei, whose enemy, Ts'ao Ts'ao, was striving to lure officers from their allegiance. Ts'ao took advice as to how he might entice Hsü Shu away from Liu Pei and, hearing that Shu was an exceptionally devoted son thought to accomplish his desire with the mother's aid. He ordered that the old lady be brought to the capital, but found her recalcitrant and most indignant that her son's desertion of Liu Pei could be suggested.

Ts'ao's adviser managed, however, to obtain specimens of Mother Hsü's handwriting and forged a letter, purporting to be from her, in which she told her son that she was in danger and begged him to come quickly, to save her. Hsü Shu showed the letter to his Commander Liu Pei, and they agreed that he must respond to the summons.

Arrived at his mother's dwelling, he entered the Great Hall and raised his hands in reverence before her. The old lady, terribly startled, and frightened that he should be at the capital among enemies, said: 'Why are you here?' Shu replied: 'I was at Hsin Yeh, received my mother's writing therefore, hastening by night under the stars, came hither.' Mother Hsü rose in great anger, struck the table, cursed him, saying: 'Disgraceful son. These several years you have whirled with the wind, have floated on rivers and lakes. I know that you entered in to learning and experience; why are you transformed: not as before? You have studied books, the arrow of your knowledge must strike the target of comprehension; you must realize that it is impossible that the heart be centred both in perfect loyalty and in filial devotion. Do you not recognize that Ts'ao Ts'ao is a brigand who insults, betrays, the Emperor? that the benevolence and right-mindedness of Liu Pei spread to the Four Quarters? Moreover, he is head of the Han Clan; you serve him, he is your Lord. Now, startled by a piece of paper which bears false writing, without examination or investigation, you discard light, give yourself up to darkness. You seize for yourself evil reputation. Verily you are a man with but a monkey's wit. How can I look at you face to face? You insult, disgrace forefathers, ancestors. Futile your life before Heaven, before Earth.'

When the cursing ceased, Hsü Shu, his two hands lifted in reverence, prostrated himself upon the ground, not daring to raise his head. His mother turned, pushed aside the door screen, entered the inner apartments. In but an instant a servant hurried out crying: 'Old Lady has strangled herself, hangs on the beam.'

Hsü Shu, terrified, hastened to save her. The mother's breath was already cut short.

Later generations praise the lady in eulogy:

Virtuous, indeed, Mother Hsü.
Fragrance of her deed wafts down a thousand ages.

She preserved honor, failing never,
Brought renown to husband's Clan.

Taught her son correct way,
Bore on body much bitterness.

The eulogy continues with a number of allusions to men and events of old. It closes with a repetition of the two first lines. While Mother Hsü's behavior is in accord with Chinese canon, my Western heart is torn with sympathy for the son, who pitifully mourned his high-minded mother.

The author of *Kuei Fan* cites first the mothers who teach sons according to the Rites, and also govern their households on correct lines. The procession is led by Mêng Mu, mother of the sage Mêng Tzǔ, 372–289 B.C., known to Westerners as Mencius, chief follower of Confucius. He studied under K'ung Chi, grandson of the sage. She is to Chinese the mother of mothers.

A lady of the Chang Clan, she was left a widow in early youth, supporting herself and little boy K'o by weaving. At first they lived near a cemetery. The child imitated funeral rites, pounded down graves, in fact centred his play on obsequies. Lady Chang shook her head and moved house. Mother and son now dwelt near the market-place. The small boy at once became a miniature trader and peddled goods from dawn till dark. Again Lady Chang shook her head, again she moved house. This time she chose a dwelling under the shadow of a school. To her joy her son became fascinated with the ceremonials carried out by students, and began to study books. She exclaimed: 'My son can really live here!' and at once decided to stay.

When small K'o one day returned from school his mother asked: 'What did you study to-day?' He answered: '*tzŭ jo yeh*,' a phrase difficult to translate. It is the equivalent of a shrug and some such words as 'crazy old stuff.' Lady Chang said no word, lifted her knife, and slit the unfinished web on her loom from top to bottom. Little K'o started in fright, trembling asked the reason. She answered: 'My son throws aside learning as I cut this web. In order to stand, Superior Man must learn.'

At this point my teacher sighed and said: 'Ah, the mother has courage, she risked their means of livelihood to correct her son.' The picture I have chosen to illustrate the incident is taken from a Ming edition of the *Lieh Nü Chuan* printed from Sung boards. It is more interesting than the illustration in the *Kuei Fan*. Little K'o, with a completely smug expression, stands in front of a building plainly marked 'schoolhouse.' His mother brandishes scissors in the air. I very much doubt that scissors were invented as early as the sixth century

B.C. but they evidently existed under the Sung who reigned
A.D. 960–1278.

Mêng K'o, profiting by the severe lesson his mother gave,
studied from dawn till dusk and often beyond the hour of
darkness. He reverently begged his teacher to make him a
great scholar. The teacher did so. Learned men wagged their
heads and told each other that the virtue of Mêng's mother lay
in developing her son step by step. They quoted lines from the
Classic of Poetry: 'The admirable One! How shall we describe
(her),' and said that she comprehended the Way of Mothers.

Meanwhile K'o married and Lady Chang showed herself
wise in the new relationship, as the following story shows.
K'o was about to enter his wife's private room at bedtime
and, to his dismay, saw that she stood there naked. He did
not speak but withdrew, evidently displeased.

The wife hurried to Mother Mêng and begged to be sent
home saying: 'Unworthy One has heard, the Way of Husband
and Wife is that in their private rooms it matters not what
happens. Now Unworthy One sat privately in the room. Her
husband, when he saw her, was much disconcerted, did not
speak. He treated Unworthy One as a stranger. The right
way for a wife is that she should not pass night alone as a
stranger. Please return her to father, mother.'

Mother Mêng called her son and spoke with him saying:
'Rites of politeness demand of a gentleman, when he is about
to open a door, he asks who is there, so that whomsoever
knows how to receive him. If about to approach the Guest
Hall, he makes a noise which will be heard; he thus warns
those within. When about to open door of inner chamber, he
should cast down his eyes, or perhaps he will see a person in
fault. Now my son has not followed the rites of courtesy, yet

demands from others the rite of politeness. Is this not far from correct?'

Mêng Tzŭ thanked her and apologized to his wife, whom he begged to remain. The tale exemplifies the saying which I have already quoted: 'Ascend bed, husband, wife; descend from bed, reserved gentlefolk.'

A few years later Lady Chang noticed that her son looked worried. She asked why; he replied laconically, 'Do not feel quick-witted.' Another day she found him clasping a pillar and sighing. Once more she asked what ailed her son and discovered that he was depressed because his mother's age prevented him from going to the capital and serving the Ruler — the obvious duty of a learned man.

Mother Mêng replied in a long speech regarding the duties of women concerned with matters inside the baton-door, duties which she had always fulfilled. She concludes her remarks by saying: 'There is also the Way of the Three *ts'ung*': — the word is generally translated as 'to follow' — 'when young, a girl follows father; when she is married, she follows husband; when husband dies, she follows son. Such is the rule of the Rites. Now my son has become a man, and I am old. My son must act according to the right way; I will act according to my ritual.'

Mêng Tzŭ became an official who preached the Way of Rightness to several Rulers. His mother has ever since been honored by artists, poets, historians, and above all by the great masses of China, who call themselves 'the black-haired people.'

Having given the lives of Mother Hsü and Mother Mêng in such detail, it seems wise to pass over the other mothers whose biographies, although interesting, are too numerous to treat appreciatively. They manifest every shade of tenderness, justice, and good sense. In all thirty-two persons are noted.

The other 'Ways,' described by the author in detail, are significant in the light they throw on the complicated structure of old style Chinese families. Each son brought his wife to the paternal home and lived there, sharing the common purse. This section of the *Kuei Fan* is an excellent sociological study, but scarcely lends itself to a summary.

The wives, concubines, sisters-in-law, and maid-servants who followed the self-sacrificing road, trodden by pattern ladies of old, must have helped to bring about the calm admired by the Chinese, whose ideal is that eight generations shall congregate harmoniously under one roof-tree!

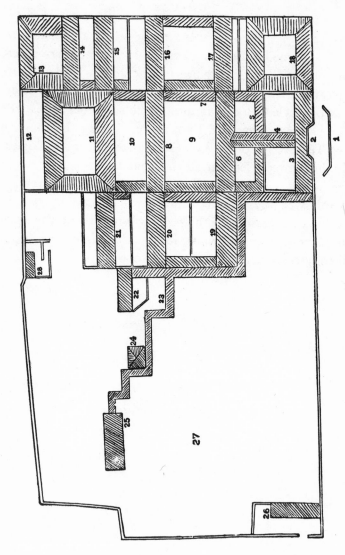

PLAN OF A TYPICAL CHINESE HOUSE OF THE BETTER CLASS

KEY TO PLAN OF A TYPICAL CHINESE HOUSE
OF THE BETTER CLASS

Shaded Sections — Buildings.
White Sections — Courtyards.

The house faces South.

No. 1. Chao Pi. — Spirit Wall. Built to protect the main entrance from the malign influence of evil spirits: these move most easily in a straight line and find difficulty in turning corners, therefore a wall before the Great Gate is an effective defence.

No. 2. Ta Mên. — Great Gate.

No. 3. Mên Fang. — Gate-keeper's Room.

No. 4. Ting Tzŭ Lang. — Covered passage leading from the Reception Hall to the Great Gate and opening on the street.

No. 5. Lang. — Covered passage-way.

No. 6. T'ing. — Reception Hall.

No. 7. Lang. — Covered passage-way.

No. 8. T'ing. — Inner Reception Hall.

No. 9. Ch'ih. — A stone-paved courtyard. It has no roof and is raised in the centre. On great occasions, such as weddings, birthdays, and so on, it can be roofed and floored, thus being made a part of the house. Trees and flowers are not planted in this court, but are set about in pots.

No. 10. T'ing. — A courtyard. In this second courtyard, to which steps lead down, trees and flowers are planted, making of it an inner garden.

No. 11. Tso Ma Lou. — Running Horse Two-Story Apartments. This is the *Kuei* so often spoken of, the Women's Apartments. It is a building in which the rooms surround a courtyard, and are connected by verandahs running round the court upstairs and down. The space in the centre is known as *T'ien Ching* or Heaven's Well. There are eighteen rooms in the upper story, and eighteen in the lower. The wife uses the front rooms; the daughters, the back.

No. 12. Hou T'ing. — Back Court. It is bounded by a 'flower wall,' or brick trellis, through which flowers can twine, and is used by the inmates of the *Kuei* as a garden.

No. 13. Nü Hsia Fang. — Women's Lower House. A house for the women servants. As in the house for men servants, No. 18, the floor is actually on a lower level than those of the master's apartments.

No. 14. Fo Lou.	Buddhist Two-Story Apartments. In the upper story, images of Buddhas, and of Kuan Yin, the Goddess of Mercy, are kept. As a rule, it is locked, and only people who have washed carefully and put on clean clothes may enter.
No. 15. Tsê Shih.	Side Inner Apartment. In this house, poor relations may live. The concubines who do not enter the *Kuei* except on invitation also live here. Guests do not go further into the house than to the wall bounding this building on the South.
No. 16. Tung Hua T'ing.	Eastern Flower Hall.
No. 17. Tui T'ing.	Opposite Hall. This and No. 16 are used for theatrical entertainments. The guests are seated in No. 16, facing South, and the stage faces North in No. 17. A cloth covering is stretched over the courtyard, and a wall divides the two *T'ing* from the rest of the house.
No. 18. Nan Hsia Fang.	Men's Lower House. A house for men servants divided as far as possible from the quarters of the women servants, also placed conveniently near the Great Gate where guests enter.
No. 19. Ta Shu Fang.	Great Book Room. This room is used as a library and study, and in it the teacher instructs the sons of the family.
No. 20. Hsi Hua T'ing.	Western Flower Hall. Here guests are entertained at meals. Flower gardens are placed on either side, and also walls which prevent either the study or the women's rooms from being seen from it.
No. 21. Tsê Shih.	Side Inner Apartment. A building used by the ladies of the house as a study or boudoir, where they embroider, paint, or write. The light is very good, whereas in the *Kuei*, on account of most of the windows opening on the court ('Heaven's Well'), it is apt to be poor.
No. 22. Ch'u Fang.	Kitchen. This is placed conveniently near to No. 20, where the men of the family dine, and No. 21, the dining-room of the ladies.
No. 23. Ch'ü Lang.	Passage-of-Many-Turnings. The superstitious belief in regard to the difficulty experienced by evil spirits in going round sharp corners governs the planning of this strangely shaped passage.
No. 24. Shu Chai.	'Books Reverenced.' The study, or students' room.
No. 25. Hsien.	A Side-room or Pavilion. This is a long, low, outdoor passage, where guests sit and amuse themselves.
No. 26. Ma Fang.	Stable. The stable is placed as far as possible

from the house. The horses, however, are kept saddled near the Great Gate for a large part of the day, in order to be in readiness should they be needed.

No. 27. Hua Yüan. Flower Garden. The gardens are arranged with hills, water, and rockeries, to look as much like natural scenes as possible.

No. 28. Ssŭ So. Privy.

A Chronological Postscript

A CHINESE hand-scroll is unrolled from right to left. To Western eyes, it seems to begin with the end.

Chinese history is, in many particulars, and not the least in this, like a hand-scroll. Modern happenings are clearly set forth, while year by year, decade by decade, the scroll, unwinding, carries the record of events further and further back.

Not until 1927 did archaeological evidence, in the shape of skeletal remains of manlike individuals, prove that members of the human family had lived in China some five hundred thousand years ago. Scientists call attention to the fact that *Sinanthropus pekinensis* had certain peculiarities observed in the jaws of modern Chinese. This is a most important point.

Heretofore it has been generally assumed that the Chinese people, in proto-historic times, wandered from the West into the valley of the Yellow River. If further investigation should prove that Chinese culture is indeed indigenous, the fact would account for the many unique phases of this culture.

The uncharted gap from early Pleistocene to proto-historic times is immense. Not until the fourteenth century B.C. can one begin to speak with certainty of the Chinese people.

At that time a kingdom called the Shang (it became later the Yin) ruled a restricted area from its capital, Anyang. The site lay in modern Honan not far north of the Yellow River.

Oracle bones, discovered in 1899, proved to be part of the royal archives. They are not yet completely deciphered, but have yielded data which throw bright light on the history of this period. Excavation, on the site of Anyang, begun as recently as 1928, reveals that the people of Shang had great artistic gifts and a culture already highly developed. The world awaits impatiently discoveries which will yet further unroll the hand-scroll of history.

☯

Shang or Yin Kingdom   *circa* 1500–1100 B.C.

Chou Dynasty: A Feudal Age.   1100–221 B.C.
    A Ruler, called the Son of Heaven, with shadowy power, presided over an aggregation of states, each governed by a Feudal Lord. Society, during this period, was organized on a basis which recognized hereditary aristocracy. It was therefore utterly different to the form which evolved after the overthrow of feudalism.
    Manners and morals were formed on the patterns laid down by the *Li Chi, Record of Rites,* and the *Chou Li, Ritual of the Chou Dynasty.* Loyalty was the chief virtue: loyalty of a son to his father and his Clan, loyalty of the official to his Feudal Lord, loyalty of the Feudal Lord to the Son of Heaven. The position and duties of woman were clearly defined. She had no property rights, nor did the Government make any provision for the education of women.
    During the later years of the dynasty organization became weak, government was not administered in accordance with traditional moral laws, and, as a result of this weakening, the 'One Hundred Schools' of Philosophy arose.
    During this period, from 551 to 479 B.C., the great leader K'ung Tzŭ, K'ung 'the Sage,' known to the West as Confucius, lived and taught. His

chief disciple Mêng Tzŭ, whom the West calls Mencius, trod in his footsteps about a century later (372–289 B.C.). The main thesis of the Confucian teaching is that enunciated by Mencius: Man is by nature good, becomes evil only through lack of correct instruction.

Ch'in Dynasty: Establishment of an Imperial
    Age.   221–206 B.C.
The leader of Ch'in, a Feudal State, overcame his rivals and established himself as 'First Emperor' of an Imperial State. His methods were ruthless. He burned books connected with the past and put to death many scholars in an attempt to break with hidebound tradition. The social revolution brought about was unparalleled until the upheaval of the twentieth century. In the interval, while China has passed through many political revolutions, the structure of the State and of society has been maintained on the lines formulated under the Han Dynasty, which succeeded the short-lived Ch'in.

Han Dynasty: Development and Consolidation
    of the Imperial Age.   206 B.C.–A.D. 221
The newly established Empire gradually opened communication with Central and Western Asia. Great artistic and literary treasures were produced. The process of paper-making was evolved. The aristocracy of intellect, which has played so powerful a part in Chinese history, as contrasted with the earlier aristocracy of birth, was established. Buddhism was introduced.

The Three Kingdoms	221–277	An Age of Partition.	
The Chin Dynasty	265–419		
Northern and Southern Empires	420–589		221–589

Sui Dynasty: Re-establishment of Empire.   589–618
T'ang Dynasty: Consolidation and Expansion
    of Empire.   618–907
    A glorious period from the cultural, artistic,
literary, and political points of view. Printing
from wooden blocks was introduced. The Forest
of Pencils, or Han Lin Academy, was established.
The examination system which had its beginning
under the Han Dynasty was further developed.

Five Dynasties: An Age of Anarchy and Parti-
    tion.   907–960
Sung Dynasty: An Age of Peaceful Imperial De-
    velopment.   960–1127
    The founder of the Sung Dynasty did not wrest
the throne from his rivals, as has usually been the
case during the course of Chinese history. A
noted general, he was chosen as Son of Heaven by
his officers and was forced, against his own inclination, to ascend the Dragon Throne. The
Sung period was one of exquisite artistic development; in addition great literary projects
were undertaken. The system of Literary Examinations, for the choice of officials, was now
given the form which it retained until its abolition in 1905.

Kin Dynasty ⎫
Southern Sung Dynasty ⎬ An Age of Partition   1127–1280
    The Kin, Golden Tartars, swept from beyond
the Great Wall and drove the rulers of the Sung
Dynasty south of the Yangtse River, where they
established the Capital at Linan, present-day
Hangchow. Eventually both the Kin and the
Sung were overcome by the Mongols under
Kublai Khan.

Yüan Dynasty: Reunification of China — as
    part of the Eurasiatic Mongol Empire.   1280–1368

A dynasty ruthless in its founding. Its great service, to the development of China, was that it established communications across Central Asia, linking Europe with the Far East. It witnessed also the development of the novel. and the theatre. In less than a century came collapse.

Ming Dynasty: An Age of Imperial Development under Native Rulers.   1368–1644

A Chinese peasant, a leader of rebel bands, established the *ta ming* or Great Bright Dynasty. In 1516 the first European vessel, a Portuguese, arrived in Chinese waters. From this time on, essentially unbroken, Sino-European relations have been maintained.

Ch'ing Dynasty: An Imperial Age, under an Alien Dynasty.   1644–1911

A Chinese General, Wu San-kuei, invited Manchu leaders to assist him in putting down a rebellion which threatened the Ming Dynasty. The Manchus accepted the invitation and, when the said rebellion had been suppressed, themselves ascended the Dragon Throne, establishing the *Ch'ing* or 'Pure' Dynasty. During the seventeenth and eighteenth centuries, under the early rulers of this dynasty, China attained a maximum of material prosperity. During the nineteenth century matters were very different. Weak rulers were faced with internal rebellions and disastrous foreign wars. At the end of this century Sun Yat-sen and his followers, among whom was numbered Ch'iu Chin, began to agitate in favor of a republic. The Manchus tried, feebly, to modernize the form of government. As a step in this direction they abolished, in 1905, the Literary Examinations for the selection of officials. In 1907 the first steps were taken in regard to governmental education for women.

The Republic of China.   A.D. 1911–

The Republican Period may be divided into four epochs.

   I. Sun Yat-sen was chosen as President of the Provisional Government in mid and southern China, the Manchus being still on the throne.

  II. The Manchus abdicated on February 12, 1912. The republican form of government was accepted for the whole country. Sun Yat-sen retired, and on February 15 Yüan Shih-kai was elected Provisional President. In October, 1913, he became Substantive President. In June, 1916, following an attempt to make himself Emperor, he died.

 III. A number of provincial military governors struggled for power. The country was kept in constant turmoil by their rivalries. Meanwhile Sun Yat-sen and his followers, forming the Kuomintang, or Nationalist Party, continued to preach social and political democracy. In September, 1923, Michael Borodin arrived from Russia to act as adviser to the Kuomintang which had its headquarters in Canton. Sun Yat-sen stated publicly: 'We no longer look to the West. Our faces are turned towards Russia.' In August, 1923, Chiang Kai-shih was sent to Moscow to study revolutionary technique, and on his return was appointed Principal of the newly established, Russian-inspired Whampoa Military Academy at Canton. In 1925 Sun Yat-sen died. Kuomintang forces, in close co-operation with the Russians, marched North in 1926–27 and, overcoming resistance, finally established the capital of the country in Nanking. In the summer of

1927 close relations with Russia were severed. Borodin and other advisers withdrew to Moscow, and the rightist wing of the Kuomintang, under Chiang Kai-shih, assumed authority.

IV. Since 1927 the Kuomintang has been in ascendancy, has been steadily extending its power, and is slowly, but definitely, creating a unified government in China. A broad educational program has been undertaken, communications have been improved, and many new laws have been passed. Those regarding the status of woman place her on an equality with man.

Bibliography

This does not purport to be a complete bibliography of the subject. It is merely a list of certain works consulted in connection with the writing of this book.

BOOKS IN EUROPEAN LANGUAGES

Mémoires concernant l'histoire, les sciences, les arts, les moeurs, les usages, etc. des Chinois, par les Missionaires de Pé-kin. (Père du Halde, S.J.) 1778.

The Chinese Classics, vol. IV; *The She King, or Book of Poetry,* translated by James Legge, D.D., LL.D. Hongkong, 1871.

The Chinese Readers Manual, by W. F. Mayers. Shanghai, 1874.

Sacred Books of the East, vol. XXVII; *The Li Ki,* translated by James Legge. Oxford, 1885.

A Chinese Biographical Dictionary, by Herbert A. Giles. Shanghai, 1898.

Typical Women of China, by Miss A. C. Safford. Shanghai, 1899.

A Manual of Chinese Quotation, by J. H. Stewart-Lockhart. Hongkong, 1902.

Things Chinese, by Dyer Ball. Shanghai, 1903.

Cantonese Love-Songs, translated with introduction and notes by Cecil Clementi, M.A. Hongkong, 1904.

Lion and Dragon in Northern China, by R. F. Johnstone. London, 1910.

Les Documents Chinois découverts par Aurel Stein dans les Sables du Turkestan Oriental, publiés et traduits par Edouard Chavannes, Membre de l'Institut, Professeur au Collège de France. Oxford, 1913.

Chinese Birthday, Wedding, Funeral and Other Customs, by Mrs. J. G. Cormack. Peking, 1923.

Chinese Lanterns, by Grace Thompson-Seton. New York, 1924.

The Invention of Printing in China and its Spread Westward, by Thomas Francis Carter, Ph.D. New York, 1925.

Humanity and Labor in China, by Adelaide Mary Anderson, D.B.E., M.A. London, 1928.

The Youth Movement in China, by Tsi C. Wang, Ph.D. New York, 1927.

The Mothers: A Study of the Origin of Sentiments and Institutions, by Robert Briffault. London, 1927.

Eminent Asians, by Josef Washington Hall. New York, 1929.

Die Kunst Chinas, Japans, und Koreas, von Dr. Otto Kümmel. Potsdam, 1929.

Far Eastern International Relations, by Hosea Ballou Morse and Harley Farnsworth MacNair. Boston, 1931.

Symposium on Chinese Culture, edited by Sophia H. Ch'ên, published by Institute of Pacific Relations. Shanghai, 1931.

China in Revolution. An Analysis of Politics and Militarism under the Republic, by Harley Farnsworth MacNair. Chicago, 1931.

La Femme dans la Société Chinoise, sa situation sociale, civile, et politique, par Wang Tsang Pao, docteur en sciences politiques de l'Université de Bruxelles. Paris, 1933.

Le Travail Industrielle des femmes et des enfants, par Wang Simine, docteur en sciences politiques de l'Université de Bruxelles. Paris, 1933.

'Early Days of Western Medicine in China,' by Dr. Wu Lien-teh, *Journal,* North China Branch, Royal Asiatic Society, vol. LXII. Shanghai, 1931.

Pan Chao, Foremost Woman Scholar of China, by Nancy Lee Swann, Ph.D. New York, 1932.

The First Wife, by Pearl Buck. New York, 1933.

Chinese Destinies, by Agnes Smedley. New York, 1933.

Letters of a Chinese Amazon and Wartime Essays, by Lin Yutang. Shanghai, 1933.

The Chinese Woman and Four Other Essays, by Sophia H. Ch'ên. Peiping, 1934.

My Country and My People, by Lin Yutang. New York, 1935.

China; a Short Cultural History, by C. P. Fitzgerald. London, 1935.

Yang and Yin, by Alice Tisdale Hobart. Indianapolis, 1936.

The Chinese Quarterly, vol. I, no. 3. 1936.

The Chinese on the Art of Painting, by Osvald Sirén. Peiping, 1936.

'Students in Rebellion,' by Nym Wales; in *Asia,* New York, July, 1936.

The Birth of China, by Herlee Glessner Creel. New York, 1937.

'Nuns of North China,' by Grace Goodrich; in *Asia*, New York, February, 1937.

'The Soongs of China,' by Geo. E. Sokolsky; in *Atlantic Monthly*, Boston, February, 1937.

Selling Wilted Peonies, by Genevieve Wimsatt. New York, 1937.

Slavery under the Han Dynasty, a paper read by Martin Wilbur before the American Oriental Society, 1937.

The bibliography used in connection with the Life of Ch'iu Chin is cited in the Foreword to the latter.

BOOKS IN CHINESE

Lieh Nü Chuan, originally compiled by Liu Hsiang of the Han Dynasty 80–9 B.C., has been frequently added to. Several different editions were consulted, notably a Sung edition with illustrations reputed to be by Ku K'ai-chih, and a Ch'ien Lung edition illustrated by the famous Ming artist Ch'iu Ying.

Kuei Fan, by Lü Hsin-wu, A.D. 1591. Reprint issued in 1927 by Li Hsi-shan.

Li Chi, an edition printed in Shansi, A.D. 1885.

Nü Ssŭ Shu, in which the seven sections of Pan Chao's *Precepts* appear.

Sou Yü Tz'ŭ, a collection of poems by Li Ch'ing-chao.

Ssŭ Shêng Yüan.

Hung Shu Lou Hsüan.

Chung Kuo Nü Hsing ti Wên Hsüeh Shêng Huo.

Ch'ing Tai Fu Nü Wên Hsüeh Shih.

Index